The Blind and Blindness in Literature of the Romantic Period

The Blind and Blindness in Literature of the Romantic Period

Edward Larrissy

Edinburgh University Press

Edinburgh University Press Ltd
22 George Square, Edinburgh

Typeset in Sabon and Futura
by Servis Filmsetting Ltd, Manchester, and
printed and bound in Great Britain by
Biddles Ltd, King's Lynn, Norfolk

A CIP record for this book is available from the British Library

ISBN 978 0 7486 3281 7 (hardback)

Contents

Preface

For many writers of the Romantic period, the blind are necessarily associated with the idea of intense inward vision. Homer, Ossian and Milton provide obvious models. The age that became so fascinated by the bardic past was also fascinated in particular by the blind bard. Yet it understood that phenomenon as an historical one. Such visions were appropriate to an earlier age: they had to give way to the abstraction, organisation and commerce of modernity. This very course of events had been foretold by the blind bard who sang 'Rule Britannia' in Mallett and Thomson's *Alfred: A Masque* (1740), an anthem in which he foresaw Britain's future commercial prosperity. Ann Batten Cristall constructs an historical account of visionary blindness from such postulates.

Yet in the Enlightenment, the blind, who are the subject of intense philosophical scrutiny, are shown to be very capable, despite the bars to sympathy and empirical learning which make them such tempting test cases. Some of the popular moral tales in which they figure make this point in a quite prosaic manner, which is nonetheless very instructive about the role they play in more polite literature. Most of all, though, they are thought to enjoy the compensations of enhanced sensitivity to music and to words. This compensation becomes associated with the loss and gain inherent in the modernity of a post-bardic age. In particular, poets may learn to value such mastery of sound and association and find a richness in these which compensates for, and even surpasses, the lost intensity of inner vision. Such was Milton's power. Indeed, it is in words and their associations that one can convey a fullness of understanding without historical precedent. Representations of blindness and the blind elucidate a tension at the heart of the Romantic period, between the desire for immediacy of vision on the one hand, and, on the other, the historical self-consciousness which always attends it.

Acknowledgements

An earlier version of part of Chapter 2 is to be found in 'The Celtic Bard of Romanticism: Blindness and Second Sight', *Romanticism*, 5:1 (1999), pp. 43–57; and part of Chapter 3 is a revision of 'Spectral Imposition and Visionary Imposition: Repetition and Printing in Blake', *Blake in the Nineties*, ed. Steve Clark and David Worrall (Basingstoke and London: Macmillan; New York: St Martin's Press, 1999), pp. 61–77. Other parts of Chapter 3 comprise revisions of a few paragraphs from my *William Blake* (Oxford: Blackwell, 1985).

I am grateful to the librarians of the British Library, the Bodleian Library, the John Rylands Library, Manchester, the Brotherton Library, Leeds, and Keele University Library. I have also profited by the advice of Simon Bainbridge, John Barnard, James McLaverty, Nicholas Roe, Julie Sanders and John Whale, for which I am immensely grateful.

Chapter 1

The Enigma of the Blind

One of the theses advanced in this book is familiar and tends to be taken for granted, namely that the Romantic period is indebted to 'the ancient topos of the blind poet or seer, a visionary whose sight, having lost this world's presence, is directed entirely beyond to the spiritual.'[1] These are William Paulson's words from his book on the blind in France in that period. However, while there is an assumption that the topos is relevant to an understanding of British Romanticism, nobody has ever claimed that it is developed in a straightforward fashion in a wide range of significant literary works. If they had, there would be books and articles which took this view; but these do not exist. Nor does my book make such a claim. On the other hand, there is a general awareness of the influence of the idea of Homer's or Milton's or Ossian's blindness, combined with a specific awareness of individual texts, such as Blake's 'Tiriel', Wordsworth's 'The Blind Highland Boy', or Keats's 'To Homer', and of individual passages, such as the encounter with the Blind Beggar in *Prelude* VII, or the De Lacey episode in *Frankenstein*. However, none of these examples is straightforward in the sense of conveying the idea of inward vision as superior to outward. Yet it is impossible to understand and appreciate fully the force of these passages without grasping their background not only in literary representations of the blind, but also in those philosophical discussions of the experience of blind people which were central to Enlightenment theories about the role of the senses in the acquisition of knowledge, and which are well known to Romantic-period authors, including those, such as Barbara Hofland or Mary Martha Sherwood, who are not known for advanced philosophical speculation. It is the figure of the blind, then, as much as the overwhelming array of tropes of blindness and insight, which is the subject of this book, for this figure palpably brings with it echoes of the philosophical and poetic contexts with which it was associated. Nevertheless, such tropes inevitably occur within and alongside literary representations of the blind, and help to constitute those representations. It would be a naïve theory of rhetoric indeed which attempted to divorce them – assuming that such a thing were possible.

This book, then, claims a significant influence of literary representations and philosophical discussions of the blind on Romantic-period writing, but does not claim that this is a matter of the frequent occurrence of the image of the blind visionary used in a straightforward fashion. Rather, it seeks to demonstrate the sometimes complex relationship which exists between this topos and other ways of representing the blind. One of these ways, it must be stressed, is even more straightforward than the representation of the blind bard. I refer to the simple stratagem of merely using blindness to figure obtuseness or lack of insight. This is the main element in the depiction of Blake's Tiriel, an early personification of tyranny in his work. Even so, a reading of the wider context shows that the figure of Tiriel possesses a relationship to the figure of the blind bard. But another influence on Romantic-period writing about blindness or the blind is to be found in one of the most prominent theories of the age: namely, that the blind possessed a compensatory sensitivity to sounds and music, and a concomitant facility at musical performance.[2] Furthermore, the idea of compensatory sensitivity to music merges with that of sensitivity to language and its resonances and associations, a notion which contributes to some of the most original thinking in Burke's *Enquiry*, and which is subtly present in those passages of Wordsworth where he laments the loss of past vision. I shall claim that the idea of sensitivity to language overlaps, especially in virtue of the concept of 'association', with a particular supposition about what is inwardly seen by those who have lost their sight: namely, that what they see are memories, rather than visions of the imagination. Other elements in the background to Romantic blindness would include the sheer mysteriousness of the experience of the blind to sighted people, and more specifically the difficulty of explaining that experience in terms of the various sense-based empiricist theories about the growth of the mind.

The account so far makes the topic of blindness and the blind seem like a Cubist collage: an assemblage of items of different kinds, some of which overlap. But my thesis will find an underlying tendency in a wide variety of texts whereby the image of the blind man is significant of the acute historical self-consciousness of the Romantic period: it carries with it not only that profound apprehension of an inner self which develops from Locke onwards, but also a sophisticated sense of the historical situatedness and relativity of that nature. Furthermore, this sense co-exists with ironic and melancholy realisation that the inwardness of modernity, acutely felt though it might be, cannot possess the power and confidence of the ancient bard's inward vision. So the figure of the blind is an index not of a decline from inwardness to externality (though that danger is certainly noted) but of an exchange, involving both gain and loss, of ancient for modern inwardness.

The Blind Seer: Classical and Renaissance Background

First, though, since it constitutes an abiding point of reference, it is worth returning to the 'ancient' topos of the blind seer. There are a number of minor qualifications and supplementary points which should be made straight away. For some have raised a question about the pervasiveness of this notion in classical and, indeed, medieval times. Panofsky quotes a medieval moralist as saying that blindness 'conveys to us only something negative and nothing positive, and by the blind man we generally understand the sinner,' and goes on to conclude that,

> Blindness is [. . .] always associated with evil, excepting the blindness of Homer, which served supposedly to keep his mind unvitiated by sensual appetites, and the blindness of Justice which was meant to assure her impartiality. Both these interpretations however are foreign to classical as well as to mediaeval thought; the figure of blindfold Justice in particular is a humanistic concoction of very recent origin.[3]

There are, however, many well-known examples which tend to a different conclusion, of which the story of Tiresias is only the most obvious. And a scholar of the classical tradition who enjoys an esteem no less notable than that of Panofsky, namely Edgar Wind, notes that blindness could be a mark of initiation into the divine mysteries.[4] Catherine Maxwell observes that there is an oscillation between two positions: 'between blindness as cost or penalty, where sight is something to be forfeited, and vision as compensation, or even reward.'[5] While one might need to introduce some balance into the account, then, it seems most judicious to observe, as Moshe Barasch does, that blindness from the classical period onwards is conceived in terms of 'a certain ambiguity or ambivalence'. As he says of the blind man,

> On the one hand, he is the unfortunate creature, deprived of what is often considered man's most precious gift [. . .] On the other hand, he is endowed, however vaguely, with an ability given to no other human being – to be in direct communication with a deity. He dwells in two worlds, or hovers between them.[6]

It does appear, however, that from the Renaissance onwards, there is a greater deployment of the figure than in the middle ages: *King Lear* is, of course, a notable example. And Homer is, in British writing after the Renaissance, occasionally referred to as a 'blind bard': an intriguing usage, for the Celtic associations of the word 'bard' were, if anything, even more apparent then than now, so that one suspects a specifically local inflection to the topos, of a kind which would later be developed very strongly.[7] Even then, one would have to note that Chapman's *Blind Beggar of Alexandria* depicts blindness only as an aid to deception. Still, by the early eighteenth century Robert Dodsley's popular poem, *The Blind Beggar of Bethnal Green,* seems to treat the idea of inward vision as an item of common sense: 'Tho' Darkness still attends me / It aids internal Sight'.[8]

Ann Batten Cristall

Moving forward towards the Romantic period, one of the most striking examples of the exploitation of the idea of inward vision is to be found in the *Poetical Sketches* of Ann Batten Cristall (*c.*1769– ?). However, one of the central claims of our book is that Romantic-period writing strongly emphasises the aural compensations from which the blind may benefit. This makes it tempting to ignore examples of the strong continuation of the 'inward vision' idea. But it is worth remembering the inward vision trope as always present alongside the compensation idea, at the very least as qualifying and inflecting it. An examination of the work of Cristall confers the further advantage that it may offer a succinct introduction to ideas about social progress and its gain and loss which were also bound up with Romantic handlings of the blind. Indeed, in the Romantic period, the idea of aural compensation becomes particularly entwined with questions about such gain and loss. Nevertheless, there is a sense in which Cristall represents the most complex literary treatment of the topic of blindness in the eighteenth century prior to that exploration of the resources of language which the major Romantic poets develop in tandem with the idea of aural compensation. The work of Milton was a powerful influence on that idea, so the argument will return to him after pursuing the treatment of inward vision in Cristall.

    Poetical Sketches (1795) contain a striking poem called 'A Fragment: The Blind Man'. The chief character, a 'reverend man', explains that 'that God which robbed my eyes of sight / Darts through my mind a ray of sacred light [. . .]', an idea in which the 'inward light' trope is made obvious and the influence of Milton is palpable.[9] Indeed, the blind man's brain is a reflection of the universe, containing 'all the grandeur of this glorious world!' (l. 16). The way in which this conception is arrived at is telling:

> 'Twas Heaven's fierce fire which swept my eyes away
> And left an orbless trunk, that knows nor night nor day.
> Yet strong ideas rooted in my brain
> From there an universe, which doth contain
> Those images which Nature's hand displays –
> The heavenly arch, the morning's glowing rays;
> Mountains and plains, the sea by tempests hurled,
> And all the grandeur of this glorious world!
>
> (ll. 11–16)

The 'ideas' in the brain, which create a universe, make the blind man seem like an echo of the God who has bereft him of his sight, and intensify the idea of mingled good and ill and of a fortunate fall. The word 'ideas' itself toys with an equivocation between a Platonic and a Lockeian conception: that these mental entities should create a universe sounds Platonic, and consorts with the echoing of God's powers; but in the end the conception is decisively Lockeian, for the blind man once possessed his sight, and knowing this we may interpret the ideas being 'rooted' as impressions that implant themselves in the mind.

The 'grandeur' of the world in the blind man's mind has the meaning of 'sublimity', and this idea is intensified by the fact that the he and his companion are in the midst of a 'rapid storm' of symbolic import. The allusion to *King Lear* enhances the sense of sublimity, and assists in opening up the topic of life's afflictions. As the blind man informs us, it is 'God's voice which urges on the storm', for the deity wills not peace but 'varied joys and pains' (ll. 24–9). The connection with the man's blindness, as part of a divinely ordained pattern of joy and pain, is obvious, and there is also the suggestion of the fortunate fall, in that his blindness may involve a compensating joy or power, and here again one feels the influence of Milton.

It is hardly surprising, therefore, that Cristall should elsewhere in her work have developed so strongly the idea of figurative blindness, and to this end should have exploited the symbolism of the privation of vision by night and darkness. That this is no mere perfunctory reference to a familiar trope is suggested, for instance, by a poem ('The Triumph of Superstition') which otherwise has nothing, on the face of it, to do with blindness. Arno, an ardent but violent young man, espies the enchanting Ianthe in the fields. His response is conveyed in terms which refer to a common Enlightenment preoccupation: the experience of the blind when their sight is restored after an operation for cataract: 'The blind restored scarce feel more strong delight / When heaven's vast orb first strikes th'astonished sight' (ll. 190–200). This developed character of the reference to blindness, or to deprivation of sight, is fairly typical.

A series of linked poems near the beginning of her collection constitutes a philosophical work in which the relationships of vision, darkness and 'creative mind' are central. (Jerome McGann argues, surely correctly, for the centrality in the poem of the concept of creative mind.[10]) She invents a number of mythological characters of her own, in ways that are reminiscent of Blake, especially in that names may contain a punning reference to the significance of the personages. The figures first encountered by the reader, Eyezion and his beloved Viza, make the topic of vision very clear.[11] Eyezion not only has his 'eyes' figuratively 'on' Viza, but also, by the same token, enjoys a vision of paradise (Zion). As for Viza, her name is a homophone of the Latin past participle *visa* ('seen'; feminine gender), and can mean 'woman seen or envisioned.' But the poem devoted to these lovers is emphatically set in the last hours of the night, 'Before Twilight' as the title has it.[12] It is emphasised that the darkness means that each must rely on 'fancy' to see the other: 'Yet fancy paints a conscious blush / O'er thy fair cheeks [. . .]' (ll. 93–4). Fortunately for him, Eyezion's fancy is remarkably strong, as he informs Viza, having enjoined her to 'Listen, whilst I describe my mental powers' (l. 52):

> A current of creative mind,
> Wild as the wandering gusts of wind,
> Mid fertile fancy's visions trained,
> Unzoned I shot, and o'er each limit strained;
> Around in airy circles whirled
>   By a genius infinite [. . .]
>
>   (ll. 53–8)

This conception of Eyezion has obvious precursors in the depiction of poetic genius in Gray and Collins. In a way that seems appropriate to the topic, these lines also help to demonstrate the relative salience of the trope of inward vision in Cristall's work as compared with poets who stress a compensatory aural sensitivity. Poetic genius is here explicitly a matter of visions present to an eye which is deprived of light.

There are other obvious overtones of the work of Gray and Collins, for the series is patently structured in terms of 'The Progress of Poesy' idea. The next section is 'Morning. Rosamonde', which is followed by 'Noon. Lysander', 'Evening. Gertrude' and 'Night'. The course of day and night is made to bear meanings about the progress of poetry, and of the evolution of individuals' conception of the role of 'fancy' in their own mental life. Considering the extent to which Cristall's idiom is still that of sensibility, and the way in which this series consciously refers to the Progress of Poesy tradition, this seems like a highly innovative work, one which verges on more typically Romantic concerns, in the way it addresses simultaneously the subjective and the public.

'Morning. Rosamonde' refers to what is ostensibly a fresh heroine who is pursued by a new lover called 'Urban'. Yet McGann is right to say that these characters are Viza and Eyezion in new guises.[13] This is partly because the appearance of Rosamonde in the early morning follows immediately on Viza's promise to appear at that time, and partly because the naming of 'Viza' and 'Eyezion' deliberately embodies the idea of conceptions which will be realised. At the same time, the oblique-ness with which the transmutation is handled (we are not told these are the same characters) itself suggests that Viza and Eyezion are indeed more akin to conceptions or potentialities than to real beings. As for the question why the new characters have the names they have, one should think again in terms of symbolism rather than literary or historical ref-erence: Rosamonde is not a reference to a courtesan of Henry II, nor to Chaucer's fair 'Rosemounde', nor is Lysander in the following section a reference to a Spartan general. 'Rosamonde' (and the French form of her name makes this clear) is the rosy world of a May morning, with all that implies symbolically; and Lysander is not a Spartan general but what his Greek name means ('liberator of man'). As for Urban, there is nothing papal about him; rather, he is one who possesses the civilised skills asso-ciated with the development of towns. It is stressed that he plays his flute with 'art' ('Morning', l. 32), unlike Lysander, who has an 'artless rhyme' ('Noon', l. 17). The very form of Cristall's poetry evokes artlessness, and was seen as doing so; she is capable of using the word 'art' in decidedly pejorative fashion, as when she refers, in 'Verses Written in Spring', to 'those who ne'er from forms depart, / The slaves of fashion and of art'.[14] The sense of opposition inherent in the contrasted connotations of Urban and Rosamonde continues that which is implied in the difference of Eyezion and Viza. Developed art is in love with artless nature. At the same time, the idea of the urban continues the reference to the ideal city in 'Zion'.

Yet the morning is too early for reconciliation: humanity is not ready for full enlightenment. The relationship of Urban and Rosamonde is characterised by alienation and deceit. She herself thinks in terms of 'tyrant Love' and is only brought to yield when 'offended Urban' employs his 'art', at which point she is ensnared 'like a bird whom fear / Has drawn within the fascinating serpent's fangs'. To mark his success, Urban takes his revenge by departing and leaving her 'weeping, and forlorn!' The artless Lysander, by contrast, conforming to his name, takes pity on a girl who admits that she 'far in vice [has] strayed'. True to Cristall's association with the circle of Joseph Johnson and Mary Wollstonecraft, Lysander is the noon-tide of human progress: politically he represents enlightened liberalism, in terms of gender politics a promise of companionate relationship and an overcoming of false and hypocritical moral notions such as the double standard. This is the Zion for which humanity may hope. No wonder that the 'damsel' for whom he feels both pity and passion should be so 'Fired by his zeal' that 'the passions of her breast' reveal 'Bright blossom of a future ripening flame!' ('Noon', ll. 120–3). On this optimistic note the section ends.

But that note is not maintained in the following section, 'Evening. Gertrude'. The sequence is indeed cyclical, and in the evening we are in less enlightened times. Gertrude is 'pensive' and melancholy. Urban appears on the scene again, and she is unhappily drawn to him. He now, however, seems reconciled with the 'sportive' Rosamonde. They consort with a motley pastoral crew, some benevolent, some not: 'neat Phillis', 'marble-hearted Rosalind', 'The loud and witty large-mouthed Madge / With her obsequious servant Hodge', 'Hebe, a blooming, sprightly fair, / With shallow Ned (an ill-matched pair)'. The dances in which these rustics engage allow them to 'forget to feel', and soon Rosamonde, triumphant but still rivalrous, encourages Urban to join with her in mockery of the sad Gertrude. It appears that everyone can join in, for soon 'wicked looks, and jests, and jeers went round'. The final note of this section is to remind us that the 'heart may blessings find / That dwell not in the eyes / But in the virtues of the feeling mind'. This relegation of what dwells in the eyes is appropriately followed by the last section, 'Night', where there is no choice but to concentrate on thought and feeling. Young Henry, pierced 'by ingratitude', roves 'forlorn'; and reminded of 'God's immeasurable power' by the innumerable stars or 'worlds' he can see in the night sky, concludes by recalling how 'man errs' when 'he to earthly passions gives dire sway, / Or mourns those joys which of themselves decay!' This might seem like a disenchanted note on which to conclude, but it needs to be recalled that this is a cyclical poem, where we might expect to entertain the possibility of going back to the beginning. Furthermore, the potential to act like Lysander does not mean giving earthly passion 'dire sway' but achieving a balance of passion, love and liberality such as is encouraged by faith in God. In this connection, Duncan Wu is right to remind us that 'despite her dissenting friends, the religious world of her poems is more conventional than that of Blake's. She is in no doubt as to the existence of an omnipresent, benevolent deity'.[15] There is no need for this reason to cut her adrift from the Locke tradition to which she, like her radical subscribers, or like other exponents of the poetics of sensibility, was indebted: God's providence allows for the possibility of developing the approved moral and spiritual state from an early life of sensation. What is striking is the degree to which she feels able to stress the idea of 'creative mind' on this basis rather than with the help of the Platonic sources to which Coleridge turned even while he was still a disciple of Hartley. In fact, Cristall's ideas are more reminiscent of Shelley, even to the extent of offering a 'quasi-pantheistic' view, as Duncan Wu puts it, referring to the way in which 'her characters deliquesce into the natural world around them'.[16]

In other ways Cristall is more typical of the kind of radical circles in which she moved in the 1790s. The Progress of Poesy always had political connotations, and Lysander's liberalism is not the only index of this. The rustics bear an assortment of names, variously of classical, romance and merely rustic connotation: 'Phillis', 'Rosalind', 'Hodge'. This mixture suggests Shakespearean pastoral comedy, with its scope for misunderstanding, which is here broadened to include cruelty and spite. Shakespeare's merry England is an object of implied criticism, the locus for social rituals of domination, exclusion and time-honoured games of courtship which are as likely as not to end in time-honoured mistrust between the sexes. In accordance with this view, Cristall is as suspicious of the medieval and the Gothic as any Paine or Godwin. 'Holbain', for instance, offers an allegory which is scarcely obscure. The elder son of a family in which Holbain is given refuge when lost in a foggy marsh has brought misery to that family by taking his mother to see a 'Gothic structure' where he has been accustomed to indulge in 'youth's romantic raptures'. When he has left her to find 'refreshments', a storm blows up and buries her under the 'tottering castle'. As it happens, there is a simultaneous disaster, for the same storm destroys the father's ships, 'loaded with wealth'. But perseverance and industry remain his guides. If this allegory seems too crude, another poem, 'The Triumph of Superstition: Raphael and Ianthe', offers a view of medieval Italy which would scarcely have been original in Cristall's circle. It begins by evoking 'Gothic times, when feudal laws obtained, / And tyranny with superstition reigned' (ll. 1–2) and proceeds to tell a sorry tale of cruelty. Lysander's 'creative mind' is best fostered in enlightened times, even as it helps to bring them about.

That creative mind, according to McGann, is also possessed by the blind man in 'A Fragment', the form of which he also rightly sees as figuring this theme.[17] The 'ray of sacred light' which illuminates the old man's mind draws him and the reader to very different conclusions from those which might be prompted by a Wordsworthian solitary. The latter might involve the reader and the poetic persona in a troubling obscurity; but Cristall's sublime tends in a different direction. The blind man accepts the speaker's proffered aid in leading him out of the storm. As McGann suggests, in Wordsworth there might have been more exploration of 'fear'.[18] For Cristall, creative mind must accept that the world is full of 'varied joys and pains', but must also accept attempts to alleviate the pains, in the way that the blind man does in accordance with the speaker's entreaties. One needs to put this acceptance alongside the praise of 'science', 'Truth' and 'Freedom' in 'The Triumph of Superstition', and that of 'industry' in 'Holbain.' Cristall's creative mind is the friend not only of liberty, but also of sober-minded, realistic, hopeful reason and industry, and here again she reveals her ideological kinship with many of her illustrious subscribers. What the series about the times of day and 'A Fragment' have in common is the idea of potential hidden in darkness: a potential which has the capacity, in the series, to find its fulfilment in the modern era. In this way, Cristall's work is the most complete inversion of nostalgia for the blind bard. But like other writings which touch on blindness in this period, it is to a high degree historically self-conscious.

Milton: The Blind Bard, the Nightingale and the Fortunate Fall

The influence of Milton on a poem such as Cristall's 'Fragment' is palpable and central, as it is on the whole development of the topos in poets subsequent to him. Of course, the success of the idea is far too important to be attributed to the accident of a precursor poet. The pervasiveness of the topos in the Romantic period, or more properly in the long eighteenth century, has to do with the development of that inwardness which Charles Taylor sees as integral to the modern self.[19] Milton provides the most pervasive image, for the Romantics, of the inspired blind poet, even allowing for the Celtic bard in his various guises. In regarding Milton in this way they were following the guidance of the poet himself. References in *Paradise Lost* to his own blindness are accompanied by those to 'Blind Thamyris, and blind Maeonides, / And Tiresias and Phineus prophets old' (III: 35–6). As Anne Ferry points out, the opening lines of *Paradise Lost* have to be seen in relation to this comparison: 'He can interpret to us Adam's story and our own share in it because, like a bird, he can soar beyond the limits of our mortal experience and our fallen vision'.[20] This is the speaker who penetrates for us the 'darkness visible' of Hell.[21]

That Milton is, for Burke and others, one of the pre-eminent sublime poets adds to the power of his image as blind bard, and gives weight to the tradition of the 'inward light' – an important influence on Wordsworth, as Nicola Trott has shown.[22] But it also involves him in a different debate: the one about the compensatory auditory powers of the blind. Of course, there are other senses than hearing which might offer compensation, and touch makes occasional appearances in this role. A fine example is to be found in Leigh Hunt's sonnet, 'On a Lock of Milton's Hair'. Contemplating this strand of the blind poet's hair, Hunt imagines Milton running his 'fine fingers' over it 'when he leant / blank-eyed, / And saw in fancy, Adam and his bride / With their heaped locks, or his own Delphic wreath'. The sense of the intimacy with oneself of toying with one's own hair is reinforced by the softness of the tactile impression. It is, however, an impression so deeply felt that it adds strength to the visual imagery in the mind's eye of the blind man, and permits him to write. In other words, the poem supplements the idea of compensation with that of assistance to inward vision. In view of this access of poetic power, it is symbolically appropriate that Milton should also be able, on the basis of feeling his own hair, to imagine the poet's laurel wreath which will adorn his brow. But the link thus established is between what might at first seem two very diverse things: the most gentle and intimate tactile sensations on the one hand, and the esteem accorded to the blind poet, with his sublime visions, on the other. As Hunt goes on to say in the sestet, 'Patience and Gentleness is Power'.[23]

If Milton can figure his blindness in terms both of loss and of compensatory inward vision, he does not invoke only the comparison of the blind bard. As Catherine Maxwell emphasises, the word of imagination in the darkness is powerfully evoked in Milton's reference to 'the wakeful bird [who] / Sings darkling' (*Paradise Lost*, III: 38–9), lines which follow on immediately from those about the 'blind [. . .] prophets old' (III: 35–6).[24] The story of Philomela, who was turned into a nightingale, is also one of compensatory musical power. Raped by her brother-in-law Tereus, she has her tongue cut out so that she cannot say what has happened to her. But by means of an embroidered picture, she is able to tell her sister Procne, with whose help she avenges herself on Tereus by serving him up a stew made from the flesh of his son Itys and then informing him of what she has done. As the sisters flee, tradition has it that Philomela is turned into a nightingale and Procne into a swallow. The pain and loss involved in the story can no longer be imparted by means either of word or picture, embroidered or otherwise: they are conveyed by the unanalysable suggestions of song. Yet the power of the song is bound up with its melancholy. As Milton says in *Il Penseroso*, 'Most musical, most melancholy!' (l. 62).

Maxwell makes the plausible claim that,

> When Milton's Romantic inheritors come to write their answering nightin-
> gale poems they do so with a specific and anxious purpose invoking the
> joyous bird in order to contest the blind poet's figure of the melancholy
> singer. In debating whether the nightingale is sad or merry, they are debat-
> ing the nature of lyric in general and its origins in loss and violence, but
> also the underlying characterisation of the poet's necessary disfiguring
> sacrifice.[25]

The most illuminating point to bear in mind is that one must place this
within the context of the Romantics' attitude to the bardic in general,
including the idea of Milton as blind bard, but very much including also
the fate of the primitive bardic vision possessed by Ossian and other
Celtic 'bards' in the modern world of commerce.

Another point to remember about Milton is that he offered an
account of himself in which the compensatory gains of blindness were
particularly strongly emphasised, being buttressed by their assimilation
to Christian imagery of fall and redemption. As Stuart Ende says, in
Keats and the Sublime, 'Though the outer landscape might have faded
with his eyesight, Milton proclaims that he "not the more" ceases "to
wander where the Muses haunt," for their locus is at least in part the
mind and "all her powers" '.[26] And in line with the Christian schema,
the poet's last condition may be happier than his first:

> Just as the poet has been granted a truer vision in his blindness, and *because*
> he is blind, so Adam and Eve are granted what the Angel calls 'A Paradise
> within thee, happier farr' (XII.587) only *after* they have lost their first
> Paradise.[27]

This schema is obviously relevant to Wordsworth's melancholy reflections on loss of vision and its compensations. It is also, I think, relevant
to Coleridge's handling of the idea of blindness in 'This Lime-Tree
Bower My Prison'. And in both cases, this inflection of the idea of the
fortunate fall is involved with thoughts about how the damaging effects
of the modern world of commerce can be overcome by means of
resources still present in that world.

One way of confronting those effects might seem to be by means of
a revolution. And here the example of Milton suggested a troubling
precedent, for the failure of his own political hopes with the demise of
the Commonwealth could be seen as furnishing an analogy with the
position of writers who sympathised with the aims of the French
Revolution after it was seen to fail. To apply and extend Milton's own
allegory, the later 1790s saw the disappointment of hopes for a
new political order often imaged as paradisal ('to be young was very

heaven'). It does not take much wit to see how Milton's blindness could take on a figurative implication whereby his inner vision, so far from being sharpened, was itself proved to be blind. In that case, perhaps the Chaos and Darkness which were antithetical to his Heaven were truer representations of the universe. These are the thoughts that are entertained, as we shall see, with different inflections, by Byron and the Shelleys: indeed, the debate between these three is partly framed in terms of the question how to conceive Milton's inheritance given the fate of the Revolution.

The world of commerce may be the cause of melancholy, for that world is also the reason for the bard's marginalisation. This point need not be illustrated by so obvious an example as Tennyson's 'Locksley Hall', where the refined, if somewhat unhinged, speaker is jilted in favour of a fool enriched by the profits of industry, relevant though this be. There is a more subtle way of conceiving the notion, namely that the question that may hover over the poet's ability to compose a harmonious vision arises partly out of the impediment posed by the world of commerce, a world consciously seen as antithetical to the ancient faculty of poetry. In the case of poets such as Keats, Byron or Shelley, who are concerned to understand what they recognise to be new political and economic realities, it is relevant to speak of what Guinn Batten calls 'the melancholy of commodity culture'.[28] If Nature, for the Romantic poet, becomes a mystery to be recorded, probed and if possible understood from individual experience, as opposed to a book of pre-established sacred emblems, something very similar is true of the experience and appearance of commerce and commodity culture. Even political economy was conscious of striving to explain something new. The poets also were pioneers in a world which, however unpoetic, by a merely apparent paradox had the ancient bard as its remote ancestor. They had something other to do than bewail their melancholy fate, for this would be merely to acquiesce in disempowerment, in symbolic castration. Here is a reason for the difference between canonical Romantic poetry and the poetry of sensibility. Sensibility pays to feeling the tribute of recognising its power while omitting to specify its cause. The major Romantic poets, by contrast, pay the tribute of recording the cause in physical or narrative detail, experimenting with the idea of letting feeling emerge by implication. In any case, much Romantic poetry differs from the poetry of sensibility in attempting to provide what Eliot was to call an 'objective correlative'.

Whatever the specific troubles they may be alluding to, the very many women poets who write about the nightingale find in it a sympathetic emblem, both of a condition of relative disempowerment, and of a specific male hostility to the woman reader and writer, to woman's words and imagination.[29] A poem such as Charlotte Smith's 'Sonnet: To a Nightingale' combines a language of sensibility (asserting and giving vent to melancholy emotion) with a not unnatural questioning of its causes: 'From what sad cause can such sweet sorrow flow, / And whence this mournful melody of song?' Or: 'Say – hast thou felt from friends some cruel wrong, / Or diedst thou – martyr of disastrous love?'[30] But when Coleridge treats of the nightingale, it is to connect it to a whole picture of what Wordsworth calls 'Nature, Man and Society', and when Keats does so, it is to invoke a refined perception of beauty that is the bitter-sweet salve of mortality: its transhistorical nature, paradoxically, can only be properly understood and appreciated within the perspective of an historically self-conscious modernity, capable of perceiving and understanding the 'march of mind' and the advancement of commerce. Only the modern mind, to put it another way, can understand the imaginative significance of the nightingale without either needing, or being able, to turn it into a myth, whether involving 'Philomela' or 'Starry Fays'. Coleridge's nightingale and Keats's are not the same bird. Coleridge's is ostensibly more joyful, and its symbolic and philosophical connections are more palpable. But both birds arise out of an impulse to make the poem a vehicle for understanding, and to make its language embody and express what for sensibility remained inexpressible. Thus, however much these poems may still register anxiety, they also represent the Romantic poet's desire to compensate linguistically for a vision that is lost.

Auditory Compensation and Poetic Associations from Blacklock to Burke

But it is auditory compensation, above all, that is something of a recurrent topos of the Enlightenment and Romantic periods. It finds emphatic expression in *The Blind Boy* (1808), a play by James Kenney (1780–1849), a popular, but not universally admired, playwright. ('Ah! where is Kenney's wit?' enquired Byron in *English Bards and Scotch Reviewers*.) In this play, the blind hero Edmond always notices what flowers are blooming. It is said of him 'How fine his sense of hearing', and he escapes death when he realises, from the evidence of his ears, that he is being lied to about his whereabouts.[31] Charles Lamb, a friend of Kenney's, wrote a remarkable sonnet about the play, or rather about their mutual friend Frances Kelly (1790–1882), the young actress who had played the boy: 'To a Celebrated Female Performer in "The Blind

Boy" ' extends the application of the topos of compensation to the actress's handling of the character:

> Rare artist! who with half thy tools, or none,
> Canst execute with ease thy curious art,
> And press thy powerful'st meanings on the heart,
> Unaided by the eye, expression's throne!
> While each blind sense, intelligential grown
> Beyond its sphere, performs the effect of sight [. . .][32]

The topos might simply be extended to the deprivation of light, as in Cristall's *Poetical Sketches*. For while Eyezion has the powerful visions of fancy, he also asserts that 'Music waited on my birth', and the poem 'Before Twilight' demonstrates the importance of his making use of this birthright.[33] It was not only Milton's imagery, but the sonorous power of his poetic language which procured for him the title of sublimity. And one of the claims of Burke's *Enquiry,* made in an especially explicit way about the blind poet Thomas Blacklock (1721–91), is that the blind may possess great facility in the employment of poetic language, which depends for its power on the exploitation of associations and not only on its capacity to make pictures.

The importance of the example of Blacklock, and what differentiates his case from that of Milton, is that he went blind at the age of six months.[34] He therefore could not have retained any clear visual ideas in his memory. This must raise questions about how he could have confected convincing visual imagery, as he was held to have done, in an age where two related convictions tended to prevail: first, that mature mental life was built up from simple sense experience; and second, that poetry, in accordance with the doctrine of *ut pictura poesis,* was essentially descriptive. In relation to the first point, nobody denied that blind people could be ingenious, learned and ethically mature. But philosophical discussions of experience, such as Locke's, including early experience, tended to emphasise the sense of sight, so that the manner of the blind person's attainment of such attributes remained a matter of philosophical debate, and harboured an element of mystery. The point about description in poetry was raised specifically in discussions of Blacklock. As Joseph Spence said, in his *Account* of the poet's life, 'The most distinguishing Character of Poetry, is to be descriptive; and it is this which gives the very near Relation that there is between Poetry and Painting'.[35] Thus, as far as Spence was concerned, 'the most difficult Part of my Undertaking' was to give an account of Blacklock's *'describing Visible Objects'.*[36] Spence makes the point that Milton only went blind when he was about fifty, and that, for all we know, Homer still possessed his sight when he wrote his epics. But we know that Blacklock went blind in infancy, and consequently whatever Ideas he may have in relation to visible Objects, must have been acquir'd only from the Characters he had learnt from Books and Conversation; and some suppos'd Analogies between those Characters, and any of the Ideas in the Stock he has laid in, either from his other Senses, or his own Reflections upon them.[37]

There was no question of any impairment of his other senses or of his intellectual powers. It is simply a fact that Blacklock was a learned man, and it went without saying that he was perfectly capable of acquitting himself well in social circles by compensating for his blindness by means of the other senses in the way that blind people were known to do. In giving an account of his experience to David Hume, he spoke of beauty, and how it was not only 'the beauty of the mind' which affected him: for 'the sweetness of the voice has a mighty effect upon me: the symptoms of youth, too which the touch discovers, have great influence'.[38] That a blind man should be affected by sweet sounds was taken for granted. But what could he mean by touch in this context? Blacklock explained that 'the girls of my acquaintance indulge me, on account of my blindness, with the liberty of running over them with my hand'. Such acquaintance permitted accuracy: he was able to 'judge entirely of their shape'. Hume remarked on 'how difficult it is even for a blind man to be a perfect Platonic'.[39] Jonathan Rée suggests, amusingly, that Hume was 'perhaps a little peeved' by the familiarity permitted to the blind poet.[40] Whatever about that, the implications of the remark (not meant entirely seriously, of course) show how natural it was to associate the blind man with abstraction from the material world; they possess a distant kinship with the idea of the blind man as prophetic visionary. But, of course, Hume was making the opposite point: Blacklock, like other blind people, was able to manage very well on the basis of his other senses and the knowledge acquired from them.

While he may not have been entirely Platonic, all are agreed on Blacklock's benevolence, which indeed may have commended itself to 'the girls of [his] acquaintance.' Spence devotes a section of his *Account* to Blacklock's '*Moral Character*', concluding that 'His Benevolence is universal'.[41] It seems appropriate that Henry Mackenzie, author of *The Man of Feeling*, should have contributed an account of Blacklock's life to the posthumous *Poems* of 1793.[42] The question about the blind man's benevolence was almost as intriguing as that about his use of visual imagery. If mature moral life was developed from the childhood operation of identification and sympathy by means of the senses, then it seemed possible that a blind child was denied one of the chief avenues for sympathetic identification, and thus for moving beyond 'solipsism' as Jessica Riskin puts it in her discussion of the blind.[43] The consensus, though, whether it be gauged from a poem such as Wordsworth's 'The Blind Highland Boy', or from some of the moral tales written by evangelical women writers for children, was that the blind possessed an unimpaired potential for benevolence. The only question was whether or not the writer wished to remind one that the blind, like the rest of us, are afflicted by original sin, as Mrs Sherwood, one of the sternest of the writers of moral tales, chose to do in *The Blind Man and Little George*. Significantly enough, there is another point of difference: Sherwood's children, unlike Wordsworth's, can be morally repugnant. But on either side of this division is a fascination with the way in which the blind can figure the integrity of the inner life of heart and spirit.

Mackenzie is on even more familiar territory when he spends some time expatiating upon Blacklock's love of music. Indeed, it seems that Blacklock was 'a tolerable performer on several instruments' and used to carry around in his pocket 'a small *Flageolet,* on which he played his favourite tunes; and was not displeased when asked in company to play or to sing them [. . .]'.[44] The pleasure the blind take in music was often stressed, but so was their proficiency at playing. Wordsworth's 'Blind Highland Boy' is a generic figure, reminding one of the myriads of blind harpers and pipers in the past of Scotland and Ireland, and probably in that of England, to judge only by Shakespeare's *Love's Labour's Lost*. Music, as Blacklock himself tells us in his article on 'The Blind' for the *Encyclopaedia Britannica,* is a proper employment for them.[45] A blind child might well be brought up to play; but equally, someone who lost their sight in adulthood might convert to the profession of music, as one is reminded by Anna Seward's *Blindness,* which was written *'at the Request of an Artist who lost his Sight by the Gutta Serena, and who was therefore obliged to change his Profession for that of Music'.*[46] Here is another way, then, in which the privation of sight might be associated as much with auditory compensations as with inner vision.

This might be a convenient point at which to return to where our discussion of Blacklock began: with words and their associations. It will be recalled that Spence deduced that Blacklock was able to form 'Ideas' of visible objects from reading and conversation, and to forge analogies between these and the data from his other senses 'or his own Reflections upon them'. Mackenzie, writing some forty years later, thinks that this is too sophisticated an argument, and dispenses with analogies and reflections. He assigns the effect to Blacklock's reading alone: 'the effect of a retentive and ready memory of that poetical language in which from his earliest infancy he delighted, and that apt appropriation of it which an habitual acquaintance with the best poets had taught him'.[47] Burke in the second (1759) edition of the *Enquiry,* introduces a discussion of

Blacklock in the chapter (V:v) called 'Examples that Words may affect without raising Images'. He is writing many years before Mackenzie, and expressly agrees with Spence on the question of analogies and reflections. He merely disagrees with Spence that Blacklock's errors in visual imagery are any more significant than those to be found in sighted poets.[48] Burke's only other example is that of another much-discussed blind man, Nicholas Saunderson (1682–1739), who had been Lucasian Professor of Mathematics at Cambridge. Since both these men had been blind from infancy, they are more useful to the advancement of Burke's radical thesis than is Milton. He asserts their respective proficiencies: Blacklock writing of visual objects with quite as much 'spirit and justness' as the sighted; Saunderson lecturing on colours.[49] On this basis he proceeds to the most revolutionary formulations of his treatise:

> When I wrote this last sentence, and used the words *every day* and *common discourse*, I had no images in my mind of any succession of time; nor of men in conference with each other; nor do I imagine that the reader will have any such ideas on reading it.[50]

Which brings him to his conclusion: 'Indeed so little does poetry depend for its effect on the power of raising sensible images, that I am convinced it would lose a very considerable part of its energy, if this were the necessary result of all description'.[51] This is Burke's answer to Spence's deployment of the traditional identification of poetry with description. Poetic words work 'rather by sympathy than imitation', and thus affect the passions.[52] Considered as a theory of poetic language, the most interesting development in Burke's argument is when he points out that 'by words we have it in our power to make such *combinations* as we cannot possibly do otherwise'.[53] In this suggestive formulation there lies compact the idea of poetic language as a network of ingeniously confected combinations which will practise upon the associations of the reader. Nevertheless, it has to be conceded that Diderot had already outlined a comparable conception of poetic language in his 'Letter on the Deaf and Dumb' (1751). Diderot notes that there is a 'spirit' flowing through the poet's words, such that

> the language used is no longer merely a succession of linked and energetic terms expressing the poet's thought with power and nobility, but also a tissue of hieroglyphics, all woven inextricably together, that make it visible. I might say that all poetry is, in this sense, emblematic.[54]

It should be noted that Diderot includes 'power' in his account, that the hieroglyphics make 'thought' visible, and that he goes on to claim that the sound of words contributes to the effect.[55] But this formulation, though laudably subtle and responsive to poetry's range, is less concise and emphatic than Burke's. The latter is more extreme in his relegation of visual ideas.

This, of course, is a very different topic from the one about the visions enjoyed by the blind seer, but it runs parallel with it in representations of the blind. It is a topic which, however, is particularly relevant to Wordsworth, who is both in thrall to the power of Milton's language and deeply influenced by associationist theories of the growth and workings of the mind. The visions which fade for the maturing poet are 'recompensed' by the 'philosophic mind' which expresses itself in reflection on the meaning of long-known and hallowed associations, and finds a supple linguistic medium capable of registering both the reflections and the associations.

The Experience of the Blind

None of this is to negate the obvious fact of the importance of vision in accounts of experience and knowledge, not least in the work of Locke, whose work is an omnipresent influence on subsequent speculations. In these accounts the blind appear as a fundamental problem and test case. The dominance of Locke means the dominance both of the sense of sight in discussions of perception, and of what is slightly different: metaphors of sight in discussions of understanding. In non-philosophical works, the idea of enhanced vision may figure the enquiry of 'the modern empiricist' as Pat Rogers puts it in his discussion of 'Gulliver's Glasses'.[56] In philosophical discussions of understanding, the use of metaphors of sight is not entirely straightforward, since it is intended to be rigorous and scientific. In his discussion of Locke, William Walsh has shown how the components of the metaphor can be further reduced to the elements of the 'mental site' as represented by an enclosed space, and a 'material body' as representing the 'mental agent': the latter is conceived as capable of being struck by the impressions of sight.[57] This is despite Locke's attempts to remove the vocabulary of impression from the psychological to the physiological arena.[58] In this we may see the germ of later developments such as Hartley's hypothesis of vibrations passing along the optic nerve into the brain. More importantly for our thesis, the idea of the enclosed mental site is consonant with the conception of the private self contemplating visual images provided by memory and imagination, a notion which is relevant to the discussion of Macpherson, the Celtic bard, spectrality and second sight. Terry Castle points out that the rationalist blurring of 'the distinction between ghost-seeing and the seemingly ordinary processes of contemplation or recollection' opened up the prospect of being ' " possessed" by the phantoms of one's own thought'.[59] But while this may have been the effect, the conditions for the later eighteenth-century literature of 'insubstantiality', as Fredric V. Bogel calls it, are already present in Locke's account of the mind.[60] This book claims that insubstantiality, and the associated melancholia which Bogel identifies, are among the reactions of writers to the progress of commerce.

It would be quite wrong, however, to place the only emphasis on insubstantiality. This subsists alongside an increasing sophistication and sensitivity in the description of things seen. There is a more straightforward side to the dominance of images and metaphors of sight. As Addison said (in the *Spectator* of 21 June 1712, No. 411):

> Our sight it the most perfect and most delightful of all our senses. It fills the mind with the largest variety of ideas, converses with its objects at the greatest distance, and continues the longest in action without being tired or satiated with its proper enjoyments [. . .] It is this sense which furnishes the imagination with its ideas; so that by the pleasures of the imagination or fancy, (which I shall use promiscuously,) I here mean such as arise from visible objects [. . .]

Such beliefs help to explain the powerful development of descriptive poetry through the eighteenth century, so that by the end of it one is offered, by Wordsworth and Coleridge for instance, something of extraordinary freshness and power. This is an aspect of what Geoffrey Thurley calls the 'Rise of Object-Dominance' in the Romantic period:

> From this time onwards, things – phenomena, objects – begin to exist in their own right and for their own sake. The poet's concern is still with meaning, we note, not with natural history. But in order to gain meaning – to be poetic – the poet now requires the thing to be itself, not the emblem of some anterior world-view [. . .].[61]

Of course, the full range of the determinants of Romantic nature poetry might be quite extensive, including domestic tourism and nationalistic landscape gardening. But as Peter de Bolla points out, such developments are inseparable from the belief that the truth of vision is worked out in visuality itself.[62] Such a belief lies behind the richness of detail in Coleridge's conversation poems, or the broad but telling sweep of Wordsworth's landscapes. It is also a concomitant of the fundamental but eloquent fact of Wordsworth's insistent language of 'sight' and 'sights'.

This brings us up against the most substantial complexity in which the blind are involved in philosophical and literary writings of the period. The blind cannot have any direct experience of vision. Those born blind, or blind from early infancy, cannot even enjoy a memory of seeing, and it is hard to describe and conceptualise the language they do in fact use about sights. So the problem is more fundamental even than the one about the blind lacking a major conduit for sympathy, and thus a major basis of moral feeling. This is an epistemological question rather than an ethical one: how do those born blind learn to function at all? These are topics which are touched on in the intense scrutiny of the experience of the blind by philosophers from Descartes onwards. The effect of Descartes's discussion, in his *Optics,* of the perambulations of a blind man with a stick, is to emphasise the role of the mind in interpreting sense-data, whether in the sighted or the blind. Certainly, no incommensurability between the senses is revealed by his discussion of the stick: 'one might almost say that they see with their hands, or that their stick is the organ of some sixth sense given to them in place of sight'.[63] On this basis, Descartes can conclude that 'it is the mind which senses, not the body [. . .]'.[64] In contrast with such rationalism, the problem of those born blind is especially urgent for empiricist philosophers such as Locke, who not only show the mature complexity of mental life as built up from early sensory experience, but in doing so have resort primarily, as we have seen, to the sense of sight. 'Molyneux's problem' was the most precise way of formulating the question, and is the source of a tradition of speculation on the senses initiated by William Molyneux (1656–98), of Trinity College, Dublin. The problem gained celebrity from its use by Locke, from the second edition (1694) of the *Essay* onwards, in his chapter 'Of Perception' (II.ix.8). The question is: Can a man born blind, if suddenly given back his sight, interpret visual experience? Molyneux's answer was, No: the blind man would have to learn to interpret visual sense-data by experience of the agreement of sight and touch. Locke was of the same opinion. The central point in this is not so much that the blind man would not at first know what he was seeing (though he would not), but that, having learnt to understand objects by touch, he will only be able to do so by sight when 'he knows how ideas from sight are related to ideas from touch'.[65] Some years later, in 1728, William Cheselden, who had been surgeon to Isaac Newton, operated on the cataracts of a boy who had been born blind, and the child's response to the sight of his surroundings appeared to confirm the conclusion of Locke and Molyneux.[66]

It was left to Berkeley to express the full implications of this conclusion in the *Essay Towards a New Theory of Vision* (1709), where he says that it is certain that 'the ideas intromitted by each sense are widely different, and distinct from each other' (*NTV,* XLVI). And in an extreme expression of the doctrine, he avers that 'the ideas which constitute the tangible earth and man, are entirely different from those which constitute the visible earth and man' (*NTV,* CII). Berkeley's intentions were different from Locke's. While Locke was happy enough to agree that the blind man could develop a complex mental life from only four senses, he wished to make the point that this life had to be built up from the material at hand, which happened to be different in the cases of the sighted and the blind. Berkeley, on the other hand, thought that Molyneux's problem revealed that there was no single object to be perceived. As Jules David Law puts it, 'Whereas Locke intends to disprove the existence of innate complex sensations, Berkeley's concern is to deny that there can be a single or unitary *object* of sensation'.[67] But whatever position one might take on this debate, the senses tended to be regarded as an almost arbitrary assortment of isolated and distinct 'windows' on the world, and this is an idea which, as we shall see, has a distinct and precise influence on Blake's thinking about the senses, and might be claimed to be a factor in the mingling of the senses in Keats or Shelley. Not that all thinkers in the Romantic period accept this separation of the senses. Hazlitt cites Locke's account of Molyneux's problem as a way of furthering his argument against the deficiencies of the empiricist tradition. He believes that the answer to Molyneux's problem is that the man who regained his sight would indeed be able to discern a conformity between the ideas of touch and those of vision:

> It appears to me that the mind must recognise a certain similarity between the impressions of different senses in this case. For instance, the sudden change or discontinuity of the sensation, produced by the sharp angles of the cube, is something common to both ideas, and if so, must afford a means of comparing them together.[68]

This conclusion is very close to that which Diderot had reached in his celebrated 'Letter on the Blind' (1749). While he admitted the difficulty of interpreting visual data at the very first moment of recovered sight, he thought that a sufficiently reflective and intelligent person, such as 'a metaphysician' would be able to recognise simple shapes on the basis of prior knowledge from touch, even though complex shapes might be more difficult.[69] His discussion of 'the blind man of Puiseaux' is reminiscent of Descartes: this blind man 'has made his arms and fingers into scales and compasses' of great accuracy.[70] It is not unlikely that Blake had read these words, but it is worth remembering that he is no true friend either to the rationalism of Descartes or to the empiricism of Locke. On that point, Blake's dissatisfaction with empiricism can be contrasted with Hazlitt's. Hazlitt thinks of himself as a philosopher of 'experience' who wishes to correct certain absurdities, as he would see them, in the empiricist account by demonstrating a process of abstraction and judgment operative in fundamental acts of perception. Blake, on the other hand, introduces a different category of cognition altogether, 'vision' or 'the Poetic Genius', but retains the separation of the senses for the fallen world.

If one needed reminding that reflection on the ideas derived from each sense need not, in this period, lead only towards scepticism, the influential treatment of the blind man in Thomas Reid's *Inquiry into the Human Mind* might instructively serve the purpose. For Reid, as for Scottish common sense philosophy in general, the most significant fact about the senses is the way that they cooperate in permitting the creature to inhabit and move around in the world. This is the reason why Reid's *Inquiry* is structured around the five senses: so that common sense can be seen as presupposed by the actions of each separate sense. Naturally, the sense of sight occupies a privileged place in this disquisition, and within the chapter devoted to it, so does the example of the blind man. The relevant section is entitled: '*Sight discovers almost nothing which the blind may not comprehend. The reason of this*'.[71] The reason is that the blind man may construct a notion of the world which is perfectly adequate for the purposes of life, and which comprehends many of the things that the sighted have learnt through the eye: 'every thing of this kind that enters into our mind by the eye, may enter into his by the ear'.[72] Indeed, so true is this, that

> a blind man might talk long about colours distinctly and pertinently: and if you were to examine him in the dark about the nature, composition, and beauty of them, he might be able to answer, so as not to betray his defect.[73]

When it comes to action in the world, despite the variation caused by changes in the light, we are able to work out the distance and position of bodies.[74] Thus, the spatial world through which we move is inferred to be the same as that which we see, and the two sensory experiences corroborate each other. For the vital thing about sensory experience is the world that can be inferred from it:

> the visible appearances of objects are intended by nature only as signs or indications and [. . .] the mind passes instantly to the things signified, without making the least reflection upon the sign, or even perceiving that there is any such thing.[75]

The Education of the Blind

The concern of the Enlightenment with education might be said to be inextricably linked with its aims – indeed, with its name. The education of the blind is a special subtopic of that concern: an engine for releasing the impoverished blind from a kind of idiocy in which they are treated as a burden on society: Mandeville's view may be characteristic of his unsentimental attitude, but it is hard to find examples of compassionate concern from his period:

> I would not encourage Beggary or Laziness in the Poor: All should be set to work that are any ways able, and Scrutinies should be made even among the infirm; Employments might be found out for most of our Lame, and many that are unfit for hard Labour, as well as the Blind [. . .].[76]

Education also had the potential to release all the blind from the dangers of that solipsism which might be encouraged by the privation of the most useful and informative of the senses.[77] But in order to found an institution capable of providing appropriate instruction on a systematic basis, a reading system for the blind would have to be invented. It is Scotland that bears the honour of harbouring the first proposal for an Enlightenment-style system of education for the blind, as can be seen from an article in the *Edinburgh Magazine* of 1744.[78] But the realisation of a plan had to wait until Paris in the 1780s. The Abbé Valentin Haüy had first been moved to ponder the assistance of the blind in 1771, contemplating the entertainment afforded by the mockery of ten blind musicians at the Café St Ovide:

> Wearing grotesque robes, dunces' caps and huge pasteboard spectacles devoid of lenses, their music sheets turned away from them, they were forced to make a living by scraping crude bows across rough stringed instruments for the amusement of the crowd.[79]

Haüy, who founded 'L'Institut national des jeunes aveugles' in 1784, also invented a reading system. This is not to say that earlier efforts had not been made, but they had been various, and those that were not *ad hoc* appear to have been primitive. Prior to this period, although there had been asylums for the blind, there is no evidence of systematic and ambitious programmes of education, so that modern historians of the subject are forced to speculate on the basis of the few remarks of earlier writers. W. H. Illingworth concludes, on the basis of such remarks, that there probably had been experiments in teaching the blind to read 'perhaps centuries before this'.[80] Thus, Haüy informs us (the translation is Blacklock's) that,

> Before our time, various, but ineffectual experiments had been tried; sometimes, by the assistance of characters moving upon a board and raised above its surface; at other times, by the use of letters formed upon paper with the puncture of a pin [. . .].[81]

They may not always have been ineffectual, for the successful use of pin-punctures by the blind Austrian pianist Maria-Theresia von Paradis probably helped to give Haüy the idea for his own method.[82] And Andrew Park, in the notes to his poem *Blindness* (1839), informs us that,

> The system of teaching the blind to read, was for a long time by the aid of a knotted cord, variously done to give the letters of the alphabet, and it was quite astonishing to see how exactly and expertly they could repeat their lessons by this mode; – but now the system is much improved through the medium of an embossed book [. . .].[83]

The embossed book is Haüy's invention. He intended 'to teach the blind reading, by the assistance of books, where the letters are rendered palpable, by their elevation above the surface of the paper'.[84] It is this system of letters in relief which, I claim, must be included in the context to Blake's relief printing method. Blake's first experiments in this are to print philosophical aphorisms with a background in philosophical speculation about the experience of the blind. His innovation is conceived in obtrusively figurative terms: 'melting apparent surfaces away, and displaying the infinite which was hid' (*The Marriage of Heaven and Hell*, 14 / E39). But there is another way in which Blake's experiment has its background in the philosophical discussion of the senses, and that is in the manner in which its results were intended to overcome the division of the senses: Blake's 'composite art', the union of word and design on the plate, is partly conceived as an overcoming of the barriers between sound and vision. This seems the more so, in that it is known that Blake had composed tunes for some of his *Songs*. Yet it would not seem necessary to overcome the division unless it were seen to have existed, and Blake's comments about the senses as 'inlets' and 'five windows' show that he is strongly influenced by the pervasive acceptance of this way of thinking about them. There is another way in which the notion was a prompt to artistic innovation, and that is in the increase in experiments with synaesthesia, of which Blake's 'London' is a good example, with its 'sigh' which is 'see[n]' running in blood down palace walls. The synaesthetic images in Shelley's poetry, for instance 'To a Skylark', have their background in his deep familiarity with philosophical speculation on the senses in the empiricist tradition. And Wordsworth's phrase about the 'mighty world / Of eye and ear' may serve not only as a succinct reminder of the way in which these two senses seem to vie with each other in his work, but also of the way in which his work can be conceived as an attempt to show that they do perceive the same world, Coleridge's 'One Life'. None of these examples is patently involved with the figure of the blind. But not only do they suggest what might constitute true perception, their being predicated on discussions in which the blind play their part becomes clearer in an adequately responsive reading of the poets' works.

The Blind and Modernity

The blind man in philosophical discussions is a problematic version of that 'punctual self' described by Charles Taylor. This figure could hardly be more different from the blind bard, who is an emphatic embodiment of the vigorous poetic faculty which was supposed to animate early societies. He represents a defunct mode of consciousness and the defunct social organisation which accompanied it. When, as in *Ossian*, the visions are of remembered past glory, he may represent nostalgia for a social system whose time has passed. Such nostalgia may or may not involve a degree of sad compromise with the progress of commerce. Certainly, the blind visionary or bard is usually contrasted with the spirit of that new world: another way of putting this would be to say that the blind bard is, in this respect, merely an extreme case of the ancient bard or primitive poet in general. But given that the blind visionary is a figure within the representations and self-representations of a period which also sees itself as having moved away from an age of poetry, the way in which he characterises an 'inner nature' is not so much by simply defining it, so much as by defining a stage in its development, both within history and the individual. And given the importance of visual experience both to the epistemology and to the poets of the period, one must always bear in mind the possibility of a degree of irony or qualification in this way of representing imagination; and that is without even taking account of the almost heavy-handed irony of Mary Shelley's depiction of the blind man in *The Last Man*. But in this case the irony is still in relation to the figure of insight and visionary power.

This schema can also be applied to the poet's need to find some sort of accommodation (not necessarily a straightforward one) with the modern world of commerce. Of course, the starting point has already been touched upon: that the world of commerce, practicality and rational enquiry has replaced one in which poetry enjoyed pre-eminence. 'Poetry and metaphysics', as Marilyn Butler puts it, 'both linked to religion, are the typical specialisms of a primitive culture'.[85] But in the development of society, according to the notions summarised by Christopher Berry in his *Social Theory of the Scottish Enlightenment*, 'language moves from obscurity to perspicuity; [. . .] figurativeness, which is suitable for poetry and oratory, gives way to the precision more suitable for philosophy and understanding'.[86] Conversely, as Adam Ferguson notes in *Civil Society*, in days when 'the bard' had the same metaphorical language as everybody else (III.viii), before '*the Separation of Arts and Professions*' (IV.i), it was common for commerce to be despised: 'It was not among the ancient Romans alone that the commercial arts, or a sordid mind, were held in

contempt. A like spirit prevails in every rude and independent society'
(II.ii). It is entirely reasonable to infer that Ferguson would include among
these the society which produced Homer: the '*blind stroling Bard*', as he
is described by Thomas Blackwell, who is an important influence on the
Scottish Enlightenment.[87] As Christopher Berry notes, Blair follows
Blackwell's principles in defending Ossian; and in the 'Early Draft' of *The
Wealth of Nations* Smith links Homer and Ossian as examples of primi-
tive poets.[88]

It is noteworthy that Blackwell, in giving an account of Homer,
emphasises, alongside metaphor, the musical properties of the speech of
early peoples, rather than the superior vividness of any visions that might
occur to the blind man.[89] Such examples serve to underscore the way in
which the blind bard might be brought in aid of reflections on the musicality of poetry, rather than represented as the possessor of inward
vision. This point leads on to an important part of the thesis of this book:
when Wordsworth or Coleridge denigrate the 'tyranny' or 'despotism' of
the eye, they avowedly do so in favour of a reflective, or indeed 'philosophic' account of experience. But what this specifically means for their
poetry is the value placed on 'association', very much including the associations of words, the associational character of language. Blake and
Keats also offer a conscious going beyond any simple conception of
poetry as ideally recording mere visual immediacy. Thomas Moore's sad
musicality can be seen in the same perspective. All of this would mean
that the notion of the blind bard is often taken in a very particular sense
in the Romantic period: that is, in line with Burke's treatise, he tends to
represent an exchange of visual immediacy for the associative and
musical power of words. This conception can be contrasted with other
ways of exploiting the topos of the blind bard: as one who has lost an
earlier vision, or as one who has made a different kind of exchange –
outer for inner vision. While these possibilities are undoubtedly alluded
to within the period, the most ambitious developments of the theme are
to do with an exchange of vision for reflection and association.

For the world had changed since the days of the ancient bard,
however one might conceive of him. There is much, of course, that
seems to support the idea of the poets' rejection of a corrupt materialist
society which had superseded the age of poetry and now threatened its
continuance. On a European stage, the most influential presentation of
the artist's predicament as a stark choice between commerce and voca-
tion is to be found in Goethe's *Wilhelm Meister*. The use made in it of
Hamlet is telling about a major significance of the melancholy and vac-
illating prince for Romantic and post-Romantic artists. More relevant
to our thesis is the song of the minstrel, 'Der Sänger', who begins his

ministrations by enjoining 'Schließt, Augen, euch; hier ist nicht Zeit, / Sich staunend zu ergetzen' ('Close yourselves, eyes; here is not the time to gaze in amazement'). Refusing the golden chain he is offered for his labour, this shut-eyed bard announces that he sings as the bird sings that lives in the branches: that is, for its own sake and not for financial reward. This song would certainly have been known to Wordsworth and Coleridge. But there is a relevance which comes from the opposite direction: Goethe, like the other German 'Romantics', was well acquainted with English literature, and the song can be seen as in part the fruit of that acquaintance. Many years later, quotations from both Shakespeare and Goethe were to buttress some of Marx's most trenchant reflections on money and commodity in *Capital*, as for instance in the reference in vol. 1, ch. 3, to Timon on 'the yellow slave' of gold.

Turning to Britain, Blake's remark that art cannot be carried on where any view of commerce exists appears to be fairly unambiguous. Wordsworth felt the hollowness of the doctrines associated with the 'wealth of nations' (*Prelude* XII: 79), and his distrust of the commercial spirit is taken as something of a critical given.[90] Coleridge worried in the *Lay Sermons* about the 'overbalance of commercial interests' in society. And it has often been mooted that Keats offers the riches of poetry as an alternative to those offered by commerce, his attitude to which is suggested by his handling of the brothers in *Isabella*. It seems fairly easy to deduce the opinions of Byron and Shelley.

But the story is not quite that simple. It is some years since I pointed out that, although Blake appeared to regret the dominance of the philosophy of the five senses, the fact that he conceded that they were 'the chief inlets of soul in this age' meant that he attributed some positive effect to that philosophy.[91] In Blake's fallen world, the choice is between no vision at all and a vision which is, to some degree, vitiated. Nor is this merely a point about epistemology, for Blake's critique of 'the cavern'd man', confined to seeing through narrow chinks in his cavern, is a political one; and his remarks about 'the selfish loves' indicate his perception of the contemporary links between theory of knowledge, ethics and political economy. More recently, Philip Connell has questioned the tendency to assume that writers such as Wordsworth and Shelley felt 'unambiguous hostility to industrial society and its apologists', and has explored 'the far more compromised and accommodating aspects of their relationships with political economy, utilitarianism, and the "spirit of commerce " '.[92] In particular, he notes for instance the complexity of Wordsworth's response to Malthus, which involved little sympathy with the latter's moral and theological grounds, but had more in common with his views of politics and society: prizing, for instance, a spirit of 'independence' among the lower classes.[93] Similar considerations apply to Keats and 'the Cockney School'.[94] It is many years now since Christopher Caudwell advanced his classic Marxist thesis about the way in which '[t]he Keatsian vocabulary is full of words with a hard material texture' in order to vie with the world of commerce by offering an alternative which mimics the strength of that world.[95] Certainly, the language of riches within the poems offers some support to this view. One does not have to believe that this was somehow dishonest or a species of trickery, nor that Keats's radicalism was somehow disingenuous. On the contrary, in so far as there is ambivalence in Keats, it is an ambivalence which questions an empty materialism even while it seeks to explore the possibility of a philosophical materialism of a mature, reflective and aesthetically aware character. In the process, it concedes the persuasive force of the luxury bred by commerce, and is constrained to register the sensibility of the age. There is, of course, a way of putting this which sounds like political suspicionism: Colin Campbell's way of putting it, for instance, in his article on 'Romanticism and the Consumer Ethic'. Speaking of the new Romantic doctrines of the self, he asserts that 'although devised as part of an overall attempt to combat or at least radically reform the newly-emerging industrial society' they actually served 'to facilitate consumerism' by 'providing the necessary cultural material for new motivational and legitimational structures and hence a new character type and associated social and cultural forms'.[96] We have already seen that there is some sense in such a view, at least in relation to Keats. However, it is only necessary to incorporate the recognition of all the other things that 'Romanticism' might be claimed to have introduced, not least by means of Keats's own work, to see how reductionist such statements must be when left unqualified.

The case of Keats is indeed instructive, and that instructiveness can in part be measured by the treatment he has received at the hands of scholars in recent years. Marjorie Levinson's ingenious work of 'deconstructive materialism', *Keats's Life of Allegory,* is a continuation of the Marxist tradition of finding Keats's work to be structured and textured by the socially aspiring ideology of the bourgeois. Nicholas Roe's *John Keats and the Culture of Dissent,* on the other hand, is the first work to offer truly rigorous and thorough-going support for the idea that Keats's poetry comprises thoughtful but unmistakable advocacy of radical political dissent. Some readers have felt that here they have a choice of opposed views. But it is probably anachronistic to think of the dissent which could attract the support of John Keats in any terms except those of an apparent contradiction – a contradiction, that is, which is more an appearance created by our own subsequent knowledge than by anything in the early nineteenth century. The age of the bourgeois revolution offers models of what is radical that can comprise at the same time the espousal of political reform and an admiration for a material luxury which should be at the command of humanity, rather than the few. This dual aspect can be discerned in Keats's poetry, and furthermore is subject to the qualification entered earlier: namely, that Keats, at least in his mature work, promotes a thoughtful and not a merely indulgent materialism, and that he is sagacious enough also to register a sense of loss, as in *The Fall of Hyperion,* a sense that there are visionary possibilities that are not available to his own age.

There is a combined effect of the poetics of verbal association and the compromise with the world of commerce: namely, that it is the reflective power of the former which enables the latter. One version of blindness with which we will often have to do in this book has not only lost an earlier intensity of vision in exchange for a wise melancholy musicality, but also possesses a wisdom which is substantially involved with that compromise. Philosophical systems which illuminate the development of modern society are themselves recognised as a product of the very modernity they seek to explain: it would not have been possible for an age of bardic poetry to develop them. And equally, those systems are not a product of the unreflective experience of the immature or merely passional self. The solitary or 'punctual' self is at the heart of the conception of the self. This is true whatever the way out of its solitude: there is the Lockeian version, whereby we learn to relate to others by a sympathetic identification in which the fundamental term is the isolated self. This is the system to which Blake refers as 'the selfish loves'. On the other hand, there is also the version of which the most influential exponent is Shaftesbury (Anthony Ashley Cooper), whereby benevolence is innate. But Shaftesbury's philosophy should not be seen as antithetical to Locke's, so much as a variant within a field where the fundamental term is the individual self. This is the aspect of his philosophy which can be related to his Whiggism: as Lawrence B. Klein puts it, 'articulating for Whiggism a cultural ideology, a politics of manners and culture' by establishing a 'positive connection between liberty and intellectual and cultural achievement'.[97] In *Characteristics,* Shaftesbury has Theocles say 'you will allow this "you" and "me" to be each of us simply and individually one better than you can allow the same to anything of mere matter'; but he does not say this ironically, nor in order to attribute a self to matter as well, but rather to establish that Nature should be allowed a 'self' on the same grounds that human individuals are. There is intelligence, purpose and a uniting principle: 'how are you then a self and nature not so?'[98] This example constitutes the largest scale – from individual to cosmos – of the Whiggish relationship described by Klein in terms of individual and culture. The benevolism essential to Shaftesbury's system was perfectly capable of subsisting with a sceptical and empiricist analysis of the acquisition of knowledge, as it did in that of his admirer, Hume. Something very like it was also capable of subsisting with a system whereby public benefits accrued from self-interested behaviour. For while Adam Smith is often understandably credited with systematising Mandeville, nevertheless he strongly believed in the power and pervasiveness of 'sympathy', to the extent that he rejected Locke's contractarianism.[99]

All this is by way of suggesting that the punctual self may have many variants. And this is without even admitting the extent to which the world-view of a period, in general, cannot be equated with any one philosophical doctrine nor accorded the systematic and precise character that the claims of a particular philosopher may possess. In accordance with this point, it is probably mistaken to set up a sharp disjunction, such as Charles Taylor proposes, between the view deriving from Locke and that deriving from Shaftesbury, such that Shaftesbury is seen as the fountainhead of 'the developing conception of nature as an inner source'.[100] According to Taylor, '[w]ith Rousseau and the Romantics [this difference] flares up into one of the deepest oppositions of our culture'.[101] There is much that lends weight to such a view; but when one considers the importance of Locke, Berkeley, Hartley and Hume to the intellectual context of Romanticism one is bound to concede that, in Romantic writing, it is not possible to consider questions about sympathy, benevolence, sense experience as influenced only by the moral sense school or as firmly aligned with a simple model whereby expressivism, inner nature and external nature all echo each other and stand at every point opposed to an analytic or sceptical view of the self or experience.

In agreement with this qualification, G. S. Rousseau is able to trace the early origins of Romanticism to Locke's emphasis on sensation. The memorable conclusion to his argument is worth quoting:

> Slowly but surely, it becomes painfully clear that Richardson, Sterne, Diderot, Rousseau, Mackenzie, and even the Marquis de Sade were the posterity of two generations of thinkers who had increasingly 'internalised' – and that is the important word – the new science of man, directing thought about man from his visible eyes and expressive face to his unseen nerves and controlling brain, from what he looks like to what he feels, and from what he feels to what he thinks.[102]

Thus, while it is true that the eighteenth century sees, as Paul Hamilton puts it, a 'competition between the visual metaphor of the empiricist epistemology and emergent alternatives', and true also that a major alternative is the Scottish common-sense school, with its emphasis on the activity of mind, in practice there is more similarity between the effects the two schools may bring about than their starting points might suggest.[103]

The solitary self of the later eighteenth century looks back to a primitive era of poetic immediacy and vision, but can no more recover the immediacy and the vision than it can return to that era. The theories which explain why that era is lost are themselves developed as part of an intellectual labour which cannot be the instantaneous possession of the isolated, experiencing subject. Philosophy, and the theories of political economy which are developed alongside it, represent another form of blindness: Adam Smith's 'invisible hand' can only be apprehended at the completion of that intellectual labour. Political economy, and the wider concerns of philosophy and science, are to work at revealing the 'hidden chains of events which bind together the seemingly disjointed appearances of nature'.[104] To return to the point at which we began, this book is very far from claiming that the blind in Romantic-period writing are typically visionaries. Rather, their very significance for the period lies in the fact that usually they are not. They provide striking figures not just for the isolated self, but for the exploration of a whole range of its problems: the possibility of sympathy, of ethics, of philosophical conviction, even of faith. The exploration may touch on any or all of these things, or indeed on the memory of vision lost. Sometimes, as in the work of Mary Shelley, the blind may represent failure across the whole range. But the blind, in providing a special, problematic case of the individual consciousness, naturally mirror the complexity of contemporary accounts of that consciousness in general, and so far from providing examples of visionary or lyrical power, are indexes of an acute historical self-consciousness. As James Chandler says, he considers, in *England in 1819*,

> figures of the sensible heart, the psyche, soul, spirit of the age, future state, national character, and the winds of historical change. In none of these instances, however, does the figure in question stand for an identification of that which is merely an affair of 'consciousness', the immaterial internality of a material externality.[105]

I agree, but would go further: the Romantic period, so far from being the location of a dehistoricising lyricism, cannot even conceive the lyrical impulse in a non-historical form. In so far as they have taken another view, contemporary scholars and critics have acquiesced in the aestheticising limitations imposed on the definition of Romantic-period writing in the nineteenth century, and accepted and attacked by modernist critics with ulterior motives.

Notes

1. Paulson (1987), p. 14.
2. See, for instance, Trumpener (1997), p. 96.
3. Panofsky (1972), p. 109.
4. Wind (1967), p. 58.
5. Maxwell (2001), p. 13.
6. Barasch (2001), p. 3.
7. Homer is the 'blind Bard' in Robert Baron's 'The Authors Motto', ll. 106–13 (*Pocula Castalia* (1650)); and in Nahum Tate's 1689 translation of Abraham Cowley's 'Flora', ll. 1–4 (Section IV of his *Of Plants*).
8. Dodsley (1741), p. 19.
9. Wu (ed.) (1997), p. 319, ll. 4–5.
10. McGann (1996), pp. 198–9.
11. Wu (ed.) (1997), pp. 276–9.
12. Ibid., p. 276.
13. McGann (1996), p. 201.
14. Wu (ed.) (1997), pp. 273–4, 298.
15. Ibid., p. 272.
16. Ibid.
17. McGann (1996), p. 204.
18. Ibid.
19. Taylor (1989). E.g. 'a turn to the self as a self', p. 176.
20. Ferry (1962), pp. 183–200, esp. p. 188.
21. Ibid.
22. Trott (1994), pp. 114–35.
23. For a very intelligent and sensitive reading of this poem, see Fairer (2005), pp. 292–309, esp. pp. 306–7.
24. Maxwell (2001), p. 22.
25. Ibid., p. 24.
26. Ende (1976), p. 1.
27. Ferry (1962), p. 197.
28. Batten (1998).
29. Ashfield (ed.) (1997), pp. xiii–xiv.
30. Ibid., p. 34.
31. [Kenney] (1808), pp. 1, 8, 30.
32. Lamb (1895), p. 105.
33. Wu (1997), p. 277, l. 61.
34. Spence (1754), p. 4.
35. Ibid., p. 28.
36. Ibid., p. 35.
37. Ibid., p. 37
38. David Hume, Letter to Joseph Spence, 15 October 1754, in Hume (1932), I, p. 202.
39. Ibid.
40. Rée (1999), p. 40.
41. Spence (1754), pp. 9–25, esp. p. 21.
42. Blacklock (1793), pp. iii–xxxii.
43. Riskin (2002), pp. 21–2, 53–4, 59–61.

44. Blacklock (1793), p. xii.
45. [Thomas Blacklock], 'The Blind', in *Encyclopaedia Britannica* (1778–83), II (1778), pp. 1188–1204, esp. p. 1200.
46. Seward (1806).
47. Blacklock (1793), p. xvi.
48. Burke (1759), p. 324.
49. Ibid., pp. 324, 325.
50. Ibid., p. 326.
51. Ibid., p. 328.
52. Ibid., p. 332.
53. Ibid., p. 336.
54. Diderot (1966), p. 36.
55. Ibid., p. 37.
56. Rogers (1985), pp. 1–10, esp. p. 9.
57. Walsh (1994), p. 93.
58. Ibid., p. 94.
59. Castle (1995), pp. 181, 175.
60. Bogel (1984).
61. Thurley (1983), p. 56.
62. Bolla (1994), pp. 89–111, esp. p. 90.
63. Descartes (1965), p. 67.
64. Ibid., p. 87.
65. Walsh (1994), p. 86. See Locke (1894), I, pp. 185–8.
66. Riskin (2002), p. 19.
67. Law (1993), p. 26.
68. Hazlitt (1930–4), II, p. 184.
69. Diderot (1966), pp. 14–30, esp. pp. 28–30.
70. Ibid., p. 15.
71. Reid (1997), p. 78.
72. Ibid., p. 80.
73. Ibid.
74. Ibid., p. 81.
75. Ibid.
76. Mandeville (1924), p. 267.
77. Riskin (2002), p. 64.
78. Farrell (1956), p. 30
79. Bates (1998), pp. 123–4.
80. Illingworth (1910), p. 4.
81. Valentin Haüy, 'An Essay on the Education of the Blind', in Blacklock (1793), pp. 217–62, esp. p. 229.
82. Farrell (1956), p. 22.
83. Andrew Park (1839), pp. 154–5n.
84. Haüy, 'An Essay', in Blacklock (1793), p. 226.
85. Butler (1985), p. 72.
86. Berry (1997), p. 180.
87. Blackwell (1735), p. 38.
88. Berry (1997), p. 179.
89. Blackwell (1735), p. 38.
90. E.g., Turner (1986), pp. 190–2.

  91. Larrissy (1985).
  92. Connell (2002), p. vii.
  93. Ibid., pp. 16–29.
  94. Ibid., pp. 188–90.
  95. Caudwell (1946), p. 95.
  96. Campbell (1983), pp. 279–95, esp. p. 292.
  97. Cooper (1999), p. xvii.
  98. Ibid., pp. 301, 303.
  99. See Winch (1996), pp. 105, 146–7.
 100. Taylor (1989), p. 265.
 101. Ibid.
 102. Rousseau (1991), p. 136.
 103. Hamilton (1983), pp. 35–6.
 104. Smith (1980), p. 1.
 105. Chandler (1998), p. 554.

Chapter 2

The Celtic Bard in Ireland and Britain: Blindness and Second Sight

Physical blindness and 'second sight' could, from the early eighteenth century, be associated with the Celtic bard and thus become markers, in polite literature, of a prophetic or poetic vision supposedly common in Celtic countries. Ossian, of course, was blind – like Homer, as it is customary to note – and was clearly possessed of 'second sight'. So that, given the ascendancy Macpherson's imitations exerted over the thoughts and ambitions of the poets and poetasters of two continents, one might ask if it is really necessary to do more than lay the association at his door. Yet, as we shall see, the association precedes the appearance of Ossian, and even subsequently is not bounded by reference to Ossian. When they occur in Romantic writing, the topics of blindness and second sight are closely linked with the development and the definition of the central Romantic ideology of poetic vision, so it is surely worthwhile to be clear and discriminating when assigning sources to their characteristic imagery.

The Blind Harper in Ireland and Scotland

Richard Stanihurst (1547–1618), one of the 'old English' in Ireland, had first introduced the notion of the blind harper to non-Irish readers in his *De Rebus in Hibernia Gestis* ('On the History of Ireland', 1584). As Edward MacLysaght points out, this was accepted as one of 'the standard books on Ireland for nearly two hundred years'.[1] Describing the customs of the Gaelic nobility, Stanihurst observed that, 'During supper there is present a harpist, often blind, who relaxes the reclining guests by striking his strings [. . .]'.[2] So accustomed were the Irish to encountering what they saw as English prejudice and calumny, that Seathrún Céitinn (Geoffrey or Jeoffrey Keating, D.D., *c.*1570–*c.*1650) felt it necessary, in his Irish-language history of Ireland (*Foras Feasa Ar Éirinn*,

'An Introduction to the History of Ireland', *c*.1640) to interpret Stanihurst's claim as one of many examples of slander procured by English bribes or pressure:

> Ní fíor dó, mar an gceudna, an nídh adeir gurab dall do bhídís urmhór aosa seanma na hÉireann; óir is follus an tan ro scríobh seisean a stáir, gurab lia neach súileach do bhí re seinm i n-Éirinn ioná duine dall, agus mar sin ó sin i leith, agus anois, bíodh a fhiadhnaise sin ar ár lucht comhaimsise.[3]

A remarkably free English rendering became available in 1723 in the handsome and heavily subscribed translation by Dermod O'Connor. He has Keating's words refer to

> . . . the Musicians of *Ireland*, whom [Stanihurst] calls a Set of *blind Harpers*; whereas if he had inquired at the time when he wrote his romantick History, he would have found, that for one Musician that was blind, there were twenty who had their perfect Sight, and could see clearly into the Malice of his rotten Heart, when he undertook to vilify and traduce the *Irish*, and represent them in the blackest Colours to Posterity.[4]

It is worth noting how easily the topic becomes involved with tropes for insight and dullness: in this case, by uncovering the supposed implications of the imputed slander, and reversing them by inverting their content.

There is plenty of evidence of the harper being blind, however, and it seems that Stanihurst's was simply an observation of fact, with which Lecky's monumental history would concur: '[B]lindness was unusually common, and innumerable blind fiddlers traversed the land, and found a welcome at every fireside'.[5] The remarks refer to fiddlers; and these, indeed, were common enough for the once-admired Scottish narrative painter Sir David Wilkie to take one of them as the subject of a characteristic picture of village life, *The Blind Fiddler* (1807), which became one of his most popular paintings.[6] But, as will be seen, the evidence is overwhelming that blindness was common among harpers and pipers, too. Furthermore, it is clear that the same tradition of training blind boys to be musicians prevailed in the Scottish Highlands. Compelling evidence that this tradition was shared by Scotland and Ireland is provided by John Gunn's *Historical Enquiry Respecting the Performance of the Harp in the Highlands of Scotland* (1807). Referring to the combination of the roles of Bard and Harper (a very important point) Gunn recalls the most famous of the blind Scottish harpers, Roderick (i.e., Ruarie) Morison: 'The offices of Bard and Harper were filled by Roderick Morison, who, being blind, was called *Ruarie Dall* . . .'.[7] In the seventeenth century, to which Gunn is referring, it is clear that the ancient association of Ireland and the Scottish Highlands not only continued, but did so along well-established lines – the exchange of harpers and, for that matter, harps, being a venerable institution. Thus, Gunn notes the visit of 'the celebrated [Irish] performer O'Kane' to Skye; he adds that, 'although blind', O'Kane could play the harp 'with great accuracy and fine effect'.[8] The list of blind Scottish musicians is impressive, and apart from Morison includes: 'John Mackay, usually called "Am Piobaire dall", the Blind Piper'; William Ross's grandfather, 'another celebrated bard, known as the blind piper'; Artúr Dall Mac Gurcaigh; and possibly Giolla Pádraig Mac Lachlainn.[9] These names were part of folk tradition in Scotland as late as the 1860s.

The best-known of the blind Irish harpers, Turlough O'Carolan (1670–1737), enjoyed some contemporary celebrity in polite English and Irish society; and in terms of the recognition accorded to Celtic bards, he occupies a place second only to that of 'Ossian' himself. Although it is a considerably less prominent place, it was one that enjoyed some European fame, since Beethoven counted himself an admirer. Maria Edgeworth and Sydney Owenson were interested in the work of Carolan, and both the interest and its sources have been clearly documented by W. J. McCormack in an appendix to the edition of *The Absentee* which he co-edited with Kim Walker.[10] This appendix also serves to remind the reader how early it was possible to encounter Carolan's work in an English library, selected in *A Collection of the Most Celebrated Irish Tunes Proper for the Violin, German Flute or Hautboy* (Dublin, 1724) – early enough, as McCormack notes, for Goldsmith to have brought it to the attention of English readers.[11] He first appears in his own right in John Lee's collection of 1780.[12] But in my opinion the most significant appearance is that which he makes in Charlotte Brooke's *Reliques of Ancient Irish Poetry* (1789).[13] More than occasional awareness of Brooke's work persisted for at least thirty years, for a 1787 account of Carolan, who is quoted in her translations, is reprinted in *The Gentleman's Magazine* for 1814.[14] In the anonymous *Anecdotes of the Deaf, Dumb, and Blind* (*c*.1800), it is remarked that 'of modern blind poets none has excelled Carolan, the celebrated Irish musician and lyrical writer'.[15] *Reliques*, which offers translations of Carolan's words without musical scores, shows a marked concentration upon him and Oisin. It is generally recognised as obvious that Brooke's title alludes to Bishop Percy's compendium, and is thus seeking to gain for the Irish tradition an equivalently romantic aura.[16] Furthermore, it has been rightly said that, 'Shades of *Ossian* crowd thickly around the *Reliques,* in atmosphere and tone but especially in diction [. . .]'.[17] From this it is clear that Brooke's *Reliques*, in a manoeuvre parallel to that in which she involves Percy, is soliciting an even more romantic comparison, and one that may benefit from the authority of a shared Gaelic inheritance. But an equally obvious point has been overlooked: the choice of poems which actually include Oisin (as opposed merely to being Ossianic in manner) is itself part of this manoeuvre. Oisin and Carolan loom large in the collection, poets as well as harpers, blind bards of Ireland.

Second Sight

The belief in 'second sight' – the ability to see visions, often premonitory, often of the dead, sometimes of spirits or 'fairies' or of a *Doppelgänger* – was part of the common inheritance of Ireland and Scotland, although similar phenomena are to be found elsewhere. Today, the best-known literary exploitation of this belief is probably to be found in Synge's *Riders to the Sea*; it is also taken for granted in Yeats's folklore writings.[18] Nevertheless, the traditions appear to have been more developed in Scotland than in Ireland.[19] But readers would once have thought first of Smollett's *Humphrey Clinker* (1771), the letters of 12 and 15 September, where the comic treatment refers to a Scottish context. In that context, second sight undoubtedly has the potential to be exploited for its Gothic potential, as it is in the case of Blind Alice in *The Bride of Lammermoor*. The capacity to see a *Doppelgänger* or *co-choisiche* (Scottish Gaelic: literally 'co-walker') is evoked in sinister form by *Confessions of a Justified Sinner*.[20] Of course, the claim of second sight may seem like a more mundane form of trickery, or at least self-delusion, as is hinted in Scott's *The Legend of Montrose* in relation to Ranald MacEagh. Or it may seem like something to be employed in serious manipulation, as in Schiller's *The Ghost-Seer*.

One of its earliest appearances in English literature relates to Scotland, and is to be found in William Collins's 'Ode on the Popular Superstitions of the Scottish Highlands' – not in strophe 3, where we encounter the oddly-named 'Runic bards/With uncouth lyres', but in strophe 4. The text that follows is incomplete in line 3, because there is no genuine complete version, and Roger Lonsdale's Longman edition uses the only authoritative text, which is a manuscript (composed 1749–50):

> 'Tis thine to sing how, framing hideous spells,
> In Skye's lone isle the gifted wizard seer,
> Lodged in the wintry cave with
> Or in the depth of Uist's dark forests dwells;
> How they, whose sight such dreary dreams engross,

> With their own visions oft astonished droop,
> When o'er the watery strath or quaggy moss
>   They see the gliding ghosts unbodied troop.
> [. . .]
> For them the viewless forms of air obey [. . .][21]

This manuscript version was first transferred to print in March 1788, in the first volume of *Transactions of the Royal Society of Edinburgh*. A suspect version, which claimed to be Collins's complete text, appeared in May 1788, published in London by J. Bell.[22] Although it appears to be a fraud, and probably committed for the same reasons that motivated other frauds perpetrated in the period, it was widely accepted as genuine. Its version of the missing fifth strophe is, at least, indicative of the sort of subject a forger might think marketable and in vogue. It refers to 'The Seer, in *Sky*', and to seers in the plural who are capable of foreseeing the bloody battles, including 'red *Culloden*', that would decide Scotland's fate. This historical prescience is clearly modelled on Gray's 'The Bard'. Instructively, the connection proves what seems plausible in any case: namely, that readers and writers were capable of confusing the seer with the bard. Collins himself had put the Runic bard and the Seer next to each other; Gray's bard corresponds with, and helps to consolidate, one of the great icons of his period and the ensuing one, an obvious source for Blake and Coleridge:[23]

> With haggard eyes the poet stood;
> (Loose his beard and hoary hair
> Streamed like a meteor to the troubled air)
> And, with a master's hand and prophet's fire,
> Struck the deep sorrows of his lyre.

The poem puts a fair degree of effort into implying that the eyes of the poet are haggard (that is, wild) because of what he can see with them; and what he sees is not present to the physical eye, but to the eye of the visionary. In this respect, the bard really is akin to the Scottish seer. It is highly relevant, then, to recall that Gray only achieved the determination to complete the poem after a visit to Cambridge by the blind Welsh harper, John Parry: 'Mr Parry has been here, & scratch'd out such ravishing blind Harmony, such tunes of a thousand year old with names enough to choak you, as have set all this learned body a'dancing [. . .]'.[24]

Gray's bard exhibits a characteristic often found in Scottish accounts of 'second sight' and in *Ossian*: he has a vision of the dead, the ghosts of ancient poet-princes of Wales ('I see them sit', l. 45). It cannot be ruled out that Gray was aware of some of Collins's sources. In any case, the best-known of these was Martin Martin's *A Description of the Western*

Islands of Scotland (1703), where he provides a passage headed, '*An Account of the* Second Sight, *in Irish call'd* Taish'. It begins thus:

> The *Second Sight* is a singular Faculty of Seeing, an otherwise invisible Object, without any previous Means us'd by the Person that sees it for that end; the Vision makes such a lively impression upon the Seers, that they neither see nor think of any thing else, except the Vision, as long as it continues: [. . .][25]

The seer, then, was, figuratively speaking, blind, and might be confused with the bard. Readers have naturally tended to assume that Ossian's blindness was indeed an appropriate indicator of his poetic vision – of his possession of the *oculus imaginationis*. They have been right to do so. And not only can Ossian see with his inward eye, but he tends also to see visions of the dead, a true indication of 'second sight'. Thus, in 'Conlath and Cuthóna: A Poem', Ossian wishes that he could see the ghost of Conlath, but then, invoking memory, he is able to perceive his former friends:

> And Ossian does behold his friends, on the dark-blue isle. – The cave of Thona appears, with its mossy rocks and bending trees. A stream roars at its mouth, and Toscar bends over its course. Fercuth is sad by his side: and the maid of his love sits at a distance, and weeps. Does the wind of the waves deceive me? Or do I hear them speak?[26]

Romantic poets might exploit the chill, uncanny potential of this capacity: uncanny in the sense that the second-sighted are aware of two scenes, one superimposed upon another, the dead on the living. Felicia Hemans elicits both the uncanniness of the idea and its sentimental corollaries in her poem, 'Second Sight':

> A mournful gift is mine, O friends!
>   A mournful gift is mine!
> A murmur of the soul which blends
>   With the flow of song and wine.
> An eye that through the triumph's hour
>   Beholds the coming woe,
> And dwells upon the faded flower
>   Midst the rich summer's glow.[27]

The eye so gifted can see through the comforting and lively phenomena of that domesticity Hemans valued so highly:

> Ye smile to view fair faces bloom
>   Where the father's board is spread;
> I see the stillness and the gloom
>   Of a home whence all are fled.[28]

Although they are of a later date (1830) and are more explicit in their relation to old superstition, these lines have the capacity to emphasise

Wordsworth's indebtedness to the tradition of second sight in *The Ruined Cottage,* where his Scottish Pedlar remarks,

> I see around me here
> Things which you cannot see. We die, my friend,
> Nor we alone, but that which each man loved
> And prized in his peculiar nook of earth
> Dies with him [. . .].
>
> (ll. 67–71)

Hemans proceeds to generalise this gift of the 'prophet-heart' as the possession of 'all deep souls'. For these, the eye, though not entirely blind to the present scene, sees more clearly what lies behind it:

> Their sight is all too sadly clear –
>   For them a veil is riven;
> Their piercing thoughts repose not here,
>   Their home is but in heaven.[29]

There is an almost Poe-like ambiguity about this 'heaven'. Is it better conceived as the inspiration of prophecy, or the abode of the dead?

The dead often gathered in group, as in the *Ossian* passage. This is part of the contemporary understanding of the nature of 'second sight'. It will be recalled that Collins referred to an 'unbodied troop'. In Martin, some seers 'find themselves as it were in a crowd of People, having a Corpse which they carry along with them'.[30] In Thomas Pennant's *A Tour in Scotland,*

> A poor visionary, who had been working in his cabbage-garden, imagined that he was raised suddenly into the air, and conveyed over a wall into an adjacent corn-field; that he found himself surrounded by a crowd of men and women, many of whom he knew to have been dead some years [. . .][31]

Hemans imparts an interesting twist to the 'host of the dead' topos by uniting it with another tradition of the seer, that of the bard as imaginative visionary. In a note preceding 'The Rock of Cader Idris', from *Welsh Melodies* (1822) she explains that

> It is an old tradition of the Welsh bards that, on the summit of the mountain Cader Idris, is an excavation resembling a couch, and that whoever should pass a night in that hollow would be found in the morning either dead, in a state of frenzy, or endowed with the highest poetical inspiration.[32]

That final idea alerts the reader to the bardic connection; and amid the darkness the speaker of the poem sees, in Romantic bardic fashion, 'the powers of the wind and the ocean'. But she also sees the dead: 'The dead were around me that night on the hill: / From their eyes, as they passed, a cold radiance they darted – / There was light on my soul but my heart's blood was chill.' If anything, the presence of that 'chill' underlines the strange collocation of the Gothic and the transcendent. We have been prepared for it by the fact that the poem gives us the larger terms which cover all the phenomena seen that night: 'I viewed the dread beings around us that hover, / Though veiled by the mists of mortality's breath, [. . .]'. These dread beings beyond the veil are, in fact, both the powers of nature and the hosts of the dead. Thus, although it may seem surprising that, when dawn breaks, the speaker finds that 'new glory all nature invested', it is actually part of the strange logic of the poem.

Hemans's language of 'piercing the veil', which was to become part of the diction of the Victorian Gothic, is also worth noting. It derives from the wider notion of crossing a boundary between one state an another, and in this form the trope is developed by Wordsworth. His friend Scott offers an example which, although it is quite late, is instructive both about the Celtic and about the trope of 'borders'.

Blind Alice, in *The Bride of Lammermoor* (1819), enjoys the expected enhancement of hearing:

> My hearing, my child, has been sharpened by my blindness, and I can now draw conclusions from the slightest sounds, which formerly reached my ears as unheeded as they now approach yours. Necessity is a stern, but an excellent schoolmistress, and she that has lost her sight must collect her information from other sources.[33]

This last remark, however, coyly hints at stranger sources of information than sensory ones. For a start, we already suspect that Alice has prophetic powers: her conviction about the tragic vindication of ancient prophecies is proved to be based on a far-sightedness much superior to a belief in old wives' tales (201). In an interesting twist, it seems that the Master of Ravenswood himself appears to suffer from the chill affliction of second sight, as it were by transference from Alice. At the moment of death she had wished to warn him, because of her own well-founded premonitions; but

> [s]he died just as the clock in the distant village tolled one; and Ravenswood remembered, with internal shuddering, that he had heard the chime sound through the wood just before he had seen what he was now much disposed to consider as the spectre of the deceased. (247–8)

Readers would not be at all surprised to find Scotland's pre-eminent author writing about second sight. The fact is, though, that Blind Alice is English. Yet it makes good figurative sense that she should be. The region in which the novel's events are set is near the Scottish border, for Ravenswood Castle is situated between Dunbar and Berwick-upon-Tweed (26), the latter in England. If second sight and the gift of prophecy are granted to those who can cross borders, it makes sense that, in this border region of a largely Celtic country, the seer should be 'from the other side'. This example, while it post-dates Wordsworth's earliest development of the trope in *The Borderers,* is clear corroboration of the figurative significance that the border could assume.

A like figuration is to be found in 'Wandering Willie's Tale' in *Redgauntlet* (1824)[34], which is even more clearly aligned with the Gothic than is the tale of Blind Alice. Wandering Willie is a blind fiddler and tale-teller. He recalls the Gaelic minstrel, 'Rory Dall' (98; blind Rory) as if to associate himself with the tradition of blind minstrels, while Scott in a footnote reminds us of the accomplishments of Blind Jack of Knaresborough, often cited, as we shall see in Chapter 4 below, as an example of the ease with which the blind may overcome their disability (406). Thus is Wandering Willie's status as the blind man, both acute and inspired, briefly suggested to us.

He is also a borderer: he inhabits the border near Cumberland: 'I am of every country in broad Scotland, and a wee bit of England to the boot. But yet I am, in some sense, of this country; for I was born within hearing of the roar of Solway' (95). And the tale involves the transgression of the border between this world and the other. Willie's grandfather, Steenie Steenson, has delivered his rent to the old Jacobite landlord, Sir Robert Redgauntlet (no Puritan he), but it was mislaid in the chaos when the latter had a fit and died, and Steenie left without a receipt. The new laird will not take his word for it, but at night a ghostly rider promises to take Steenie where he can find proof of his payment. This turns out to be a great house in every way like Redgauntlet Castle, except that Steenie knows that it is ten miles from there, in the thickest part of the wood. Here he sees Sir Robert with his old friends, all of whom should be dead, as well as 'the savage Highland Amorites' (112), carousing as merrily as they did in life. Steenie manages to extract a receipt on the promise that he will return to the castle in a twelvemonth to pay homage for his protection, thereby no doubt sealing his fate as one bound by contract to the powers of hell. When Steenie returns to this world, he offers the receipt, which is dated the day before. Sir John opines that he must have obtained it in hell and promises to denounce him as a warlock; but Steenie says he will go to the Presbytery to have his experiences explained, and the threat to his father's reputation persuades Sir John to accept the receipt.

It is fitting that Wandering Willie should tell a tale that contains an example of second sight. The tale itself presents a Jacobitism roundly identified with the feudal in terms of Satanic imagery, and converts the romance of Faery (a castle full of good things in the forest) into the ghastly vision of a *danse macabre*. In this way, Scott marries Scottish subject-matter to the mainstream Gothic presentation of feudalism as bloody, tyrannous and haunted by a violent history. The tale is also confirmation that Scotland's future lies with modernity. Ingenuity may impose fair dealing on the oppressive laird, and in any case, he belongs to an age of superstition. A vision such as this is appropriate to a minstrel who inhabits the border between Scotland and England: the nation that harbours feudal longings and fairy tales, and the nation that has ensured that these things are of the past.

But there is no reason to tie literary references to second sight to some restrictive definition which would have to include visions of crowds. Although it was sometimes conscious of one or more of the phenomena described above, the polite world accepted a bold and sketchy picture of visionary and prophetic second sight which overlapped with the image of the bard, and in this it was to a certain limited extent in sympathy with its sources, or at least with Martin, who was arguably the most important of them. John MacInnes points out that in parts of Scotland the phenomenon of second sight could embrace 'both precognition and telecognition', and that Martin's discussion of the Isle of Skye shows that there it was not even as restricted as that in the seventeenth century.[35] One of the most interesting characteristics of Scottish second sight in the Jacobite period was that it could encompass political prophecy. MacInnes summarises the situation thus:

> Tómas Reumair, as he is known in Gaelic [i.e.,Thomas the Rhymer], has a unique status as prophet of the messianic hope of the Gaels: one day we will regain our rightful place in Scotland. By the mid-seventeenth century it was already well known, judging from allusions to it in Gaelic poetry; in the songs of the Jacobite campaign of 1715 it had a prominent place: one of them begins with the words: 'This is the time when the Prophecy shall be fulfilled.' This messianic theme has always appeared to me to be an important element in the cultural life of Gaelic Scotland and psychologically important in the Jacobitism of the eighteenth century. Conventional historians disregard it.[36]

The realisation that visionary bards might still be carrying political messages raises in an especially acute form those questions that people have always asked about Macpherson's political meanings. But if anything, it only serves to underline how sharp would be the fact and the feeling of decline in the Gaelic tradition in the period from 1715 to 1745, up to the time in which Macpherson was writing. As Peter T. Murphy points out, with the suppression of Gaeldom in the period after Culloden, there is a sense of loss in writings about the Highlands which is shared by, but not confined to, Macpherson's Ossian poems.[37] It is in this light that one has to read Fingal's questioning of the value of living on in song.[38] Who will now be left to hear the bard's time-honoured recitation of past heroism?

Yet even though the sense of loss is pervasive, melancholy sentiment and spectral insubstantiality are not the whole story with Macpherson, as a highly original chapter in Jerome McGann's *Poetics of Sensibility* makes clear. Ossian does indeed possess the eye of imagination, and there are reasons for thinking that in some respects it is a very clear eye. Noting the way in which commentators refer to the mental and the sentimental in Macpherson, McGann observes that such views obscure 'the tendency of Macpherson's writing to collapse the distinction between the mental and the physical'.[39] McGann links Macpherson's view of 'materialized mentality' to Scottish philosophy's 'key ideas, that passion and feeling are the basis of human action'.[40] In accordance with this view, language is 'more performative than referential', with the result that 'the gap between *res* and *verbum*, assumed in an informational model of language, begins to close, and may collapse altogether, as happens when Macpherson generates a phrase like "son of song"'.[41] McGann proceeds to emphasize the materiality involved in 'material-ized mentality'. In Book II of *Fingal*, for instance: 'But who is she that, like a sun-beam, flies before the ranks of the foe. It is Degrena, lovely fair, the spouse of fallen Crugal'. McGann refers to Macpherson's note that 'Deogrena signifies *a sun-beam*', and claims that the point is 'to establish the *literal* truth of this field of representations'.[42] Yet although McGann has redressed the balance in an admirable way, it remains the case that his excellent formulation, 'materialized mentality', implies complexity, a complexity that includes the mental, be it affective or intellectual. Furthermore, the very fact that readers feel compelled to debate the insubstantiality or otherwise of Ossian is in itself significant. These points may help to reveal a paradoxical state of affairs: the liter-alness, the concreteness, to which McGann refers are attributes of the past. In the present, the blind bard is reduced to sentimental nostalgia about those clear and distinct visual data which still occur to him, but only in memory. It is instructive to combine this realisation with an extremely astute point made by David Hill Radcliffe to the effect that Macpherson converts lyric into epic.[43] To put it another way, this is not only what he literally attempts with the fragments of Gaelic lyric he encountered, but what he attempts in terms of genre. And the point is that he cannot conceal the lyric origins of what he confects. There are traces of this 'intensity of the past' (so to speak) in Thomas Moore, and even in Wordsworth.

Social Progress: From the Bardic Age to Britannia's Rule

The thinkers of the Enlightenment saw that intensity as something which was exchanged, in the progress of society, for abstraction and commerce. From this modern perspective the intensity merged with superstition. Collins's 'Ode' may present us with an excited bard, but he figures in a poem on 'Popular Superstitions'. If the bardic age is distant for Highlanders, how much more so for modern 'Britons'. Yet stories about the primitive past can be made to illustrate progress, and the gain and loss involved: the exchange of past energy and immediacy of experience for the philosophic mind and eye which are concomitants of material and commercial advance. Furthermore, allusions to Celtic bards may be used to demonstrate the sad necessity of merging Celtic and English identities. The 'Runic' bards of Collins confuse the associations of Celtic and Teutonic. In Thomson's *Alfred: A Masque* (1740), a like confusion is made the basis of a vision of a future Britain espied from a barely nascent England. Throughout the masque, which is set in his exile in Athelney, Alfred is seen as a king of England, albeit only *de jure*. The Hermit, inspired by the 'Genius of England', is able, in a passage which is indebted to *Macbeth* (a play replete with Scottish second sight) to summon prophetically the spirits of future kings.[44] These are implicitly recognised as Alfred's successors. Edward III and Elizabeth appear, and finally, William III 'arises' in recognition of the Glorious Revolution, and for the first time 'Britain' is referred to, with accurate reference to the post-Stuart arrangement.[45] The 'Superstition' of Catholicism and James II flies from before him. The climax of the masque, though, occurs when 'our venerable bard, / Aged and blind', sings 'An Ode' ['Rule Britannia'].[46] The word bard, with its Celtic associations, looks odd in an Anglo-Saxon setting;[47] but it is appropriate in some ways to a future Britain which includes Scotland and Wales. The blindness of the bard evokes a past of vivid, primitive visions in terms which were familiar enough to a Scot such as Thomson. Indeed, the 'bard' is a frequent enough figure in his works; and this is not the only place where he possesses inner vision. Thus, in *The Castle of Indolence*, the bard of Baghdad 'Cheer'd the lone midnight with the Muse's lore; / Composing music bade his dreams be fair . . .' (I: xlii).[48] On the other hand, this oriental poet raises the question whether the use of the word 'bard' really does carry any memory of Celtic associations elsewhere, as in *Alfred*. Certainly it can in a British context: thus in *Castle of Indolence* Canto II the bard is 'a little Druid wight'. Taking Thomson's Scottish background along with lines such as this, it is more likely that the usage is quite self-consciously Celtic, as is certainly the case with Blackwell's provocative description of Homer as a 'blind stroling bard'.

It is precisely a past inhabited by bards more or less Celtic which will be superseded in the new Britain, just as their exceptional vigour was a necessary first stage of progress. The new Britain, however, will be a realm of modern commerce, not of primitive poets, as the blind bard in *Alfred* prophesies:

> *To thee belongs the rural reign;*
> *Thy cities shall with commerce shine:*
> *All thine shall be the subject main;*
> *And every shore it circles, thine.*
> 'Rule, &c.'[49]

But in such a society it appears that material progress mocks the anxiety provoked by doubt about the tenability of the traditional framework of agreed myth. The insubstantial and the spectral offer ways of asking questions about the sacred, and of representing the suspicion that the transcendent does not exist, since at the very least they may suggest that the sacred is no better than the most arrant superstition: this is a stratagem of which Shelley was to make self-conscious use ('God and Ghosts and Heaven'). More subtly, they may suggest that whatever lies beyond is actually, in some sense, more dead than alive: in this way, representations of the dead may half-conceal the suspicion that even the dead are not really around to haunt us any more. There is a certain amount of eighteenth-century and Romantic poetry which answers 'Rule Britannia' with blind visions that work in the opposite direction: exchanging rhapsodic glimpses of the future for elegiac visions of the past. In so far as such poetry, like 'Rule Britannia' itself, ponders the fate of a nation, it may make use of the topos of the host of the dead to figure what a nation has lost.

Blindness and Second Sight in Wordsworth, Blake and Keats: The Celtic Influence

Wordsworth, something of a Scotophile, quotes from Robert Heron's *Journey through the Western Counties of Scotland* (1793) in the Preface to the second edition of *The Excursion*.[50] In this there is to be found a concise but indubitable reference to second sight: 'It is common among them, to fancy that they see, the *Wraiths* of persons dying, which will be visible to one, and not to others present with him'.[51] *The Excursion*'s wandering pedlar is Scottish, as are some of his precursors in *The Ruined Cottage* and *The Pedlar* (1802).[52] Wordsworth was also perceptive enough – and interested enough – to doubt the authenticity of the added sections of Collins's 'Ode'. Indeed, he was sufficiently indignant to attempt single-handedly to have them expunged from an edition of Collins's works.[53] These interests leave their mark on his work.

The topic of second sight makes a memorable appearance in *The Prelude*, in Book Seventh, 'Residence in London', where the poet, in one of the earliest registerings of the experience of 'the big city', evokes the chaotic anonymity of the flowing crowds, comparing them to 'A second-sight procession, such as glides / Over still mountains, or appears in dreams . . .' (1805 version, VII: 595–603).[54] Not only is the crowd clearly identified as spectral, it is also described in terms of a particular genre of the spectral: the evocation of a host of the dead, to which we have recently referred. '[D]reams' refers to visions; but 'mountains' identifies the characteristic location of the visions which were granted to Ossian and other Celtic seers. Wordsworth might not be convinced by *Ossian*, of course; but he was demonstrably interested in the whole phenomenon of second sight. Furthermore, his attitude to *Ossian* is less clear-cut than is often imagined. It has been plausibly maintained that, rather than being a complete rejecter of *Ossian*, Wordsworth constantly alludes to the Ossianic in his melancholy evocations of the darkness that gathers around a visionary faculty once strong.[55] Wordsworth submits the Ossianic to a naturalising revision analogous to that which he imposes upon 'the Gothic', revealing the human and imaginative truth which lay behind the imagery of the fantastic and supernatural, though a thorough examination of the workings of that revision will have to await a later chapter.

The reader will be anxious lest I should be about to claim that the Blind Beggar, the sight of whom accosts the poet in the ensuing lines of *The Prelude* (1805, VII: 608–23), is a Celtic bard. But such heavy-handed interpretation is unnecessary to establish the point that the juxtaposition does indeed allude, though in no mechanical fashion, to a body of imagery in which blindness could be associated with imagination: a faculty about whose operations, in the case of a sighted person, it is possible to speculate, while, in the case of a blind person, these must remain mysterious. So that all I have done is to note another nuance to the way in which the passage contrasts the spectral inauthenticity of the city crowd with the irreducible individuality and separateness of humans – qualities that, famously, are also mocked by the biographical label on the beggar's chest. 'The Blind Highland Boy', in Wordsworth's ballad of that name, provides a clearer example of a blind Celtic visionary, the conception of whom is formed out of the context I have been sketching. The narrative tells how the boy, though blind, 'neither drooped nor pined, / Nor had a melancholy mind' (ll. 21–2).[56] This is a good sign in Wordsworth. He is playful, and moreover musical, being a blind piper:

> And then the bagpipes he could blow;
> And thus from house to house would go,
> And all were pleas'd to hear and see;
> For none made sweeter melody
>   Than did the poor blind Boy.
>   (ll. 41–5; Wordsworth 1983: 222)

The last two lines rehearse the common belief upon which the musical training of blind children in Scotland and Ireland was based: namely, that they had acquired a compensatory proficiency and sensitivity – an idea which, as Katie Trumpener points out, was also the premise of a certain amount of Enlightenment theorizing about the condition of blindness.[57] Within *The Blind Highland Boy; with Other Poems,* the sequence of which this poem is first, we also have 'Power of Music', in which the information that the popular musician is blind is casually imparted only at line 31, as if it was so much to be expected as to be hardly worth mentioning.

But the boy's auditory imagination is stronger even than this might suggest:

> Yet he had many a restless dream;
> Both when he heard the Eagles scream,
> And when he heard the torrents roar,
> And heard the water beat the shore
>   Near which their Cottage stood.
>   (ll. 46–50; Wordsworth 1983: 223)

It is this faculty which leads him off on a typically Wordsworthian adventure in the pathetic mock-sublime, for he takes to the river in 'A Household Tub'. His boat is compared to a traveller's balloon (l. 138; Wordsworth 1983: 226), and this begs comparison with the opening lines of *Peter Bell.* The strangeness, to the sighted, of a blind boy's experiences can be compared with the inspired lunacy of 'The Idiot Boy' when he describes his experiences in his wild ride on the pony: 'The cocks did crow to-whoo, to-whoo, / And the sun did shine so cold' (ll. 460–1).

The most important characteristic of the Blind Highland Boy is 'that inward light / With which his soul had shone so bright' (ll. 171–2; Wordsworth 1983: 227). Although filled with disappointment at being rescued from his boat, the applause and the welcome which he receives from the people overcome this feeling, and he is 'reconciled / To live in peace on shore' (ll. 204–5; Wordsworth 1983: 228). This is possibly one of the most bathetic expressions of the characteristic Romantic structure of a widening of consciousness, followed by a reconciliation with a now altered mundane. It may be significant that after 1827 the subtitle of this poem became 'A TALE TOLD BY THE FIRE-SIDE, AFTER RETURN-ING TO THE VALE OF GRASMERE' (Wordsworth 1983: 221). The original layout of *Poems in Two Volumes* (1807), volume II, had placed *Poems Written During a Tour in Scotland* first, followed by *Moods of My Own Mind*, followed by *The Blind Highland Boy; with Other Poems*. Many of the poems in that third section in fact relate to places or persons in the Lake District, as if to emphasise the interpenetration of the familiar and the uncanniness of vision.

In much of Wordsworth's poetry, the idea of reconciliation can bear tormenting witness to a forced renunciation of intensity, as in 'Ode: Intimations of Immortality':

> What though the radiance which was once so bright
> Be now for ever taken from my sight,
>   Though nothing can bring back the hour
> Of splendour in the grass, of glory in the flower;
>   We will grieve not, rather find
>   Strength in what remains behind . . .
>   (ll. 177–83; Wordsworth 1983: 276)

What 'remains behind' is the recompense, the reconciliation, of the 'philosophic mind', a sober substitute which nevertheless required the visionary experience for its preparation. The lines above follow on from the celebrated evocation of the imaginative spirit of the child – an evocation which (I do not believe that this has been noted hitherto) is placed in a designed relationship with 'The Blind Highland Boy'. This relationship has been made more evident to the modern reader by Jared Curtis's Cornell edition of *Poems, in Two Volumes, and Other Poems* (1983) and by the ready availability of Alun R. Jones's edition of *Poems, in Two Volumes*, under the title *Wordsworth's Poems of 1807* (1987), especially to the reader who pays heed to Jones's advice that 'Wordsworth took pains with classifying the poems under their headings'.[58] As we have already observed, the whole of the third section of the second volume is entitled *The Blind Highland Boy; with Other Poems*. 'The Blind Highland Boy' is the first poem in this section, and the 'Ode' is the last, which means that Wordsworth intended the reader to notice that the 'Ode' came under that heading, and that it provided a fitting conclusion to the section.

The lines in the 'Ode' which particularly suggest the relationship are these, about 'the Child':

>   thou Eye among the blind,
> That, deaf and silent, read'st the eternal deep,
> Haunted for ever by the eternal mind, –
>   Mighty Prophet! Seer blest!
>   (ll. 111–14; Wordsworth 1987: 136)

The eternal world seen by the Child is equally open to the Highland Boy, and has nothing to do with the superficialities which exercise the crowd, to whose hubbub the Child is figuratively deaf. Both are 'Seer[s]', and both are 'Haunted' by imagination – rather than by a procession of ghosts. The latter is an image which Wordsworth was happy to use as a comparison with inauthentic existence. But he is never happy to give assent to the supernatural conceived as a spirit world, and always wishes, as here, to harness supernatural terms and imagery to some more refined purpose, as he would see it. This would be equally evident from the various versions of the story of Margaret in *The Ruined Cottage*, *The Pedlar* and *The Excursion*, for the Scottish wanderer is not just a natural poet ('Oh many are the Poets that are sown / By Nature': *Excursion*, I: 77–8); his ability to evoke the memory of the dead Margaret in each detail of her ruined cottage is an example of a kind of second sight, or, if you like, of Wordsworth's naturalised Gothic – or Celto-Gothic. Wordsworth is the most obvious example of a Romantic poet who is influenced in a quite detailed way by the imagery associated with blind Celtic bards and second sight. But he is not the only one to respond. Blake's tyrant deity, Urizen, is a type of fallen bard. As the 'primeval Priest', he is a corruption of the poet, and his flowing white hair and beard are deliberately made indistinguishable from those of the Ancient Bard, in 'The Voice of the Ancient Bard', so that we shall be reminded of how perilously easy it is for inspiration to degenerate into 'imposition'. Some versions of *The Book of Urizen* make Urizen's closed eyes look so blank as to suggest blindness. On its own, this fact is not especially cogent; but it must be remembered that the development of Blake's mythology is clearly bound up with his reading of *Ossian*.

Keats provides a clearer example, though its significance can only be fully appreciated in the context of the importance of the imagery of vision and blindness in Keats's work as a whole. The poem in question is 'There is a joy in footing slow', which is subjoined to his letter to Benjamin Bailey of 18 and 22 July 1818.[59] This was written from Scotland, and includes an account of some of his travels in the Highlands. It evokes the experience of forgetting one's surroundings as one tramps along, 'the forgotten eye . . . fast wedded to the ground'. It goes on to suggest the danger that, when the 'Spirit' thus goes forth 'To find a Bard's low Cradle', it may, in going 'beyond the Bourn of Care', be detained in the supernatural realm ('forget his mortal way'). The poem ends, in a somewhat awkward and extemporary manner, by suggesting a typical Keatsian compromise:

Yet be the Anchor e'er so fast, room is there for a prayer
That Man may never loose [*sic*] his Mind <on> Mountains bleak
    and bare;
That he may stray league after League some great Berthplace to find,
And keep his vision clear from speck, his inward sight unblind –

Losing one's mind is equivalent to joining the spirits 'unaware', as he
had put it earlier in the poem. But the conclusion does not reject the
'inward sight' which might have been blamed for this danger; rather, it
seems to indicate that there are two forms of 'inward sight' – one
malign, spectral and in some sense blind, the other benign and clear-
seeing. The benign imagination looks like a predecessor of that which
(for instance) in 'Ode on Melancholy' is instructed to remain 'wakeful'.

Thomas Moore and the Shadow of the Blind Bard

As we have seen, 'The Ossianic' in reality comprised rather more than
reference to Macpherson alone. There is complexity attending the way
one should sum up this broad category, however. On the one hand, there
is much evidence to show that the Ossianic can in part be related to the
broader category of inspired poetic vision. But on the other, there is
much that is about loss of vision. If one attempts to attend disinterest-
edly to the tone of Macpherson himself, what one finds is a mixture of
the melancholy of loss – lost vision, lost strength and lost companion-
ship – with the contrasting sense of the possibility of inspired prophecy.
Wordsworth could broadly be seen as affording parallels with this tonal
and thematic contradiction. But the popularity of such works as *The
Pleasures of Imagination* and *The Pleasures of Memory* should remind
us that there is a strong tendency in the eighteenth century to think of
the visual 'ideas' both of imagination and memory as flickering on the
screen of an isolated consciousness. This way of conceiving of private
experience – an inheritance of the Locke tradition – is as important
a consideration in understanding the Ossianic craze as is the idea of
inspired blindness. Nevertheless, blindness seems an appropriate way of
troping both ways of thinking about inward vision.

The topic of blindness, being interwoven with that of the bard, may
also induce reflections on the development of what Katie Trumpener has
called 'bardic nationalism'. Her book shows how this kind of expressive
primitivism about the nation, while it could become an engine of liber-
ation for colonised peoples, could also be recuperated and exploited by
imperialism. Howard D. Weinbrot has made a closely parallel point,
and one which he develops more specifically in relation to the poetry of

the eighteenth century and of the Romantic period. The new, constitutional, Protestant and supposedly Anglo-Celtic dispensation in Britain is open to the visionary wisdom of the Druids, and able to expunge and indeed reverse the wrongs done by the medieval tyrant, Edward I, when he slew the bards (as Gray had related in 'The Bard'), or those done by the Romans when they imprisoned Caractacus, while young Britons yearned for 'liberty' (as William Mason had dramatised in *Caractacus*, 1759).[60] A complex web of imputed affinities was supposed to link ancient Hebrews and Scots with modern British Protestants and thus help to validate the new, prophetic poetry of Britain.[61]

These were relationships which could not cast the Irish in an especially favourable light. Although their traditions had helped in a small but significant manner to foster the imagery and ideology of the visionary bard, they could not join the family. Their Catholicism and their supposed barbarism (the two might be linked in anti-Irish rhetoric) usually meant that they had to stay where they had always been: beyond the pale. Wordsworth's Scotophilia is balanced by something close to Hibernophobia, for although he is ready to acknowledge some flaws in British policy, his characterisation of the Irish seems little short of intemperate.[62] Southey is sensitive enough to recoil from the systematic and thorough employment of torture in Ireland in 1798 (itself a little-noted phenomenon) but concedes that he has 'a most evil opinion of the half-christened herd'.[63] He writes this at a time when he was composing *Madoc*, a poem which might have been made to illustrate the harnessing of bardic nationalism to a slightly displaced fantasy of imperialism, albeit in a liberal and pantisocratic form.[64] We expect a bard and are not disappointed:

> Then, strong of voice,
> The officer proclaim'd the sovereign will,
> Bidding the hall be silent; loud he spake,
> And smote the sounding pillar with his wand,
> And hush'd the banqueters. The chief of Bards
> Then rais'd the ancient lay.[65]

Figuratively speaking, there is blindness in the attitude of Southey and others: aware of the suffering of bards in lands that participate fully in the British polity, or were part of its history, but blind to them in the case of Ireland. But although, as we shall see, there is a connection between the ideology of visionary imagination (in which the blind bard is an important topos) and selective blindness in the figurative sense, that connection does not necessarily operate via individual cases such as this one.

Nor should one engage in facile generalisation about the exclusion of the Irish: the extraordinary celebrity of Moore's *Irish Melodies* may stand as a warning against this. Nevertheless, his methods involved an indirection intended in part to conceal the true nature of his political wishes from most British readers, and in part to suggest the likeness of Irish sentiment to that which was found in the celebrated songs of Robert Burns. We noted the combined force of Ossian and Carolan in the background to Brooke's *Reliques*. Moore's *Irish Melodies* profits by the same associations. At Trinity College the eighteen-year-old Moore essayed an 'Extract for a Poem in Imitation of Ossian', which not only assumes an Irish provenance for the ancient bard, but introduces 'a note of angry defiance that is utterly missing in the Scottish poet':

> O! children of Erin! you'r robbed; why not rouse from your slumber of Death? – Oh! why not assert her lov'd cause, and strike off her chains and your own – and hail her to freedom and peace! Oh! that Ossian now flourished and here; he would tell us the deeds of our sires, and swell up our souls to be brave! – for his Harp flow'd a torrent around, and incitement enforc'd as the stream! – but silence now reigns o'er the wires.[66]

The Ossianic note is pervasive in *Irish Melodies*. The mute and abandoned harp of 'The Harp that Once' or of 'My Gentle Harp' ('Thou hang'st upon the willows still'); the bittersweet praise for courage in a lost battle ('After the Battle'); the listing of exotic Gaelic names from the remote past: all these are familiar.[67] Memories of the dead may be conveyed in spectral terms:

> Oh, ye dead! oh, ye dead! whom we know by the light you give
> From your cold gleaming eyes, though you move like men who live,
>> Why leave you thus your graves,
>> In far-off fields and waves,
> Where the worm and the sea-bird only know your bed,
>> To haunt this spot, where all,
>> Those eyes that wept your fall,
> And the hearts that bewailed you, like your own, lie dead?[68]

In the context of *Irish Melodies* it is clear that this is meant to evoke a specifically Gaelic capacity for second sight, part of the definition of which was to be able to see the dead, and that 'we' are a goodly proportion of the people of Ireland. At least as relevant to our thesis, though, is the evocation of visions or memories that occur at night, such as the half-heard song of the dead lover in 'At the Mid Hour of Night', or, most of all, the 'light' of former years in 'Oft in the Stilly Night', a song which originally appeared in *National Airs* as a 'Scotch Air', but which became such a favourite that it was often included with the *Irish Melodies* and even lent its title to a selection of Moore's poems:[69]

> Oft in the stilly night
>> Ere Slumber's chain has bound me,
> Fond Memory brings the light

> Of other days around me;
>   The smiles, the tears,
>   Of boyhood's years
> The words of love then spoken;
>   The eyes that shone,
>   Now dimmed and gone,
> The cheerful hearts now broken![70]

Taken together, all these characteristics establish the influence of Ossian clearly enough. That of Carolan is definite and avowed, even though his are by no means the only traditional airs of which Moore made use. Moore was chiefly indebted to Edward Bunting's *General Collection of Ancient Irish Music*, which began life as a transcription of airs played at a famous festival of the remaining harpers of Ireland in Belfast on 10–13 July 1792, dates deliberately chosen to coincide with the celebration of the fall of the Bastille. The first collection was published in 1796, and there were subsequent collections in 1809 and 1840. Sixteen of the sixty-six airs in the first collection were by Carolan. In the 'Letter on Music', originally appended to the third number of the *Melodies*, but later used as a preface, Moore praises Carolan for not 'sacrificing his native simplicity' to the imitation of Italian ornament.[71]

The undoubted and identifiable presence of the two blind bards in the background to the *Melodies* renders appropriate Moore's notable concentration on musicality, of which the 'Letter on Music' is only the most definite avowal. Here we have an example of the way in which the idea of compensatory hearing could actually influence and lend authority to innovation in poetic style. It has often been suggested (recently with some thoroughness by Terry Eagleton) that Moore is a proto-symbolist.[72] Certainly his musical poetic is more than an unpondered predilection: Moore's hope that the humble nature of his endeavours would exempt them from 'literary criticisms' itself sounds as if it might be merely humble.[73] But it finds echoes in the negative depiction of the 'critical and fastidious Fadladeen' in *Lalla Rookh*.[74] Literary criticism is antipathetic to the unanalysable musicality of poetry, which has an affinity with inexpressible essence: as it is said at the beginning of the second section of that poem, 'Paradise and the Peri',

> One morn a Peri at the gate
> Of Eden stood disconsolate;
> And as she listened to the Springs
>   Of life within, like music flowing,
> And caught the light upon her wings
>   Through the half open portal glowing,
> She wept to think her recreant race
> Should e'er have lost that glorious place![75]

There is no doubt but that intellection is well dissolved in sentiment in Moore. But it is worth remembering that the dissolution is hardly complete, and that the language of tears, regrets and the heart does not come from nowhere: it is that of sentimental poetry, strongly influenced by the Ossianic, and this conjunction would itself have suggested a kind of political decoding to his readers, even if only in terms of sympathy. Further, Moore patently remains more indignant than Macpherson. All those critiques which claim that the salon emasculated Moore are offering little better than prejudiced fiction. As Jeffery Vail points out, Moore's experience of 'misrule' in Ireland meant that he was not 'propelled towards conservatism'. Contemplating the failure of radicalism both in France and Ireland, Moore wished to use his art 'to persuade rather than confront, to undermine rather than uproot, and to stimulate reform rather than revolution'.[76] Nevertheless, there is nothing politically mysterious about 'Revenge on a tyrant is sweetest of all!', especially if the context suggests that the person in question is the Prince Regent.[77] And scores of lines like this can be cited. So that even politically, *Irish Melodies* are not entirely 'decontaminated', as Robert Welch points out, adding that Moore wished to have it 'both ways' in his polite milieu.[78] This 'both ways' has parallels in Moore's Whiggish politics, as we shall see.

There is, of course, a straightforward political meaning to the fundamental method of the *Melodies*. Moore provides old Irish airs with modern poetic words; and despite his surprising claim in the 'Letter on Music' that most Irish music is not very ancient, he himself claims that there are, indeed, ancient airs still extant, and the implication is that it is these which he is restoring.[79] The act has two parallel resonances: he is translating the old Irish spirit of the music; and he is enacting the immemorial association of poetry and music in Ireland.[80] But the indirection of his technique is itself politically motivated. For he has to hand, in the shape of the allegorical poetry of the Jacobite era, a model of political verse which conveys the full political secret of its music and imagery only to those in the know.[81] Yet it must be remembered that the secret cannot be divorced from the suggestive techniques which convey it: this is what conduces to that powerful union of nationalism, passion and music which was to make Moore so influential even on national movements outside Ireland. Arguably, this development would not have surprised him, since his own *National Airs* (with subtitles such as 'German Air' and 'Italian Air') could be said to offer them a prospectus. Hemans borrows the notion in her 'Lays of Many Lands' and 'National Lyrics', just as she borrows the specific form of nationalist expression in her *Welsh Melodies*.[82]

An important component of this idea is that a nation's music, in the strictest non-verbal sense, embodies the national spirit more effectively than words. Under this heading, Moore is not alone in harnessing nationalism to some of the most ambitious themes of Romanticism. Mangan does something comparable in his association of paradisal music with Ireland's glorious past in 'A Vision of Connaught in the Thirteenth Century'. Ireland has nothing to learn from Germany in this respect – though it is instructive to note Mangan's immersion in German poetry, and his bizarre setting of 'A Vision' in Germany. In accordance with the logic of the Romantic ideology of the Ideal in the particular, Ireland possesses her own distinctive music, frequently melancholy, sometimes gay. The harp itself comes to represent that music, and in view of Ireland's national submission and the decay of her past glories it is sometimes said to be asleep. To Lady Morgan belongs the honour of first popularising this idea, in *The Lay of an Irish Harp, or Metrical Fragments* (1807). 'The Irish Harp', from this collection, is prefaced by an epigraph from Ossian, '*Voice of the days of old, let me hear you. Awake the soul of song*'. The poem begins with a line to which Moore is indebted: 'Why sleeps the harp of Erin's pride?' Moore develops this idea in several of the *Irish Melodies* including, of course, 'The Harp that Once'. Morgan noted that her own poem derived from a visit to Ireland in 1805, the same visit that supplied her with much material for *The Wild Irish Girl* (1806). A striking episode in the twenty-seventh Letter reveals the almost literal force that the idea of the sleeping harp might possess. Horatio visits 'the last of the race of *Irish bards*', whom he discovers in bed, where he has lain down 'from debility'.[83] When he gets up to greet them, 'we perceived that his harp had been the companion of his repose, and was actually laid under the bed-clothes with him'. There is a sense of a tradition on its last legs and requiring the sort of tender care that only a patriot might feel. In one of those lengthy antiquarian footnotes with which Morgan, like Edgeworth, sketches a national cultural history, we discover that this description is based on fact: on an account, that is, of a visit by the Rev. G. V. Sampson to the home of Dennis Hampson, who 'lost his sight at the age of three years by the small-pox' and had been trained by 'John C. Garragher, a blind travelling harper' (200). This Dennis Hampson had 'played at the famous meeting of harpers at Belfast, under the patronage of some amateurs of Irish music' – the occasion at which Bunting noted down the tunes for his collection: the same collection from which Moore derived many of the melodies to which he put words.

It is true, of course, that there is another side to Moore's recovery of tradition, as one would expect from a man of 'many mediations'.[84] His act of cultural translation not only finds a modern verbal idiom, but in relation to Ireland's past expressly disavows anything more than sentimental nostalgia. The 'Letter on Music' engagingly asserts that 'it is possible to love our country very zealously, and to feel deeply interested in her honour and happiness, without believing that Irish was the language spoken in Paradise'.[85] Moore shows that the past is indeed gone, and that there is potential gain in this. Without expressly exonerating 'the tyrant', he implies, in accordance with his Whiggish propensities, that Ireland's spirit, if it is to be revived, will have to find a modern form of life: this is one meaning of Moore's professed admiration for Burns. Thus it is that, like Macpherson's bard, he 'occupies a historical middle ground, handing the past to the future by virtue of his verse'.[86] But unlike Macpherson, he has as yet no settlement on the basis of which to abjure indignation. This is the true meaning of what one might call 'the shadow of the blind bard' in Moore's verse: images of the past occur to the mind's eye, but the melancholy musicality carries with it not only the sense of loss, but a lack of clarity about the future.

Moore is not alone in his position in the nineteenth century. Politically, he has much in common with O'Connell, despite his reserve about the latter's methods. Technically, as Welch suggests, he can be seen as a pioneer of the 'Irish Mode' in versification.[87] This in itself is an important point, for it suggests that a poetic influenced by the idea of blindness has developed and helped to foster a proto-symbolist poetic of musicality. Combined with this, Moore's use of evocative imagery in a patriotic cause makes him a forerunner of Yeats. Even a nationalist poet who felt that Moore was too indirect was capable of continuing the same methods: Thomas Davis's poem of the 1840s, 'Blind Mary', like a number of Moore's, provides a lyric for the blind Carolan's music (the air *Máire Dhall*, or 'Blind Mary'). The whole context of Davis's work makes it very clear that this is an *aisling* poem of broad political import, which, like many another of that genre, accords symbolic status to a woman (Cathleen ni Houlihan, Dark Rosaleen), who represents Ireland. In other words, in this poem, at least, he is doing something very close to what Moore attempted:

> There flows from her spirit such love and delight
> That the face of Blind Mary is radiant with light –
> As the gleam from a homestead through darkness will show,
> Or the moon glimmer soft through the fast falling snow.
> [. . .]
> Ah! grieve not, sweet maiden, for star or for sun,
> For the mountains that tower or the rivers that run –
> For beauty and grandeur, and glory, and light,
> Are seen by the spirit, and not by the sight.[88]

The 'homestead', along with the evocation of the landscape, establish her intimacy with her native country, and while she cannot see them, they are securely a part of her spirit. Her name, a favourite of the Catholic common people, is also significant.

The idea of blindness allows the Celtic to be assimilated in especially powerful form into the post-Lockeian world of memory and association. As much as early society, it is the early self that appears strong and close to materiality in Macpherson, and while this emphasis is not so emphatic in Moore, all the eighteenth-century interpreters of the Celtic are fascinated by the contrast between an early bardic society and modern commercial society. This fascination means that questions about translation and the character of true 'originals' come to the fore, but this is only the textual aspect, so to speak, of an idea of exchange, the most striking instance of which is to be found in Mallet and Thomson's 'Rule Britannia', where the blind bard foresees Britain's commercial and enlightened future, for which she must exchange her bardic past.

Notes

1. MacLysaght (1979), p. 19.
2. Lennon (1981), p. 150. The quotation is from Lennon's translation of *De Rebus . . .*, the title of which he translates as 'On Ireland's Past'.
3. Céitinn (1902), p. 40.
4. Keating (1723), pp. xi–xii.
5. Lecky (1892), I, p. 317.
6. Sir David Wilkie, *The Blind Fiddler* (1807). Oil on canvas. National Gallery. Exhibited in the RA, 1807. Repro. in Wilkie (1868), No. 3. It is described as the work that 'fully established' his fame (p. iv) and as being on a 'national' (i.e., Scottish) subject (note to No. 3).
7. Gunn (1807), p. 98. Walter Scott refers to this book in *Waverley*.
8. Ibid., pp. 48, 60.
9. For the first two names, Campbell (1862), IV, pp. 200, 185; for the second two, Watson (1937), pp. 6, 106.
10. Edgeworth (1988), Appendix II, 'The Tradition of Grace Nugent', pp. 276–81. ('Grace Nugent' is the title of one of Carolan's songs.)
11. Ibid., p. 277. See Goldsmith (1966), 'The History of Carolan, the last Irish Bard', III, pp. 118–20: from the *British Magazine* (July 1760).
12. Lee (1780).
13. Brooke (1789).
14. Anon. (1814), pp. 29–31, 121–3.
15. Anon. (c.1800), p. 31.
16. Welch (1988), p. 3.
17. Ibid., p. 43.

18. For an anthology of interesting seventeenth-century texts on second sight, see Hunter (2001). On the variety of phenomena covered by second sight, see Davidson (1989), editor's introduction, p. 4, on Columba: 'Besides perceiving happenings in the future and at a distance, he could also see invisible beneficent powers, here called angels, and mischievous and destructive ones, here called demons . . .'. These demons may be identified with the fairies seen by other seers in Celtic countries.
19. John MacInnes, 'The Seer in Gaelic Tradition', in Davidson (1989), p. 20.
20. Ibid., pp. 19–20, for the 'co-walker'.
21. Lonsdale (1969), pp. 505–7.
22. See Lonsdale's discussion, ibid., pp. 492–501.
23. At the same time, the figure of the bard becomes involved in, and helps to sustain, claims about the character of primitive poetry and mythology. The classic short treatment is in Abrams (1953), pp. 78–84. See also Butler (1985), pp. 57–76.
24. Lonsdale (1969), p. 179.
25. Martin (1703), p. 300. 'Best-known', not only because it is the most obvious source for some of Collins' ideas, but because it seems to have been a book of first resort for Johnson in his 'background reading' for his trip to the Western Isles: see Johnson (1985), references in the index to Martin and to second sight. Johnson's (unprejudiced) reflections on second sight are at pp. 89–91.
26. Macpherson (1996), p. 124.
27. Hemans (1849), p. 483. (See also Wu (1998), p. 1003.)
28. Ibid.
29. Ibid., p. 484.
30. Martin (1703), p. 304.
31. Pennant (1774), p. 96.
32. Hemans (1849), 152. (See also Wu (1997), p. 507.)
33. Scott (1991), p. 198. Future references are given in parentheses in the text as numbers referring to the page.
34. Scott (1985), pp. 102–17. Subsequent page references are given as numbers in parentheses in the main text.
35. MacInnes in Davidson (1989), p. 18.
36. Ibid., p. 22.
37. Murphy (1986), p. 573.
38. Ibid., p. 574.
39. McGann (1996), p. 35.
40. Ibid.
41. Ibid., p. 38.
42. Ibid., p. 39.
43. Radcliffe (1992), pp. 213–32, esp. p. 221.
44. Mallet and Thomson (1740), pp. 28 et seq.
45. Ibid., pp. 30, 32, 34.
46. Ibid., pp. 41–2.
47. See Kersey (2001), p. 38.
48. Thomson (1787), p. 169.
49. Mallet and Thomson (1740), p. 42.
50. Wordsworth (1936), p. 727; Heron (1793).

51. Heron (1793), II, 227. Nicola Trott is undertaking a study of the wide implications of the idea of 'second sight' in Wordsworth.
52. In 1801–2, the Wordsworths provided 'additional material about the Pedlar, giving him a new name – Patrick Drummond – and a Scottish rather than a Cumbrian background'. Wordsworth (1979b), p. 26.
53. Wordsworth and Wordsworth (1939), I, pp. 313–16, and 345–6, Letters to Alexander Dyce.
54. Wordsworth (1979a), p. 258.
55. Stafford (1991), pp. 49–72. See also Moore (1925), pp. 362–78.
56. Wordsworth (1983), p. 222. For quotations from poems, henceforth cited in the main text as Wordsworth 1983 with page number.
57. Trumpener (1997), p. 96, in her sub-section, 'Savage Nations and Second Sight', pp. 96–100.
58. Wordsworth (1983); Wordsworth (1987), p. xiii.
59. Keats (1970), pp. 138–40.
60. Weinbrot (1993), pp. 398, 393; Mason (1796), p. 14.
61. Weinbrot (1993), pp. 419–25, 485–91.
62. Wordsworth and Wordsworth (1979), pp. 42–6.
63. Letter to C. W. Williams Wynn, 15 July [1798], in Southey (1965), I, p. 171.
64. For an interpretation which is positive about the liberal character of *Madoc*, see Pratt (1996), pp. 149–63. For one which is less positive about it, and about other forms of Enlightenment proselytising, see Muldoon (1990).
65. Southey (1909), p. 466.
66. Flannery (1997), p. 24.
67. Moore (1872), pp. 427, 452, 437.
68. Ibid., p. 458.
69. Moore [18??].
70. Moore (1872), pp. 413–14.
71. Ibid., p. 434.
72. Eagleton (1998), pp. 140–57.
73. Moore (1872), p. 434.
74. Ibid., p. 52.
75. Ibid., p. 81.
76. Vail (2004), pp. 41–62, esp. pp. 41, 60.
77. Flannery (1997), p. 159.
78. Welch (1980), p. 25.
79. Moore (1872), pp. 433–4.
80. Moore (1835–46), I, pp. 312–13.
81. Tessier (1981), pp. 34–5; refers to the influence of the Irish Jacobite poets and especially those *aisling* poems in which 'an unidentified young woman, the allegorical representation of Ireland, gives voice to patriotic or political feelings'. The woman might well be unidentified in the earlier part of the period: the fairy woman in Aodhagán ó Rathaille's (Egan O'Rahilly's) 'Gile na Gile' ('Brightness of Brightness') is anonymous. But the popular tradition gave rise to named figures, such as Cathleen ni Houlihan, or Róisín Dubh (the latter becomes James Clarence Mangan's 'Dark Rosaleen').
82. Hemans (1849), pp. 338–53, 534–8, 145–53.

83. Owenson (1999), p. 199. Future references by page number in brackets in the text.
84. Chandler (1998), p. 289.
85. Moore (1872), p. 433.
86. Murphy (1986), p. 571.
87. Welch (1980), p. 41.
88. Davis (*c.* 1911), p. 361.

Chapter 3

Blake: Removing the Curse by Printing for the Blind

Empiricism and the Blind

In Blake's work, the imagery of blindness and the blind is normally related to his debate with empiricist epistemology, although there are some exceptions to this rule. Since the publication of my study in 1985, there has been further support for the idea advanced therein, that Blake's attitude to empiricist theories of knowledge, chiefly as represented by the Locke tradition, is quite ambivalent, and that it cannot be described as one of simple rejection. In any case, his response to that tradition is closely bound up with his attempts to define his own point of view, which means that the aim of analysing the latter can go in tandem with that of analysing the former. The links between blindness, the critique of empiricism, and the analysis of the growth of tyranny are strongest in the 1780s: in 'An Island in the Moon' (c.1784), *All Religions Are One* and *There Is No Natural Religion* (c.1788), and 'Tiriel' (c.1789).[1] Indeed, it seems that some of Blake's most characteristic themes were first developed in close relationship with the imagery of blindness and in the light of philosophical debates about it.

As it happens, one of the earliest uses of the imagery of blindness, 'Blind Man's Buff', is one of the exceptions to the rule proposed above. Nevertheless it could be seen as implying a lighthearted critique of Locke's theory of government and civil society, if not of his epistemology. As Nick Rawlinson points out, 'There is a great deal of flirtation in the poem, but all unsuccessful: their blindness seems to mock Cupid's and their passion is not allowed direct expression [. . .] thwarted sexual desire is forced to emerge as suppressed violence'.[2] The sexual element is made clear by means of double entendres: 'The lasses prick the lads with pins', Dolly's bottom 'kiss[es] the ground', 'titt'ring Kate / Is pen'd up', and 'Sukey is tumbled on the ground'. The participants seek to win by cheating. The poem ends with the prototype of those ironic morals which Blake was also to employ in 'An Island in the Moon' and the *Songs*:

> all those
> Who on the blinded man impose,
> Stand in his stead; as long a-gone
> When men were first a nation grown;
> Lawless they liv'd – till wantonness
> And liberty began t'increase;
> And one man lay in another's way,
> Then laws were made to keep fair play. (E423)

Something about the abrupt flatness of that last line, in particular, suggests that Blake's critique is really of a society that instils the repression which thus issues in violence and warfare, and that this society is blind and the cause of blindness.

Whatever the date of composition of this poem, *Poetical Sketches* (1783) is close to being contemporaneous with 'An Island in the Moon' (*c*.1784), where Blake's tongue-in-cheek poems and endings offer a parallel: 'The hungry poor enter'd the hall to eat good beef & ale / Good English hospitality O then it did not fail' (E461); or the first version of 'Holy Thursday', with its ending about 'cherish[ing] pity lest you drive an angel from your door' (E463). 'An Island in the Moon' also contains references to shortsightedness and partial blindness which certainly do relate to the critique of empiricist epistemology. The best-known of these references is to be found in the re-phrasing of the title of Locke's *Essay on Human Understanding* as 'An Easy of [. . .] <Huming> Understanding by John Lookye Gent' (E456). The suggestions of facility, burying (the opposite of exhuming) and narrow vision ('Lookye') take in Hume as well as Locke. The idea of shortsightedness recurs in the little verse about that natural empiricist, Samuel Johnson:

> Lo the Bat with Leathern wing
> Winking & blinking
> Winking & blinking
> Winking & blinking
> Like Doctor Johnson. (E458)

Reynolds had painted five portraits of Johnson, who complained that the second made him look like 'blinking Sam'.[3] Blake is clearly using the remark to reinforce his point about the narrowness of empirical reasoning. The verse also refers to Collins' 'Ode to Evening':

> Now air is hushed, save where the weak-eyed bat,
> With short shrill shrieks flits by on leathern wing.

The bat, like the Owl of Minerva, flies when the sun of life is setting: empiricist reasoning is myopic, and associated with the decline of energy.

However, a reading of the whole of 'An Island in the Moon' suggests that Blake has more concepts of reason in his sights than the empiricist one alone. This is perhaps not surprising, given the wide application of one of the puns involved in the name 'Urizen' (admittedly a later coinage, as far as we know), namely 'Your reason.' This last phrase, however, is not a later coinage, but derives from a passage in 'An Island in the Moon' itself (E450), where the 'Philosophers' are quarrelling about the merits of Voltaire. Obtuse Angle proceeds to claim that Voltaire was a fool 'because he understood nothing of the Mathematics', and proceeds with the quarrel by 'shutting his eyes & saying that he always understood better when he shut his eyes'. The Antiquarian agrees with the low estimate of Voltaire, claiming that 'Voltaire was immersed in matter, & seems to have understood very little but what he saw before his eyes' (E451). This is a reference to the kind of mischievous and extreme popularisation of Lockeian empiricism to be found in Voltaire's *The Ignorant Philosopher*. At the beginning of this work, Voltaire issues this invitation:

> In this narrow circle by which we are circumscribed, let us see what we are condemned to be ignorant of, and what we gain a little knowledge of.[4]

In sum, the overall impression gained from a reading of 'An Island' is that he thinks of both rationalists and empiricists in terms of a narrow and short-sighted reason: both are immersed in the classical problem of knowledge – the confrontation of reason and brute matter, which, by Voltaire's admission, gives rise to the conviction that reason is shortsighted.

Blake's tractates, *There Is No Natural Religion*, [a] and [b], are intended to prove the necessity of 'the Poetic or Prophetic character' (E3) to any kind of knowledge. It is acceptable to translate this 'Poetic Genius' (to use the term of the contemporaneous tractate *All Religions Are One*: E1) as 'imagination', as long as one does not equate it at all points with Blake's later concept of 'Imagination'. The Poetic Genius is the true cognitive faculty. It brings about all advances in knowledge, and is in contradiction of Newton's boast that 'Hypotheses non fingo'.[5] Blake does not think of knowledge as something essentially uniform and immutable which has to be unveiled, but as part of the historical process: 'Reason or the ratio of all we have already known. is not the same that it shall be when we know more' (E2).

The first series of *There Is No Natural Religion* concentrates on the limitations of the natural man. Blake accepts the Pauline doctrine that 'the natural man receiveth not the things of the spirit' (Corinthians 2:14); and it is plain from his annotations of Swedenborg that he also accepts the latter's elaboration of this theme: 'Observe the distinction here between Natural & Spiritual as seen by Man', and 'Man may comprehend [the Divine]. but not the natural or external man' (E603). However, Blake goes far beyond this acceptance in extending the application of the term 'natural' to empiricist thinking. His first tactic, then, and it is of some moment, is to accept a thorough-going empiricism for what Christians had been accustomed to call the natural man. Thus,

> I Man cannot naturally Percieve. but through his natural or bodily organs
> II Man by his reasoning power. can only compare & judge of what he has already perciev'd. (E2)

The second aphorism answers Locke's concise definition of knowledge:

> *Knowledge* then seems to me to be nothing but *the perception of the connexion and agreement, or disagreement and repugnancy of any of our ideas.* In this alone it consists. Where this perception is, there is knowledge; and where it is not, there, though we may fancy, guess, or believe, yet we always come short of knowledge.
>
> (Locke 1894, IV.i.2)

There is also a reference to Bacon's scientific method of accumulating data for comparison (*Novum Organum*) of which Locke's definition is, among other things, a refined philosophical justification.

The third aphorism is particularly interesting: 'From a perception of only 3 senses or 3 elements none could deduce a fourth or fifth' (E2). This refers to a tradition of speculation on the senses initiated by William Molyneux (1656–98), of Trinity College, Dublin. What came to be known as 'Molyneux's problem' became celebrated because of its use by Locke (from the second edition of the *Essay* onwards) in his chapter 'Of Perception' (II.ix.8). The question is: Can a man born blind, if suddenly given back his sight, interpret visual experience? Molyneux's answer was, No: the blind man would have to learn to interpret visual sense data by experience of the agreement of sight and touch. Locke was of the same opinion.

It was Berkeley who drew out some radical implications of this conclusion in the *Essay Towards a New Theory of Vision* (1709), where he says that it is certain that 'the ideas intromitted by each sense are widely different, and distinct from each other' (*NTV*, XLVI). In a notably trenchant expression of the doctrine, he states that 'the ideas which constitute the tangible earth and man, are entirely different from those which constitute the visible earth and man' (*NTV*, CII). As a result of this kind of thinking, the senses tended to be regarded as an almost arbitrary assortment of isolated and distinct 'windows' on the world. There had already been playful speculation about different numbers of senses, with which the more rigorous philosophical work of Locke and Berkeley might become associated. Fontenelle, for instance, in one of the most popular books of the eighteenth century, *A Conversation on the Plurality of Worlds* (1686 – this translation 1777),

> Here it is thought we want a sixth sense, that would teach us many things, of which we are now ignorant; this sixth sense is apparently in another world, where they want one of the five which we enjoy; nay, perhaps there is a much greater number of senses, but in the partition which we have made of them with the inhabitants of other planets, there are but five fallen to our share, with which we are well contented for want of being acquainted with the rest: Our sciences have bounds, which the wit of man could never pass. (78)

There are several reasons beyond the mere popularity of this work which give grounds for suspecting that Blake had read this translation.[6] But on the subject of the senses alone, it is noteworthy that he associates the idea of 'numerous senses' with a transcendence of the bounds (a word with Blakean connections) of the 'philosophy of the five senses':

> The ancient Poets animated all sensible objects with Gods or Geniuses, calling them by the names and adorning them with the properties of woods, rivers, mountains, lakes, cities, nations, and whatever their enlarged and numerous senses could percieve.
>
> (E38)

In *The First Book of Urizen* (1794), the Eternals are similarly endowed:

> Earth was not: nor globes of attraction
> The will of the Immortal expanded
> Or contracted his all flexible senses.
> Death was not, but eternal life sprung.
> (*Urizen*, 3, E71)

The isolation of each sense is described in *Europe* (1794):

> Five windows light the cavern'd Man; thro' one he breathes the air;
> Thro' one, hears music of the spheres; thro' one, the eternal vine
> Flourishes, that he may receive the grapes; thro' one can look.
> And see small portions of the eternal world that ever groweth;
> Thro' one, himself pass out what time he please, but he will not;
> For stolen joys are sweet, & bread eaten in secret pleasant.
> (iii, 1–6; E60)

In Blake's aphorism about '3 senses' he is using our ignorance of other possible senses as a metaphor for knowledge not given by sense. Exactly the same device had been employed by Voltaire, with opposite intent. In a supplement to *The Ignorant Philosopher*, there is 'A Short Digression' about a hospital which had some blind pensioners:

> They distinguished perfectly by the touch between copper and silver coin; they never mistook the wine of Brie for that of Burgundy. Their sense of smelling

was finer than that of their neighbours who had the use of two eyes. They reasoned very well on the four senses; that is, they knew every thing they were permitted to know, and they lived as peaceably and as happily as blind people could be supposed to do. But unfortunately one of their professors pretended to have clear ideas in respect to the sense of seeing; he intrigued; he formed enthusiasts; and at last he was acknowledged the chief of the community. He pretended to be a sovereign judge of colours, and every thing was lost.[7]

This dictator chose a council and proclaimed that the pensioners were clothed in white, though in fact this was not the case. Those who disagreed were called 'heretics'.[8] But violence ensued, and to appease the warring factions the dictator issued a decree saying that all the pensioners were dressed in red, though in fact none of them was.[9] There were more quarrels until finally, toleration was introduced. Voltaire adds:

> A deaf man, reading this little history, allowed that these people being blind, were to blame in pretending to judge of colours; but he remained steady to his own opinion, that those persons who were deaf, were the only proper judges of music.[10]

In reality, Blake is not speculating on the possibility that the poetic character would reveal further senses, or their perceptions: that would be a mistakenly literal-minded interpretation. Rather is he emphasising the limitations of the senses, and, in effect, answering the thrust of Voltaire's little satire. In other words, in using the notion of numerous senses, he is doing more than merely suggest that one might go on piling up or aggregating further senses. He is suggesting an organising and unifying power, broadly akin to Coleridge's concept of Imagination. In effect, this is how he has extended the meaning of *perception*. The purpose of this is pointed up by a remark of Hazlitt's in the 'Lectures on English Philosophy'. Discussing Locke, he remarks:

> The great defect with which the 'Essay on the Human Understanding' is chargeable is, that there is not really a word about the nature of the understanding in it, nor any attempt to show what it is or whether it is or is not any thing, distinct from the faculty of simple perception. The operations of thinking, comparing, discerning, reasoning, willing, and the like, which Mr. Locke ascribes to it, are the operations of nothing, or of I know not what.[11]

Blake sets out to prove that we perceive more than is given in sense: in other words, he starts with the concepts of Locke and Hume and subverts them by altering the meaning of the word 'perception': 'Mans perceptions are not bounded by organs of perception. he percieves more than sense (tho' ever so acute) can discover' (*NNR* [b], I; E2).

The 'Conclusion' of the second series of *There Is No Natural Religion* is the statement of Blake's answer to those tendencies he later sums up as 'Bacon & Newton & Locke': 'If it were not for the Poetic or Prophetic character the Philosophic & Experimental would soon be at the ratio of all things, & stand still, unable to do other than repeat the same dull round over again' (E3).

The Blind Tyrant: From Tiriel to Urizen

It is worth considering the proposition that Blake's first known extended symbolic poem, 'Tiriel' (*c*.1789), is actually a kind of companion to the aphorisms of *c*.1788 that we have been discussing. If these involve an intervention into Enlightenment discussions of the blind in order to support the 'Prophetic character', then 'Tiriel' has a blind protagonist who is associated with the corruption of prophecy, and, incidentally, is an obvious forerunner of Urizen. It is in 'Tiriel' that Blake first suggests a conformity between the personal and the institutional, and begins to draw together the various threads that contribute to a social and personal *malaise* which seems to have its roots in the distant past of humanity – a fact symbolised in the outlandish names and 'primitive' architecture of the setting of 'Tiriel'.

Tiriel is portrayed in the designs as an old man with a 'shrivel'd beard' whose eyes are 'blind as the orbless skull among the stones'. By contrast, Har's beard is luxuriant. The designs thus lend support to the text's identification of Tiriel with a relatively desiccated form of authoritarianism. But Har, Tiriel's father, and father of all men, also gives laws: at the end of the poem Tiriel addresses him:

> He said. O weak mistaken father of a lawless race
> Thy laws O Har & Tiriels wisdom end together in a curse
> Why is one law given to the lion & the patient Ox?

Har may be identified with Adam: his consort is Heva, whose name is the Hebrew form of Eve. Har has given laws consonant with the belief in an omnipotent God of Love and has expected, in his conviction that all men are alike, that his sons shall keep them. But Blake represents the differences in the 'lawless race' of men by 'the lion & the patient Ox'. Har's sons have left him, unable to keep his laws, and Tiriel in turn gives laws to his own children. This is the blessing that his children interpret as a curse: 'His blessing was a cruel curse. His curse may be a blessing' (1:17). Tiriel has cursed his children at the beginning of the poem for a reason that is not at first clear. A fair and highly probable inference is that they had disobeyed his laws. Kathleen Raine thinks that 'Tiriel' has such a direct relationship to the Oedipus story that it seems unexceptionable to her to say:

tò [Blake] it was perfectly clear; it is the curse which lay upon the house of Cadmus, condemning Oedipus to the murder of his father and a marriage with his own mother, from which were born the sons whom he himself curses with such terrible passion before his death [. . .][12]

Now 'Tiriel' does have some resemblances to the story of Oedipus; but these are rather in the nature of resemblances in the characters and some of their actions than of a wholehearted adoption of the Greek narrative and its setting. The poem is designed as a vehicle for Blake's emerging thinking about the corruption of humanity: the curse is surely the one mentioned in the lines quoted above, and is the indirect result of giving one law to beings whose nature is held to be alien to it – whose individuality is not reflected in a code of laws uniformly applied. It is not uncharacteristic of Blake to avoid making an overt statement that this is so. On the other hand, crucially, he makes no mention of a marriage of Tiriel to his mother, nor of his having killed his own father. For Tiriel could only be taken not to be the son of Har if his words to Har on the subject are taken seriously. But Blake indicates that Tiriel's words are dissembling at this point.

If Tiriel's curse is indeed caused by the law and by his 'wisdom', then he and Har are both comparable to Urizen and to figures like him elsewhere in Blake's work. The presentation of Har in the designs, with flowing white hair and beard, supports this interpretation. That Har also resembles Adam does not contradict this, since Blake had not yet evolved his myth of the Four Zoas and their fall. Har is a fallen Adam, like Urizen in so far as he gives laws. The original man, according to Blake, was a maker of mythologies: 'the Poetic Genius is the true Man' (*All Religions Are One*; E1). In *The Marriage of Heaven and Hell* (1790–3), Plate 11, Blake describes how the myths of the true man were gradually perverted into belief in transcendent deities: having asserted, in lines we quoted above, that 'the ancient Poets animated all sensible objects with Gods or Geniuses', he goes on to describe how 'a system was formed, which some took advantage of & enslav'd the vulgar by attempting to realize or abstract the mental deities from their objects; thus began Priesthood'. An alternative description of the same process of corruption is then provided: 'Choosing forms of worship from poetic tales'. Har, being comparable to both Adam and Urizen, represents the 'Poetic Genius', the 'true Man', when he has fallen into the error of making the deities that reside in the human breast into Gods above who make laws for men below. A deleted line, 'Thy god of love thy heaven of joy', in Tiriel's speech to Har, refers to this error.

This false and debilitating love is memorably depicted in the illustration of Har and Heva nestling in senile innocence against one another under the staring gaze of their nurse Mnetha, whose name is partly traceable to the Greek *Mnemosyne*, memory: the innocent perception of divinity in Man and the things of Nature has become a distorted memory.

The setting for this scene of fallen innocence is pastoral, as for so many of the *Songs of Innocence*. But Har's fallen nature makes him strikingly similar to 'the Father of the ancient men' in 'Earth's Answer', one of two related poems introductory to *Songs of Experience* (1789–94). Here the Earth has been imprisoned by the laws of 'the Father': she refers to him thus: 'Selfish father of men / Cruel jealous selfish fear'. 'The Father' appears first in the 'Introduction', where he attempts to regain the 'lapsed Soul' of nature:

> Hear the voice of the Bard!
> Who Present, Past, & Future sees
> Whose ears have heard,
> The Holy Word,
> That walk'd among the ancient trees.
>
> (E18)

These lines identify the Father with the fallen Poetic Genius and thus with Har. And this interpretation is aided, though it be slightly, by an illustration which expands the sense of Har to be taken from the words alone.

Another design, *Tiriel Supporting Myratana*, helps to enlarge our notion of the poem. This contains things not described in it: Tiriel's palace, and its background, a treeless expanse with a featureless, white pyramid in the distance. One is reminded of the Neo-classical architects' regression to the use of the simple Doric order, and even to the 'natural' order that some thought had come before the Doric. A few sought the essential beauty of the cube, pyramid, cylinder, sphere and cone. In this search Claude-Nicolas Ledoux (1736–1806) and Etienne-Louis Boulée (1728–99) were very advanced.[13] It was Boulée who designed a gigantic, plain, hollow globe (*c*.1780–90) to be a monument to Newton. The point of such experiments was partly in their connotations of the natural, primitive, rational society which late eighteenth-century thinkers believed they could see in prehistory; and partly in the related belief that geometry would provide the basic structural notions of a rational architecture.

Blake thought that such a rational standard constricted the imagination. He probably already thought that an order like the Doric represented what he was later to call 'Mathematic Form'. His Opinions about Egypt were constantly unsympathetic, being derived from his reading of the Bible. His opinions about Egyptian Art, in particular, may well have been influenced by his friend Barry, who considered that the Egyptians, 'much as they had practised in the art, yet never rose to any perfection above that of practical mechanical conduct [. . .] Their figures appear neither to act nor think, and have more the appearances of dead than of animated nature.'[14]

And so to the pyramid in the illustrations of *Tiriel Supporting Myratana*: the setting places Tiriel's kingdom after the corruption of the art of the Patriarchs of Asia and pre-Biblical Egypt.[15] It is a kingdom of rational materialism, and evidences the effects of Har's laws, and the meaning of Tiriel's 'wisdom' as reason. Thus Tiriel himself is, as it were, a later version of Har: the father of a later, more corrupt age.

These connotations of one design add considerably to our sense of the things that Tiriel stands for. There are, then, two mistaken patriarchal figures in 'Tiriel', and Blake attempts to show that the different errors of each are closely connected. If Har is a degraded 'Poetic Genius' or 'Spirit of Prophecy' (to quote from the nearly contemporaneous *All Religions Are One* (E1)), this is as much as to say that he is a fallen and false prophet. And Tiriel also is a false prophet. As Elizabeth Stieg has demonstrated, his appearance, with beard and long garments, and his denunciations of error all support this interpretation; and he even acts like a true prophet in that his prophecies of doom are fulfilled, so that his falsity consists in leading others to follow his mistaken 'wisdom'.[16] Har has given laws in ignorance of the energy to which they would be fetters: though he may seem benevolent, the stultified 'innocence' which prevents him from seeing that all men are not alike is dangerous. Tiriel, unlike Har, lives in the world, and must act upon the laws which Har has invented. This is another aspect of the mistaken 'wisdom' with which he, rather than Har, is particularly associated. He is forced into violence and is therefore peculiarly fitted to see that Har's laws are mistaken.

The respective attributes of Har and Tiriel are united, to a high degree, in Urizen.[17] Urizen is very much this combination of the violent and tyrannical with the pitying law-giver, who cannot understand the torments of energy. The combination of these attributes is also to be found in *Songs of Experience*, some first versions of which date from 1792, at the latest.[18] Thus, in 'Earth's Answer', the 'Starry Jealousy' who has imprisoned Earth is said to be 'Cold and hoar / Weeping o'er' – an aspect of jealousy we encounter again in 'A Little Girl Lost': the girl returns to her 'father white'

> But his loving look,
> Like the holy book,
> All her tender limbs with terror shook.
> Ona! pale and weak!

To thy father speak:
O the trembling fear!
O the dismal care!
That shakes the blossoms of my hoary hair. (E30)

Since 'Starry Jealousy' is referred to as 'the Father of the ancient men' we may conclude that, like Har, he is a 'weak mistaken father', a fallen Adam. Certainly 'Jealousy' inherits Har's maundering incomprehension of energy, though now this seems a more sinister attribute, since it consorts, in the same character, with overt tyranny: the connection of Tiriel and Har is embodied. 'Jealousy' directly anticipates the Urizen who says, in bewilderment at the fires of energy,

I have sought for a joy without pain,
For a solid without fluctuation
Why will you die O Eternals?
Why live in unquenchable burnings?
                    (*Urizen* 4:10–13; E71)

And, like Har, Urizen formulates

Laws of peace, of love, of unity:
Of pity, compassion, forgiveness.
Let each chuse one habitation:
His ancient infinite mansion:
One command, one joy, one desire,
One curse, one weight, one measure
One King, one God, one Law.
                    (*Urizen* 4: 34–40; E72)

Ernst Cassirer points out that 'One king, one law, one faith' was the motto of the Enlightenment epoch.[19] By the time of the writing of 'Tiriel' Blake has already grasped the principle, in Enlightenment philosophical thinking, of the reduction of phenomena to simple unities. Tiriel, when he has finally gained insight, asks, 'Why is one law given to the lion & the patient Ox?', an idea for which Blake did a pencil study,[20] and which is repeated at the bottom of Plate 24 of *The Marriage* (E43).The reference is to Isaiah 11:7 and 65:25: 'The lion shall eat straw like the ox'. This phrase occurs in the middle of a well-known passage which was traditionally interpreted as a vision of paradise:

The wolf also shall dwell with the lamb, and the leopard shall lie down with the kid; and the calf and the young lion and the fatling together; and a little child shall lead them. And the cow and the bear shall feed; the young ones shall lie down together: and the lion shall eat straw like the ox.

(Isaiah 11:6–7)

This, then, is the 'heaven of joy' which Tiriel refers to slightingly in the deleted line which comes just before his mention of the lion and the ox:

Blake implies that contraries cannot be reconciled simply by reducing them to one principle, that of enforced innocence.

In Plate 24 of *The Marriage* Nebuchadnezzar is shown crawling on his hands and knees above the motto 'One Law for the Lion & Ox is Oppression' (E43). This plate must date from 1790–3, and there is an early version in the Notebook (N44). It will be recalled that Nebuchadnezzar 'did eat grass as oxen' (Daniel 4:32–3) when he was driven from men by God. Blake is making an oblique link with the idea of the lion eating straw like the ox. I think it would be wrong to identify Nebuchadnezzar with the lion's energy: on the contrary, I think that Blake is attempting to imply that Nebuchadnezzar is a tyrant in the same way that Tiriel was, and has come to feel the ill effects of the laws he himself has promoted.

In the pencil drawing, which dates from around the time of 'Tiriel', there are not only a lion and an ox, but an old man with long white hair and beard holding a crook or a crozier, with two children at his knees. Geoffrey Keynes identifies the figure as Tiriel with a whip, and the two children as Har and Heva, claiming that the drawing is 'clearly' intended for 'Tiriel'.[21] However, the bearded figure, if it is any personage from 'Tiriel', is surely Har: he does not look in the least like Tiriel; nor are Har and Heva portrayed as children anywhere in the 'Tiriel' designs. The object in the old man's hands is surely a shepherd's crook. The drawing shows, yet again, that Blake associated the growth of the law with the attempt to remain in a state of innocence when faced with the terrifying power of energy for creation and destruction. The picture evokes a sense of the pastoral for the same reason that Har and Heva are said, though old, to behave like this: 'Playing with flowers. & running after birds they spent the day / And in the night like infants slept delighted with infant dreams' ('Tiriel', 2: 8–9, E277). The imagery recalls *Songs of Innocence*. But Har and Heva have outlived the time when they should have put away the reliance on this kind of innocence.

The idea of One Law is closely related to that of the 'bounded' which restrains Energy and Genius. It arises from fear and incomprehension – the same fear and incomprehension which drive Thel to run shrieking from the vision of Experience back into the vales of Har. The question is: How precisely is Blake using the term 'Law' at the time of the writing of 'Tiriel'? In *The Book of Urizen* the term clearly refers to several types of law which Blake wishes to link: when he writes 'One King, one God, one Law' he is referring to his belief that the laws of Priest and King are closely related, and have the same object: oppression on both personal and social levels. It also refers to his belief that eighteenth-century thought was consolidating, rather than relieving, this oppression, by reducing so many diverse phenomena to the principle of unity. Law, for instance, as 'Natural Law', was now firmly based in universal Reason: its dictates were uniform and immutable and grasped by the Reason of Mahometan and Turk no less than of Jew or American Indian. In religion, Socinianism was merely the forceful expression of what had always been central to Deism.

In *An Essay on Man* Pope avers that, 'Each individual seeks a sev'ral goal; / But HEAV'N'S great view is One, and that the Whole [. . .]' (11: 238–9). Blake's image of the Lion and the Ox is intended to counter just such a view: the Deist, who wishes to reduce everything to one principle, discourages the individual genius. But Blake defends the 'sev'ral goal': the Lion is not the Ox: 'How can one joy absorb another? are not different joys / Holy, eternal, infinite!' (*Visions of the Daughters of Albion*, 5: 5–6, E47).

For Pope's editor, Warburton, Church and State existed to perfect man's ability to live according to the Natural Law: Church and State are 'ordained to one end, to perfect Man's nature; yet, as they pursue it by different means, they must act in conjunction, lest the diversity of the means should retard or defeat the attainment of the concurrent end.'[22] Warburton proposes a 'politic ALLIANCE' of Church and State.[23] For Blake both Church and State are corrupt institutions which take their common source from an undivided Poetic Genius, of which Religion and Legislation are corrupt systematisations. 'Tiriel' concerns the period after the Fall of the Poetic Genius. Har, with his God of Love and Heavens of Joy, corresponds to Warburton's 'RELIGION'; and Tiriel, king of the west, to his 'GOVERNMENT'.[24]

Warburton is not claimed to be the necessary source of Blake's allegory in 'Tiriel': rather his *Alliance Between Church and State* is taken as the most striking example of a kind of thinking which was very common in the eighteenth century (for instance in Montesquieu). But State and Church for Blake are 'The Beast & the Whore'. We are now in a position to answer the question, What is Blake saying about the Law at the time of the writing of 'Tiriel'? It is clear that he already uses the term with the same implications that it has in *Urizen*, of the constriction of Energy and individual Genius, born of the fear of these; acting on the level of the political and religious, but internalised by the individual. Priesthood, Legislation, Kingship are, like 'Fable or Allegory', corruptions of what was originally one, undivided function, the 'Poetic Genius'.

To say that 'Law', systems, limitation in general are derived from a fear of Energy may not sound very interesting. The interest in what Blake is saying may be more apparent if the assertion is phrased in a positive way: system-building begins as the need for security, almost for tidiness, in the face of the unpredictability of Energy. This is an opposition which is central to the conception of *Songs of Innocence and Experience*.

Blindness and 'London'

Of course, *Songs of Innocence and Experience* involve figurative blindness in their very structure and its embodiment. The 'two contrary states' of the human soul have mutually exclusive visions: one reads black where the other reads white. Even the contrasting designs embody this idea. Indeed, one feature of the designs involves a further reference to figurative blindness and vision: the full foliage of some of the borders of the *Innocence* designs contrasts with the leafless trees of some of the borders in *Experience*, and this contrast models that between joyful ignorance and joyless knowledge (one may see through leafless branches) .[25] But one of the *Songs of Experience*, 'London', makes reference to a blind man in its illumination, and, furthermore, an 'ancient curse' is referred to two pages away from 'London' in the *Notebook*, in a poem ('An ancient Proverb') that also refers to a 'blackning church' and a 'marriage hearse'.[26] This suggests that 'London' links blindness and corruption in ways which are worth comparing with 'Tiriel'. The illumination shows an old bearded man, leaning on sticks, being led through the streets by a little child. The Notebook identifies this figure as 'London blind & age-bent', and this identification is supported by Plate 84 of *Jerusalem*, which shows a closely similar design (though reversed), glossed in the text by lines about 'London blind and age-bent, begging through the streets / Of Babylon, led by a child. his tears run down his beard' (84:11–12; E243). It is significant, therefore, that perception – specifically the senses of sight and hearing – should be so emphasised in the poem. The nature of this emphasis, however, is by no means straightforward. In the first stanza, an important layer of meaning is that the speaker scrutinises and is able to interpret the 'Marks of weakness, marks of woe' he encounters in the passers-by. In the second stanza, the emphasis moves to the sense of hearing, but again, the speaker's capacity to interpret is emphasised, and in this case it is even more powerfully analytic ('in every ban, / The mind-forg'd manacles I hear'). The third stanza sees a synaesthetic process whereby the speaker converts sounds into complex visual imagery, the vehicle for which is a densely metaphorical language. On hearing 'the Chimney-sweeper's cry' the speaker is able to 'hear' how it 'appalls' every 'blackning Church', where the antithesis between 'blackning' and the etymological sense of 'appalls' (to make pale) emphasises the unliteralness of the image: such strange perceptions, made of mingled sight and sound, occur only to the mind of the poet-prophet. The notion of an 'inner eye' is certainly an influence on this poem. But that tradition is powerfully enhanced by Blake's use of synaesthesia. This reading is supported by the next two lines, in which the speaker hears how 'the hapless Soldiers sigh / Runs in blood down Palace walls', and by the almost conceited language of the final stanza, in which he hears how 'the youthful Harlots curse / Blasts the new-born Infants tear / And blights with plagues the Marriage hearse'. In all of these cases an analysis of the structure of oppression, and some of its worst effects, is conveyed. The associations of the words take the effect beyond mere synaesthesia: the young prostitute's venereal disease becomes a metaphor for a plague akin to a curse sent by God. Yet synaesthesia is not merely an important component, but also in itself a sign of a speaker who can transcend the boundaries normally set between the senses, and also between the 'Philosophy of the Five Senses' and the 'Poetic Genius.' That London should be blind suggests the impercipience which accompanies and causes its fallen condition, a limitation for which a parallel is offered in 'the mind-forg'd manacles'. An important irony of the poem is thus the antithesis set up between the blind man with long white hair who represents London, and the bardic prophet who condemns it and possesses a faculty akin to that inner eye possessed by blind visionaries. The antithesis is the more striking in that both are London wanderers, and the old man ('London') possesses the long white hair and beard which may also adorn the prophet. In this way, the poem offers a supreme reworking of the theme of bardic vision lost in the world of commerce.

The Divided Self

In his facsimile edition of the *Songs*, Geoffrey Keynes speculates that this 'bearded figure may be the creator, Urizen, himself crippled by the conditions he has created'.[27] One does not have to state categorically that he is identical with Urizen (whatever that would mean) in order to see that there is some relationship, for Urizen is a figure of multiple reference, and *The Book of Urizen* makes it clear that he is indeed a victim of his own perverted imagination. Furthermore, one of its chief themes is the decline of human vision, as is particularly evident from Plate 25, where the inhabitants of the 'thirty cities' of Urizen's creation find that their senses shrink, 'Till the shrunken eyes clouded over / Discernd not the woven hipocrisy' (E82). In this condition they mirror that of their creator, whose own formation has involved his eyes being placed 'On high into two little orbs / And fixed in two little caves / Hiding carefully from the wind'

(Plate 12; E76). Such lines are supported by those designs in which Urizen's eyes are closed, notably the title-page of *The Book of Urizen* itself. That title-page, however, insists in its iconography that the curse is as much to do with division of the self as it is with the imposition of tyrannical law: or rather, the iconography insists that these phenomena amount to the same thing, for the division between the two tables of the laws points down to the centre of Urizen's head, symbolising the divided self.

This is a point also made in the 1795 colour prints. *The Good and Evil Angels* contains one of Blake's most striking images of blindness: the Evil Angel looms forward with sightless eyes, manacled, as we may learn from *The Marriage of Heaven and Hell*, by Reason. Indeed, this design is a version in reverse of that on Plate 4 of *The Marriage*, where we are reminded of the 'Errors' of 'Bibles or sacred codes' which teach that there are 'two real existing principles Viz: a Body & a Soul' (E34). On the contrary, 'Man has no Body distinct from his Soul' and 'Energy is the only life and is from the Body'. The figure of the Evil Angel in Blake's print, therefore, represents the degraded conception of the body consequent on an erroneous dualism. Its terrifying aspect is a reminder of the dangers of repression. The symbolic attributes of the design are well described by Robin Hamlyn in the catalogue of the 2000 Tate exhibition: 'The Angel's senses are incomplete: the Evil Angel is sightless, the closed mouth suggests that he cannot be heard and the sensation of touch must remain unknown to him because he is chained.'[28] But, of course, both poles of the dualism are infirm: as Hamlyn points out, 'The androgynous forms of both Angels also imply that touch, through sex, is impossible.'[29] In line with the critique of 'Reason' and 'Good', the most obvious colour print of 1795 to put alongside this one is *The House of Death*, which shows the figure of death as an old man with long white hair and beard, casting arrows of lightning, but with his eyes closed like Urizen's on the title-page of *The Book of Urizen*. Indeed, his hands rest on two round cloud-shapes which vaguely evoke the domed tops of the tablets of the law in a manner which is perhaps more obvious from the image of Urizen in *America*. The figure in *The House of Death* is another version of Urizen. It is entirely appropriate that he should appear in a series with the blind figure of the Evil Angel, and of course with that design of *Newton* which bears such a close resemblance to the figure with the compasses in *There Is No Natural Religion*.

Printing for the Blind

To rescue the body and to rescue imagination are, in Blake's earlier work, interrelated endeavours. His desire to 'cleanse the doors of perception', announced in *The Marriage of Heaven and Hell*, is well known, as is the fact that this ambition was to be realised by his innovative methods of printing. Not all the implications of the printing metaphor in *The Marriage* have been noticed; and, in any case, I shall claim that they need to be gauged in relation to the idea of printing for the blind. Not only does a sullied 'door of perception' suggest obstruction of vision, but there were experiments with 'relief printing' for the blind going on in the early 1780s, and since the idea of relief printing is so unusual, we must count these as part of the context for Blake's own experiments. Of course, Blake also considers the figurative implications of his techniques, and with printing these would include matters to do with the meaning of repetition and the reversal of images. These figurative implications need to be studied in tandem with any consideration of the processes themselves.

I have adverted elsewhere to the implications of the words 'imposition' and 'impose', suggesting that they comprise, for Blake, the assertion of vision by means of that 'firm perswasion' which is itself an inseparable attribute of the visionary character.[30] In *Historicizing Blake*, I further suggested that 'self-imposition' was an opposed category, embodying the idea of internal division and 'Self Contradiction'.[31] But there is another aspect of Blake's usage of the word 'impose', related to printing, which has never been noticed. For the word 'impose' means 'to lay pages of type or stereotype plates in proper order on the bed of a press and secure them in a chase'. The word is a staple of printers' and compositors' terminology, and it would be an easy but otiose task to demonstrate that it normally receives a separate section, for which it provides the heading, in compositors' manuals: thus, in Moxon (1683) we have the section '*Of* Imposing'.[32] Furthermore, at least in the days before offset (and now electronic) printing, this usage was well enough known to the non-expert. It still appears in recent editions of popular dictionaries such as *Chambers*.

Now this usage refers to the printing of books or journals, and in implying 'proper order', does so because it refers to the need to print a number of pages onto the folio at once, in such a way that the versos, rectos and juxtapositions are in the right places, so that when the folio is folded and cut, the pages will be consecutive. Blake is not producing a book by the conventional method, and thus he does not produce large folded signatures requiring the cutting of pages. Nevertheless, it is perhaps significant that we know from J. T. Smith's *Nollekens and His Times* that Blake would have accepted the designation 'stereotype plates' for his own relief-etched plates; and conventional books could indeed be produced from stereotype plates.[33] Furthermore, Joseph Viscomi has conclusively shown that Blake often printed in gatherings: in the case of *Innocence*, for instance, he printed editions of the book by impressing pairs of plates onto both sides of the folio.[34] For this reason, Viscomi is content to refer to Blake's 'printing plates in forms' (form being another word for chase) and to his use of 'folio *imposition*' (my emphasis).[35] In other words, Blake's invoking of 'the idea of the book' does extend to the practical question of their printing, and this invoking was chiefly constituted by *imposition*.

It is not surprising, then, to find that Blake himself employs the word 'imposition' in the context of printing. The word first appears in *The Marriage*, Plate 12, where Blake dines with Isaiah and Ezekiel. This is quite close to the place where the printing metaphor is made very explicit in Plate 14, in the passage about the 'infernal method'. One may grant, of course, that the word 'impose' in this context possesses other connotations, those of 'deceive' (a now almost defunct sense) and 'impress'. The first connotation, when unravelled, would imply that those whose visions are opposed may well experience their opponents as deceivers: Angels are likely to feel this way permanently; Devils will feel this way about Angels; but among themselves, Devils will recognise that 'Opposition is true Friendship'. The second connotation is itself congruent with a reference to printing. Both connotations would sit comfortably with a metaphor derived from the printer's sense of the word 'impose': referring as it does to the order in which plates are laid down, it suggests that what is essential to Blake's vision has something to do with its being unfolded over a plurality of plates, and with juxtaposition of plates as a concomitant of that unfolding.

But there is yet another meaning with which Blake would have been familiar. Repetition and plurality may suggest the arbitrariness of the sign. This, of course, is a condition of the fallen world for Blake. Nevertheless, it is one with which he has to struggle; and he is undoubtedly aware of the semiotic debates about arbitrariness in which the word 'imposition' had a venerable place. Thus Aquinas, taking a hint from Aristotle's *De interpretatione*, refers to signification under two kinds: *impositio secundum naturam* ('imposition according to nature') and *impositio iuxta arbitrium humanae voluntatis* ('imposition according to the judgement of the human will').[36] The former is more indicative; the latter more arbitrary (*arbitrium*). Urquhart's translation of Rabelais, in the scholastic tradition, also makes use of the idea of *impositio*:

All Speeches have had their primary Origin from the Arbitrary Institutions, Accords and Agreements of Nations in their respective Condescendments to what should be noted and betokened by them. An Articulate Voice (according to the Dialecticians) hath naturally no signification at all; for that the sence and meaning thereof did totally depend upon the good will and pleasure of the first Deviser and *Imposer* of it.

(III: 19; my emphasis)

And in Locke's *Essay* we are informed that 'Words [. . .] come to be made use of by Men as the *Signs of* their *Ideas*; not by any natural connexion [. . .] but by a voluntary Imposition, whereby such a Word is made arbitrarily the Mark of such an *Idea* (III.ii.1)'. The point Blake would have accepted here, as Robert Essick makes clear, is the difference between an Adamic language on the one hand, and the arbitrariness of the conventions of the fallen human world on the other. (My argument does not depend on any of the possible beliefs about what Saussure intended in his own doctrine of arbitrariness.) If we bring together the associations cited so far, including that which would simply comprise the idea of 'impressing' or imposing a plate on the paper, we might suggest the following conclusion: imposition refers to Blake's sense that, by his 'infernal method', he is, with a hint of paradox, asserting a 'firm perswasion' through a medium characterised by succession, difference and juxtaposition. But in view of the fact that there is some contemporary dispute about the character of the 'difference' intended by Blake's method, it will be necessary to be fairly precise about what does and what does not seem to be supported by a parallel consideration of that method and of his language about it. Stephen Leo Carr has argued strongly for the marked significance of the facts of variation in different printings, in terms both of different ordering of plates, and, even more, of different approaches to colouring.[37] He has connected this variability to Derrida's concept of *différance*, especially in relation to the way in which that concept comprises the notion of 'iterability': the inevitable capacity of the utterance to be repeated, which entails that it is constituted by significative elements which can never be reduced to an original context.[38] Robert Essick and Joseph Viscomi have offered disagreement with this analysis, largely on the evidence of Blake's actual production, and of its artistic context, rather than in repudiation of its theoretical treatment.[39] Robert Essick suggests that the actual variation, though present, is not nearly as significant as the persistence and continuity, which he relates to Blake's avowal of the 'Eternal' character of his designs: 'My Designs unchangd remain' (Blake 1977: 87).[40] Both Essick and Viscomi refer to the prevalence of variation in the market for eighteenth-century prints, though Essick concedes that the 'degree of variation' is greater in Blake.[41] This seems to me to be a significant concession. But what features of Blake's books are emphasised by the idea of 'imposition' as both a literal and figurative use of a printing term?

The term surely has everything to do with juxtaposition of plates (several plates are printed onto one folio), and nothing intrinsically to do with variation in the order or colouring of them. And if it be said that imposition is a feature of all book printing, it must surely be conceded that Blake is trying to derive significance from emphasising what is involved in it in a context where he has also drawn attention to the union of word and design. In other words, what Blake is indicating as a novel and radical feature of his method is the potential for a composite art on lines the most ambitious analysis of which remains that of W. J. T. Mitchell. This, rather than anything about variability of colouring or order, is what can be strictly inferred from a consideration of the prominence of the word 'imposition' in *The Marriage*. The point remains radical enough: the 'firm perswasion' of the honest prophet is not characterised by the univocal, but by the polyphonic, and by the overcoming of barriers between genres and senses. Furthermore, while nothing can be strictly inferred about variability, Essick's concession is not only significant but surely correct: there is a high degree of variability on Blake, and while this is not referred to by the word 'imposition', it does possess an affinity with what that word is pointing to. At the same time, there is something very assertive about the combination of the ideas of 'imposition' and 'firm perswasion', and relief etching is figuratively appropriate to such assertiveness.

The infernal method is also essentially characterised by the use of relief etching, as opposed to intaglio. It seems likely to be profitable to assume that a figurative meaning, a 'spiritual sense', attaches to this choice and to its effects. I believe that there is such a figurative meaning, and that it is especially associated with another sense of 'imposition' which I earlier called 'impressing'. Now the method was in part devised in order to permit what Ackroyd calls 'painting rather than engraving the copper plate', and this was a means towards the end of combining design and text.[42] Given that this combination (however we may wish to conceive its effects) was intended to 'expunge' the 'notion that man has a body distinct from his soul' (*The Marriage of Heaven and Hell*, 14), we must read Blake's intention of 'melting apparent surfaces away' (including its figurative aspect) as referring not to any type of engraving, but specifically to his own method of relief etching. Two further questions follow: how much of the body is referred to in any aspect of the new method or its effects? To put it another way: we know that the sense of vision (and vision in more than a limited corporeal understanding) is invoked by the co-presence of text and design. We also know that the auditory was important to Blake, both from stories of his composing melodies for the *Songs* and from the discussion of 'cadence' and 'numbers' in the address 'To the Public' at the beginning of *Jerusalem*. To come to the point, relief printing for the blind was intended for them to touch: is the sense of touch alluded to in any way? A number of critics and scholars have noticed connotations and effects which suggest that it is. Robert Essick has been the most explicit about this possibility:

> Blake's illuminated texts ask us to see the individual, ever-various shapes and textures of designs and autograph letters through an eye integrated with, and thus expanded by, the sense of touch. In this way, relief-etching is itself a stimulus to 'the improvement of sensual enjoyment' and cleansing of the senses to make them 'enlarged and numerous'.[43]

The reason why we may feel that the sense of touch is invoked has to do, I would claim, both with the connotations of the printing method, and with the effects procured by it. Thus Joseph Viscomi speaks of the 'infinite' being 'displayed' because it is 'made prominent, as it literally would be when the design was etched into relief'.[44] And Vincent De Luca speaks of the appearance of 'a wall of words' on a large scale as figuring 'the energy of the sublime experience'.[45] Neither of these last two critics invokes the sense of touch, but both of them adduce the considerations which lead Essick to do so. It is also worth recalling that Blake may be assumed to have been serious in his desire to equate body and soul in the most comprehensive way, and that in several well-known passages he refers to the body by referring to each of the senses.

I have already suggested that Blake is specifically relating touch and sight by reference to a precisely contemporary phenomenon: the invention of relief printing for the blind. As we have already seen, it was the Abbé Valentin Haüy who in 1783 devised this aid in its first true form. An account of the technique was provided in his book of 1786, *Essai sur l'éducation des aveugles*. The blind Scottish poet, Thomas Blacklock, made a translation which appeared posthumously in his collected works. The technique involved the creation of books with relief text by punching relief plates into the cards which made up the pages. Despite earlier haphazard efforts at the use of relief letters, this was the first example of systematic relief printing, and was recognised as such.[46] One of the assertions made by Blake is that the experimental is not dependent on the senses as we know them. And the new, experimental method he employs to print this text is also intended to let us discover more than the senses as we know them could inform us about. Blake is providing an analogue of relief printing for the blind, one that exploits the figurative senses of blindness and vision, in that it makes relief etching a means of access to imaginative vision among those who require their 'doors of perception' to be cleansed. As we have seen, his first experiments with his new method, *There Is No Natural Religion* and *All Religions Are One*, are of texts which take off from Enlightenment discussions of the blind.

The figurative associations we have already been explicating take on a new significance once this is realised. Indeed, there are further such associations to consider: namely, all that is involved in what Viscomi refers to as the design's being 'made prominent'. In view of Blake's espousal of 'Opposition', the mere fact that his method is 'a simple reversal of intaglio' (as Morton Paley puts it) is surely significant.[47] For intaglio could scarcely be described as a method involving the sense of 'prominence'. Where Blake extrudes design and text, intaglio incises them. The figurative advantage accorded to relief etching is that, by virtue of an energetic extrusion of the sign, it is both 'honest imposition' and 'firm perswasion', and these two concepts involve what I earlier called 'impressing'. (I use the word 'sign' as Essick does in *William Blake and the Language of Adam*, in the wide sense according to which it may refer not only to words but also to significative icons, indices and figures, and thus also to Blake's engraved plates considered in their totality as significative entities – considered, that is, in a term which has gained some currency, as 'hieroglyphs'.) The commercial version of intaglio, on the other hand, is an incision into the self, which Blake associates with the absence of 'firm perswasion': with the doubt which he would later equate with self-contradiction. If this be accepted, it becomes worth enquiring as to whether or not 'self-imposition' also implies the printing metaphor. The word is to be found in *Milton*, in Palamabron's characterisation of Satan:

> You know Satans mildness and his self-imposition,
> Seeming a brother, being a tyrant, even thinking himself a brother
> While he is murdering the just.
>
> > (7:21–3: E100)

It is surely worth entertaining the hypothesis that self-imposition comprises a reference to the prevalent method of commercial engraving. Support for this idea can be found in the line at the centre of the tables of the Law which descends onto the centre of Urizen's head on the title-page of *The Book of Urizen*, where, significantly, he is holding writing instruments. There is, then, a type of book creation which is characterised by division of the self. The later reference to his 'book of Brass' (3:44: E72) lends credence to the idea that such book creation may comprise the creation of books through the agency of etched metal plates, even if we may not share the confidence of Erdman and Mitchell that all, or indeed any, of the versions of the title-page show Urizen holding a burin.[48] *The Book of Urizen*, thus, begins to address the topic of how what is termed the

Spectre in Blake's later work is 'the ghostly double of imaginative vision, haunting and tracking it with its negative self-image'.[49] And we can easily conceive how this large general topic might already comprise the subordinate topic of the spectral quality of Blake's labours 'as working engraver', labours which include the use of intaglio.[50] This technique, which Blake, as Paley points out, reverses, is itself a 'reversal' of imagination, and would be congruent with the Spectre's being himself a 'reversal': 'the Almighty hath made me his Contrary / To be all evil, all reversed' (*Jerusalem* 10:57; E154); 'as a distorted & reversed Reflexion' (*J* 17:42; E162). The topics of reversal and reflection are bound up with the practical task of engraving in the most essential manner. The need to reverse the design on the copper plate, like any practical task for the true craftsman, was not a matter (it should not need saying) for complacent inadvertence or idle guesswork, but for explicit precept and rule; and a time-honoured means of procuring reversal was with the use of the mirror. A manual which makes this very clear, since it provides many subheadings, is Maxime Lalanne's of 1866, in which a section called 'Reversing the Design' is followed by 'Use of the Mirror'.[51] This will remind Blakeans of the piquant fact that the result of George Cumberland's engraving experiments was to produce a reversed text: he averred that his works might be read with 'the looking glass' because 'reversed', and that therefore they would be 'none to the crowd', that is, inaccessible to the *profanum vulgus*.[52] Albion, who sits in despair in the illumination to *Jerusalem* Plate 37, seems unable to read the reversed mirror-writing, on the scroll to the left of the design, which would tell him the way in which Humanity escapes the power of the Spectre.

Extrusion versus incision can be seen as exuberance versus prudence and timidity. But they can also be seen as positive and negative, with the negative shadowing the positive. Thus, when Blake says to the Angel 'we impose on one another', we may read this one way as 'we print on one another', but alternatively as 'each of us prints on the parts the other leaves out' ('But thou read'st black / Where I read white'). Furthermore, if one visualises the way in which the same shape would be treated by relief etching on the one hand and intaglio on the other, one can see how the line of intaglio might look as if it were providing an outline for the line of relief engraving ('Reason is the bound or outward circumference of Energy', *MHH*, 4, E34). Translated into terms more related to printing, this perception suggests some such thought as the following: 'Your printing, which seems to provide a line for my conceptions really only offers weakness and recessiveness, where mine offers boldness and salience.' Blake identified the fall with blindness to the Spirit of Prophecy. He sought in his very medium to overcome that fall and that blindness. As part of this endeavour, he included a critique of other forms of engraving.

Notes

1. For dates see the relevant Textual Notes in Blake (1988). Quotations from Blake are from this edition, cited in the text as E followed by the page number. For an account of Blake on empiricism, see Green (2005).
2. Rawlinson (2003), p. 79.
3. Griffiths, Clifford and Royalton-Kisch (1978), No. 11.
4. Voltaire (1767), p. 16.
5. Modern philosophers of science, like Popper, would reject Newton's idea of himself, and the eighteenth-century idea of him. Particularly useful is the discussion in Rée (1974), pp. 151–7.
6. Vortexes, not vortices, are discussed on pp. 88ff., particles ('little balls') of light, pp. 41–2; inhabitants of the moon, pp. 40–71; microscopic life: 'A mulberry leaf is a little world, inhabited by multitudes of these invisible worms, which, to them, is a country of vast extent' (p. 76); 'fancy then millions of creatures to subsist many years on a grain of sand' (p. 77).
7. Voltaire (1799–81), unnumbered vol., *On Toleration* (1779), Book 2, p. 76. Different issues of this work vary considerably in pagination, translation, and even number of volumes.
8. Ibid.
9. Ibid., p. 77.
10. Ibid.
11. Hazlitt (1930–4), II, p. 146.
12. Raine (1969), I, p. 36.
13. Honour (1968), p. 127; Rosenblum (1967), pp. 149–51.
14. Barry (1831), pp. 345–6. The lectures were delivered much earlier than this date, however: Barry began lecturing in 1784 (though appointed Professor in 1782): *DNB*.
15. Cf. Bogen (1970), pp. 153–65; and Hall (1970).
16. Stieg (1990), pp. 273–96, pp. 278–80.
17. It is interesting to note that Tiriel's name stands for the intelligence of mercury, the element which, I shall claim, in good company, belongs also to Urizen: see Beer (1978), pp. 251, 256.
18. In the Notebook. See Blake (1977), p. 7 for dating.
19. Cassirer (1932), p. 23.
20. *Why is one law given to the lion & the patient Ox* (*c.*1788. Prof. C. A. Ryskamp, Princeton, NJ). Repro. in Keynes (1970a), Pl. 5.
21. Ibid., facing page.
22. Warburton (1748), pp. iii–iv.
23. Ibid., p. iv.
24. Ibid., p. iii.
25. Larrissy (1985), pp. 11–13, 46.
26. Blake (1977), N107 (where N refers to a page in Blake's Notebook.)
27. Blake (1970b), Plate 46 commentary.

28. Phillips and Hamlyn (2000), p. 218.
29. Ibid.
30. Larrissy (1985), p. 10.
31. Larrissy (1994), p. 70.
32. Moxon (1962), p. 223.
33. Smith (1828), II, p. 461.
34. Viscomi (1993), pp. 112–18.
35. Ibid., p. 117.
36. Aristotle is presumably responding to the distinction unfolded in Plato's *Cratylus*, but unlike Plato takes the view that language is essentially composed of conventional signs. For a discussion of the whole question of the debate about convention and motivation, as it might have influenced Blake, see Essick (1989), pp. 28–103.
37. Carr (1986), pp. 177–96.
38. Ibid., p. 187.
39. Essick (1986), pp. 197–217; Viscomi (1993), pp. 163–76.
40. Essick (1986), p. 204.
41. Ibid., p. 202.
42. Ackroyd (1995), p. 112.
43. Essick (1980), p. 120.
44. Viscomi (1993), p. 81.
45. De Luca (1991), p. 93.
46. Haüy 'invented the art of printing in relief for the blind', according to *The Penny Cyclopaedia* (1833–6), IV, p. 517.
47. Paley (1978), p. 14.
48. The design is reproduced in Blake (1995), p. 63. The Editor, David Worrall, points out (p. 26), that the confidence about the burin once possessed by Mitchell is hard to maintain, and that Mitchell himself is now less sure. See Mitchell (1969), p. 84. Compare Blake 1974, p. 183: Urizen is holding 'an etching needle'.
49. Vine (1993), p. 46.
50. Paley (1983), p. 253.
51. Lalanne (1880).
52. See Lister (1975), p. 66. Michael Phillips also discusses Cumberland, placing his experiments in the context of the atmosphere of suspicion prevalent in Britain during the Terror (and also placing the local and small-scale character of Blake's production in that context): Phillips (1994), pp. 263–97.

Chapter 4

Edifying Tales

The condition of the blind may furnish good matter for a story. There are many possibilities: their capacity to act as competently as the sighted, or learn to do so; their retention of a good heart when struck blind, or possession of one despite being blind from birth; the tricks that the sighted may play upon them, or the compassion they may demonstrate or elicit. All of these fundamental narrative opportunities may become involved with contemporary reflections on the value of work, the existence or otherwise of innate benevolence, or the way in which spiritual insight may be attained. A straightforward example is provided by a very popular and oft-repeated tale of blind competence and industry. The chapbook, *The Life of John Metcalf*, appeared in the late eighteenth century and was reprinted many times.[1] Metcalf, commonly known as 'Blind Jack of Knaresborough', was a renowned figure. He also makes an appearance in the anonymous *Anecdotes of the Deaf, Dumb, and Blind* (1800?), alongside various figures, some obscure; some, like Carolan and Blacklock, less so.[2] As we have seen, he is mentioned by Scott in a footnote to 'Wandering Willie's Tale'. He had been blinded by smallpox when six years old, but, as the title of the book makes clear, he engaged competently in many exploits of 'Hunting, Card Playing, &c.', as well as building roads and erecting bridges. Not surprisingly, he proved expert at music, and entertained the 'nobility and gentry' with his skill.[3] The booklet contains a number of stories which demonstrate his ability to find his way around, and include people's surprise at discovering that Metcalf is blind. Thus he guides a gentleman from York to Harrogate at night. On arrival, the gentleman is told of his companion's disability, upon which he exclaims, 'Had I known that, I would not have ventured with you for an hundred pounds'.[4] Jack enlists in the campaign of 1745, playing marches on his fiddle and 'hautboy'.[5] Questioned by an officer as to how he 'durst venture into the service, blind as he was', he replied, referring to a frequent cause of blindness, that 'had he possessed a pair of good eyes, he would never have come there to have risked the loss of them by gunpowder'.[6] It is interesting to speculate that the many casualties of the war who were blinded in action rendered a tale such as this of even greater interest to the public. In conformity with this piece of repartee, Jack is seen as a good, bold fellow, though not pedantic in his pursuit of virtue, with his card-playing and dealing in contraband.[7] Nevertheless, the booklet ends with a little rhyme asserting that 'The bright sun beams of virtue will turn night into day'.[8]

Charles Lamb's *A Tale of Rosamund Gray and Old Blind Margaret* (1798) is also relatively straightforward in its handling of blindness, if not of moral implication, not least because Margaret has only gone blind in old age, a not uncommon occurrence. Rosamund Gray, young and innocent, is defiled by the wicked Matravis, and dies shortly afterwards. The topic of unmerited misfortune echoes the calamities of Lamb's own recent experience, and the theme, if not the manner, suggests a link with Coleridge's more optimistic handling of a like subject, partly in relation to Lamb, in the version of 'This Lime-Tree Bower My Prison' he had revised to include the topic of blindness by 1800. Allan Clare, Rosamund's unfortunate lover, reflects upon what has occurred:

> I gave my heart to the Purifier, and my will to the Sovereign Will of the Universe. The irresistible wheels of destiny passed on in their everlasting rotation, and I suffered myself to be carried along with them without complaining.[9]

This uncomplaining attitude is foreshadowed in the description of Margaret's reaction to going blind at the beginning of the tale: 'Margaret retained a spirit unbroken by the calamity. There was a principle *within*, which it seemed as if no outward circumstance could reach. It was a *religious* principle, and she had taught it to Rosamund [. . .]' (377). Blindness is indeed an appropriate affliction with which to emphasise 'a principle within'. Margaret's attitude is underlined by her attitude to thunder:

> There had been *thunder* in the course of the day – an occasion of instruction which the old lady never let pass. She began –
> 'Thunder has a very awful sound: some say God Almighty is angry whenever it thunders, – that it is the voice of God speaking to us; for my part, I am not afraid of it' –
> And in this manner the old lady was going on to particularise, as usual, its beneficial effects, in clearing the air, destroying of vermin, &c. [. . .] (393–4)

The presence of Margaret also provides occasions for Rosamund to exhibit and practise benevolence. Thus she gathers wild flowers and places them 'in the bosom of her old blind friend', so that she may smell them (383). One day she has been taking great pains with drawing a landscape, but while she is out, Margaret, taking it for waste paper, had torn it in half and twisted it into 'thread-paper' (383–4). On returning, Rosamund, though giving her grandmother 'a roguish smile', refrained from comment, knowing how the old woman would fret. The practice of benevolence to our fellows supersedes the demands of the most disinterested and lovely of the arts. The inner life, of which the blind so immediately remind us, is more important than a representation of beauty; and the beauty that we (unlike the blind) may see – and represent – is contrasted with an inward harmony beyond any one of the senses.

How an old blind lady responds to the sound of thunder; how she tore up a landscape drawing by mistake: these are the kinds of incident which make up much of Lamb's tale. Indeed, one of the most striking things about it is how little action it contains in proportion to its length. Many pages are devoted to the humble aperçus of old Margaret, or to unpretentious examples of benevolence. This is a book which has learnt from Wordsworth's assertion that 'The moving accident is not my trade', or his pronouncement in 'Simon Lee' that 'It is no tale, but should you think / Perhaps a tale you'll make it'. Of course, the wicked seduction of Rosamund is indeed a 'moving accident', but it appears, as it might in a Wordsworth narrative, oddly displaced and reduced by matter which is meant to remind us of the quiet persistence of human benevolence in the midst of a suffering which will always be with us.

The blind make a compelling subject for the evangelical and other writers of moral tales for children who flourish from the late eighteenth century into the early nineteenth. The contrast and relationship of inner and outer, and the possibility of the blind showing fortitude, present ready opportunities for the vivid dramatisation of ethical and spiritual questions. The evangelical writers we shall have to deal with are all women. As Gary Kelly explains, citing one of the writers we shall discuss, 'Representation of subjectivity and silent suffering in everyday life continued to be a prominent topic in writers such as [. . .] Barbara Hofland [. . .] Domesticity of a sentimental, socially nurturing, and ameliorative kind was also considered "proper" matter for women writers.'[10] Some of these writers would have been well aware of the philosophical debates surrounding the experience of the blind: Mrs Sherwood (Mary Martha Sherwood), the most celebrated of them, knew the Lichfield circle – Anna Seward, Richard Lovell Edgeworth, Thomas Day.[11] Elizabeth Pinchard (*fl.*1790) casts much of her most popular tale, *The Blind Child, or Anecdotes of the Wyndham Family* (1791), in the form of dramatic dialogues, and indeed this is the description she gives to some of her work.

Put this alongside her invoking of Barbauld and the Countess de Genlis in the introduction, and one feels not only the desire to edify, but the influence of liberal ideas about encouraging a form of fiction that would be direct and easily assimilable by the child.[12] But this influence does not extend to a trust in the child's innate goodness. The idea of casting moral tales in the form of dramatic dialogues is specifically indebted to Genlis (1746–1830), the author of *The Child of Nature*. Her *Théâtre à l'usage des jeunes personnes* (1779–80), sometimes known as *Théâtre d'éducation* or *The Theatre of Education*, acquired considerable esteem among writers for children. As her English translators say, this was 'universally considered as her *chef d'oeuvre*', and was conceived in the Rousseauesque spirit that 'LEARNING by heart detached pieces of prose and verse would not produce the same effects'.[13] The collection consists of a series of plays on moral subjects, mainly for children, though some of them are suitable for 'Ladies' women and shop girls'.[14] The English translation went into several editions, and would probably have helped to promote the use of blind characters in improving tales, since the second volume started with 'The Blind Woman of Spa'. This play shows how the family of M. Aglebert, the shoemaker, look after old blind Margery. The children are depicted taking delight in the exercise of compassion, and debating about its proper expression. Thus Mary looks forward to the time when she will be grown up, and can dress Margery and 'lead' her 'about'; but Jane is troubled by the thought that this might be adverting too bluntly to Margery's disability: 'Hold your tongue; you vex her. I do believe she cries'.[15] This was not Genlis's only foray into the subject of blindness: she also wrote a story called 'The Blind Girl' in which the heroine, the fair Herminia, undergoes a successful operation for the restoration of her sight. When she looks in the mirror, she thinks she sees her mother. Her lover, Durmance, is captivated by 'the pleasing innocence' of this response, which, we may infer, demonstrates the goodness of a heart whose emotions, in a blind person, might seem mysterious.[16]

Like Herminia, the nine-year old Helen Wyndham, heroine of Pinchard's *The Blind Child*, bears a superficial, but highly significant, resemblance to those subjects of philosophical discussion who had gone blind in infancy:

> when she was about a year old, she had the misfortune of losing her sight by a violent cold, so that she was now entirely blind, her fine dark eyes turned mournfully round without receiving a single ray of light. She had become blind so young, that she had no idea of the objects before her; she knew not what was meant by the sun, the moon, or any thing that was talked of as beautiful; and what still more affected her tender heart, she knew not the countenance of her father and mother! (15)

When, towards the end of a fairly lengthy book, Helen's sight is restored by an operation (it appears that the cold had caused cataracts), she behaves like a textbook example of Molyneux's predicted answer to his problem:

> By degrees she became familiar with the objects about her, which at first she knew not how to avoid in walking across the room; nor was it for some time she could enjoy the beauties of nature, scarcely understanding the meaning of her own sensations. (175–6)

But this predicament is not made the subject of any fundamental philosophical speculation or lesson to do with the nature of experience, and she rapidly discovers her joy in the visual world. Most of the book has been concerned with different matters. Thus, although the privation of sight is dwelt upon, it is partly with the intention of encouraging sympathy and compassion in the young reader.

The following examples also give some idea of how important simple dialogue is in the book: a reflection of the influence of Genlis's *Théâtre* on prose narrative, and one which is motivated by a desire to induce children into the imagining of social situations and debates with which they could readily identify. A simple example is Helen's exclamation about her inability to understand what 'a glorious morning' is: 'But, Emily, you said just now, it is a *glorious morning*; why cannot I have any notion of a *glorious morning*?' (25). A more philosophically interesting example is provided by Helen's inability to understand what being 'handsome' means. Her sister Emily had claimed that one Mr Thomson had said, merely for politeness' sake, that she herself was handsome, and indeed their Mamma had agreed that he was merely being polite. Helen is puzzled: 'But how is that? Would Mamma be pleased with you for being handsome, why then are you not?' (27). She means, 'why then are you not handsome?' Clearly she imagines that one can choose. The emphasis, though, is on duty and true sensibility: how fine it might be to choose to be handsome in order to please one's mother, since that should always be a consideration. Emily proceeds to inform Helen that people 'frequently become vain or proud with their beauty' (28). This is something we can see that Helen would be unlikely to do even were she sighted, and something Emily will never do:

> In the mild countenance and elegant manners of Emily you might read the excellence of her temper and the intelligence of her soul. In her eyes, as in a mirror, you saw reflected every motion of her heart; she was without disguise, and her natural graces were infinitely preferable to any which art and affectation could have taught her. (13)

But although true sensibility is the good opposite of affectation, as it might be in Genlis, Pinchard's moral universe is rather more bracing: Mrs Wyndham roundly asserts later in the book that '*duty* is superior to *feeling*' (72).

The book contains several episodes, unconnected with Helen's blindness, designed to support this assertion. Mrs Somerville, for instance, has a 'nervous kind of sensibility' and never restrains her tears: this is something against which Mrs Wyndham warns Emily, describing it as an example of 'over indulgence of our best feelings' (73–4). This example is juxtaposed with that of feckless parenting and the uncontrolled childish cruelty and selfishness to which it may lead. Mrs Sidney can 'never keep [her children] in order'. Her daughter, Harriet, however, has a charge of her own: a bird which she keeps in a cage, and which, significantly, has been blinded with a red-hot knitting-needle by her brother Ned in order to make it sing better (a remote reference to auditory compensation). Emily makes an instructive connection: 'Alas! I have a sister who is blind!' Harriet admits that she 'should be sorry for her', but as for the blinding of the bird, protests that 'nobody ever told me it was cruel, so how should I know?' (91–2). The implied lesson is driven home by the example of Ned, who gives a live mouse to the cat to torment and kill; having contemplated Ned's cowardly behaviour, young Arthur Wyndham opines that 'his father did not teach him better', and Mrs Wyndham that he is therefore to be pitied (93, 102). The tale thus makes cunning use of examples of moral questions that would be familiar to children from their own experience in order to induce in them the acceptance of clear moral instruction. In conformity with the doctrine of original sin, we are being reminded that human feeling is not innately compassionate or morally developed: true sensibility is guided by a sense of duty, which must be inculcated.

It should by now be clear that Pinchard wishes to dissent from any simple symbolic schema whereby the blind child possesses an innate goodness which prevails over any difficulties in communication. She also introduces a symbolically significant Gothic tale within the tale, a fairy story, designed to denigrate the idea of the visionary acquisition of knowledge. Part of the significance resides simply in the juxtaposition of this topic with that of physical blindness, part in the Gothic and fairy-tale associations themselves, which together add up to the thought that the subjectivity of inward vision carries no conviction. It is a point that Pinchard feels well worth making in a period when Gothic and romance modes were becoming more fashionable. The implied critique is assisted, at least for the adult purchaser, by the common contemporary mistrust specifically of fairy tales for children, a mistrust which sought authority in Locke.[17] Thomas Day disapproved of them, and Maria Edgeworth claimed in 1798 that they were 'not now much read'.[18] Pinchard is not being courageously controversial in introducing a specimen of the genre into her tale. Rather, she is employing self-conscious artifice to impart her own evangelical inflection to widely-accepted post-Lockeian ideas about the fairy story. 'Elfrida, or the Mirror. A Fairy Tale' is set in the reign of Edward III and concerns the eponymous young girl, who, when her father is summoned to the Scottish wars, wishes that some 'beneficent Being' would tell her how he is faring: a turbanned figure, scarcely a foot in height, appears, with an ivory wand in one hand and a mirror in the other (127, 129). The fairy tells Elfrida to take the mirror three times a day and she will see what her father is doing; but she must leave an interval of at least half an hour between these seances (133). On the first viewing she sees her father falling from a horse, on the second she sees him lying pale and languid on a couch, as she does again on the third (135–7). Letters from her father arrive, but they afford no comfort, since she knows what has happened subsequent to their dispatch (137). Although the next day the mirror reveals that her father has made a recovery, she asks the fairy to take back the mirror, which it does, drawing the moral that there are some wishes best not granted (139–40). But Pinchard has already prepared us for this conclusion, in advance even of the story, by prefacing it with reflections on the 'limitation of man's knowledge' and by inviting us to consider 'the narrowness of our capacity in this state of our existence as one great source of the comfort we enjoy' (122–4). The lesson is that, even were we to be granted such capacity (and the prefatory remarks make it clear that this is not a normal occurrence) we lack the wit to interpret it.

But if visionary powers would delude us, even if they existed, no less are we inclined to be too impressed by what strikes the outward eye. This theme is introduced through the discussion of 'handsomeness' to which we have already referred. It is reintroduced, significantly, soon after the tale of Elfrida, when Mrs Darnford is cited as an example of one who chooses friends for superficial reasons related to their appearance: 'A fine face, an interesting figure, are recommendations sufficiently powerful to win the heart' (160–1). It also helps to be '*good natured*' with people like her – another dig at the idea that true sensibility can be founded in human inclinations free of moral and spiritual instruction.

In sum, the blind Helen has suffered a terrible privation, for which we should feel compassion, though there is no guarantee in mere human nature that we will do so without a Christian education. Her privation is not compensated for by any visionary capacity, nor could it be. It might be said that in one sense she is fortunate in not being tempted to judge by superficial notions of what is 'handsome' or beautiful; but without the guidance of a good Christian family, no doubt even she might have found some other superficiality in which to indulge. Fortunately, however, she has benefited by such guidance, and in its spirit she has borne her privation with fortitude. Such are the lessons to be drawn from Pinchard's dry but highly self-conscious moral tale.

Blindness persevering in duty is an even more central theme in *The Blind Farmer and His Children* (1816) by Barbara Hofland, 'a prolific writer for children'.[19] The theme of a connection between the national love of industry and the national pre-eminence in commerce is announced on the title-page, by means of an epigraph from Thomson: 'A simple race! yet hence Britannia sees / Her solid grandeur rise; hence she commands / Th'exalted stores of every brighter clime'. In some ways, the point is the more striking in that the tale of blind Farmer Norton has so little to do with brighter climes, and everything to do with fortitude, stoicism, perseverance, industry and the education of children to survive and prosper. Possibly it was this last theme, most of all, which procured the approbation of 'Mr. and Miss Edgeworth', as announced in the *Advertisement*. (Hofland was also a friend of Mary Russell Mitford.)[20] Farmer Norton has cataracts (or 'crackertons' as the groom calls them), but it is subsequent to their encroachment that he arranges the education of his children.[21] Since his eyes are not quite bad enough to be operated upon through most of the book (21), much time is devoted to the heroic efforts of the family. Ultimately, though, his sight is restored by an oculist in Oxford (98). The story is certainly an example of 'Mrs Hofland's belief that the practise of Christian virtues in business affairs can lead to financial security'.[22] But as with Pinchard, one discerns the influence of philosophical discussions of the blind in a passage such as this:

> The Farmer was surprised to see how much his children were grown, and he confessed that he had formed no idea of it, having not attained that accuracy of feeling which is frequently remarkable in those who were blind from infancy, which was probably owing to his having had some trifling perception of objects, until within a short time. (102–3)

The point is a subtle one, based on a good understanding of the philosophical debates: Norton had not had time to unlearn the acquired perception of the connection between the data derived from the different senses. Thus his blindness results in a kind of temporary complacency which prevents him learning to interpret the tactile world with the sensitivity of those born blind.

What we have found, then, are ideas of fortitude and a sense of duty being brought together with themes from the philosophers' discussions of the blind, and a similar union can be found in a very different work for children, Samuel Roberts' *The Blind Man and his Son* (1816). Samuel Roberts of Sheffield (1763–1848) was a tireless campaigner for working people and the poor, and an abolitionist. A characteristic specimen of his many works, *Tales of the Poor, or, Infant Sufferings* (1813), contains 'The chimneysweeper's boy'. This indicates an approach to the representation of the blind rather different from that which is to be found in Pinchard or Hofland, namely one that emphasises compassion for the afflicted. There is an interesting religious context for this, for Roberts is not properly speaking an evangelical. It is interesting to note that Charles Lamb sent to Roberts's close friend James Montgomery (1771–1854) a copy of what he refers to as Blake's 'Sweep's Song'.[23] Montgomery was a member of the Moravian community, as we now know that Blake's mother had been.[24] Roberts himself is the author of a poem, 'The Song of the Poor Little Sweep', which is undoubtedly influenced by both the *Innocence* and the *Experience* 'Chimney Sweeper' songs of Blake. Thus the scene is set with the sweep calling out amid the snow-drifts, as in the *Experience* poem; but a gentleman reminds him that he has 'a father in Heaven, / Whose care never slumbered, whose eye cannot sleep; / Whose pity to children is constantly given'.[25] These lines contain echoes of both of Blake's poems. Although Roberts persisted in the Anglican communion, he was moved in his youth by Methodist preaching.[26] His mother attended Methodist services, but transferred her sympathies to the Quakers, though she never joined the Society of Friends, remaining an attender.[27] Hers, remarks Roberts, 'was truly the *religion of the heart*', a phrase which, significantly, was often applied to the faith of the Moravian community.[28] With these connections, Roberts was unsympathetic to the harsh emphasis on original sin to be found in the evangelical tradition, a note which is struck in the title of one of his works, *Vital Christianity Opposed to the Reformation Society* (1839). His mistrust of evangelicalism extended to sympathy with Catholics, and a subordinate concern of the earlier *The Blind Man and His Son* is to encourage that sympathy in the context of the incipient debate about Catholic Emancipation.

The blindness of the 'venerable looking blind man' whom we encounter at the beginning of the book, led by his young son Henry, appears like a punishment for fecklessness and inattention to duty, for he has been improvident with his inheritance.[29] His own father, as he tells the boy, had built a church and a model village called Zoar, in which the poor were employed in 'improving the estate, and cultivating the lands' (16, 17). But after his father's death he lost the estate through his incompetence, as a result of which he was unable to discharge his debts

(29). His devoted and pious Catholic wife dies, and soon his blindness comes upon him, while little Henry is still only three. Yet again, we encounter the trope of loss and compensatory gain: the idea of blindness is used to emphasise the importance of the inner guidance provided by the 'Holy Spirit' (66). A lengthy passage harnesses this theme to ideas derived from the philosophical discussion of the blind, specifically the question of whether one can 'deduce' (as Blake puts it) senses one does not possess from those one does:

> if I had been blind from my birth, and you had still told me of this wonder-ful and useful facility which you possess, I might deny that either you, or any body else, possessed it, and I might continue to grope my way in darkness, fully convinced, and asserting, that every one was as blind as myself. This might be called stupid incredulity. But if an oculist of great fame were to arrive and to make it known publicly, that he could and would cause every blind man to see who would be at the trouble of only asking him so to do; and if many who had before been as blind as myself, assured me that they had been to him, and that they could now see as well as their neighbours; if I still persisted in refusing the gift of sight, and in denying that any one *could* see, nobody would hesitate in declaring me to be *worse* than stupidly incredulous.
>
> Such, however, appears to me the man who denies the operating influence of the Holy Spirit of God. (67–8)

It is to be noted that the ground of conviction offered here, unlike what it would be for Pinchard, lies in the direct experience of those who testify to the existence of the Holy Spirit. Ultimately, then, as in Blake, deduc-tion is not enough; but fortunately its deficiencies are supplied by some-thing more direct.

What the blind man cannot see is also, as so often, figuratively sig-nificant. The setting of Henry's grandfather's estate was the wild coun-tryside of Roberts' native Yorkshire, where it borders the old county of Westmorland. Indeed, in contemplating the estate, 'a superficial specta-tor would have concluded that *picturesque effect* had been his *sole object*' (17). Sole object it may not have been, but this is only a partial concession to utility: clearly its landscape, an example of the rough pic-turesque which contains elements of the sublime, has a part to play. The grandfather had 'loved its mighty rocks, its pathless mountains, its gloomy dales, its wild heaths, its dashing waterfalls, its lonely glens, its gliding streams, and its wide-spread lakes' (15). At the beginning of the tale we can see the sun hanging over Skiddaw (5), and the proximity of the Lake District to this area of Yorkshire is intended to remind us, by reminding us of the Lake poets, that Nature gives indications of God's sublimity. Nor is such a view denigrated. Of course, all of this is invisi-ble to the blind man who is at the centre of the scene. But he feels the evidence of God's spirit in the place where, however it arrives there, it must in the end establish itself: within. This topos, of the blind man sensing benignity of which he cannot acquire visual evidence, is present also, as we shall see, in Shelley's prose fragment, 'The Coliseum'.

The subordinate theme, about the potential goodness of Catholics, is made to carry a similar message. From the piety and dutifulness of the blind man's deceased wife we are warned not to be prejudiced against them. A possible objection is dealt with: they may be fond of outward forms and ceremonies, but they still have spiritual worship. This is the important thing, and it appears that one may have it with or without the forms. Here the trope of seeing through appearances is given an interesting twist: the outward forms really are subtended by the inward life of the spirit. Those who insist that Catholics are blinded by outward forms are in fact thus blinded themselves.

There could scarcely be a sharper contrast, at least within the confines of this genre, than that between Roberts and 'Mrs Sherwood' (Mary Martha Sherwood), who was not only 'very popular for Sunday reading', but also 'deeply conscious of the Roman peril'.[30] Her Calvinistic outlook was settled in the view that 'the child's nature was determined by original sin'.[31] But the child is father of the man, and that includes the blind man. Her brief tale, *The Blind Man and Little George*, offers a variation on the conventional Protestant theme of spiritual blindness, where the misguided youth of the chief character, blind Richard, is rewarded by physical blindness. When he was a boy, and sighted, there were no Sunday schools. Sunday schools were a considerable concern of evangelical writers for children, notably Sarah Trimmer.[32] Nevertheless, he had a pious grandmother who used to invite him to her house on the Sabbath day in order to teach him his duty to God, but this was of no interest to him.[33] The immediate cause of his blindness was the same as that which affected many others in this period, warfare (7); but the true explanation was that 'the Lord punished me in my own way; for I would not admit light into my heart, and therefore the Lord deprived me of the light of my eyes' (8). Or, to be even more explicit about the metaphor, 'I chose to be spiritually dark – I would not receive knowledge; and now have I lost sight for ever, not only of Him I would not see, but of that glorious sun which is his emblem' (9). He had ended up boarding with an old woman who, the opposite of his grandmother, could give him no 'instruction' (8). In the end, though, the Holy Spirit moves him 'to cease grieving for the loss of my bodily eye-sight, but rather to mourn on account of my spiritual darkness' (10). In ascribing this great moral change to the workings of the Holy Spirit, Sherwood is effectively equating the workings of the Holy Spirit with those of an unmerited grace, in true evangelical fashion.

Nevertheless, as with Pinchard, the message is that proper guidance in youth has the potential to lead to the right path. But Sherwood's message is bleaker: she wishes to remind us that some may shun guidance until God's grace predisposes them to do otherwise. Sometimes this may never happen.

As if to underline these points, she includes two children of differing natures in her tale. They are, significantly, playing truant together from Sunday school (3). The eponymous George is receptive to the wisdom of the redeemed blind man, whereas his companion Jack is already bound on a course of wickedness and disaster. George is less committed than Jack to truancy, being worried about the possibility that he will be denied 'his new hat' if he does not attend (4). His interview becomes overtly catechistic:

> 'What kind of blindness have we by nature?' said Richard.
> 'Spiritual blindness,' replied the child; 'for we all hate to be taught, and that is the reason why it is such hard work to get boys to church and school.' (13)

The introduction of catechism into a children's tale is indeed an imitation of evangelical catechisms, which, as Gary Kelly notes, were promoted 'to ensure that the right "principles" have been internalized in the pupil's subjective being'.[34] In this case, the teaching is about teaching itself, and constitutes an especially crucial piece of the instruction which leads George to salvation: 'Thus was the discourse of poor blind Richard blessed to George, in bringing him, with the divine favour, from the state of spiritual darkness in which we are all by nature, into a state of light and happiness' (15). The same cannot be said of Jack, who mocks the teachings of the blind man, departing with a wink to George, and putting his finger in his mouth to signify that no attention should be paid to what they had been hearing (11). In later life, 'he fell from one bad course to another, till at length he died in great misery' (15).

Stories such as we have been examining may not exhibit the philosophical ambition of many of other treatments of the blind from this period. Nevertheless, they also bear witness to the contemporary fascination with the blind and their experience. They are very much of their time, and they ask the questions that the time wished to have answered. How can the blind feel sympathy? Does the acknowledged goodness of some blind people offer proof of innate benevolence? Can the blind be industrious citizens? These questions are very similar to the ones that are addressed in the many of the more ambitious works of the period.

Notes

1. Anon. (1814).
2. Anon. (*c*.1800?), pp. 24–7, 31.
3. Ibid., p. 9.
4. Ibid., p. 13.
5. Ibid., pp. 38–9.
6. Ibid., p. 45.
7. Ibid., p. 53, for the contraband.
8. Ibid., p. 72.
9. Lamb (1924), IV, p. 420. Subsequent references are given in the text as page numbers in parentheses.
10. Kelly (1993), p. 178.
11. Meigs (1969), p. 77.
12. Pinchard (1793), p. iv. Subsequent references are given as page numbers in parentheses in the text.
13. Genlis (1787), I, pp. iv, viii.
14. Ibid., IV, p. ii.
15. Ibid., II, p. 15.
16. Genlis (*c*. 1820), pp. 23–8, esp. p. 28.
17. See Pickering (1981), pp. 40–3, for Locke's critique of tales about bugbears and the supernatural, and its influence in the late eighteenth century: the most relevant work of Locke is his *Some Thoughts Concerning Education* (1693).
18. Meigs (1969), p. 145; Pickering (1981), p. 41.
19. Muir (1954), p. 125.
20. Darton (1982), p. 211.
21. Hofland (1816), pp. 2–3. Subsequent references are given as page numbers in parentheses in the text.
22. Hunt (1995), p. 79.
23. Lucas (1907), p. 526.
24. *Montgomery* (1856), VI (1856), p. 80. For Mrs Blake and the Moravians, see Davies and Schuchard (2004), pp. 36–43.
25. Roberts (1849), pp. 54, 55.
26. Ibid., pp. 14–15.
27. Ibid., p. 15.
28. Ibid.
29. Roberts (1816), pp. 5, 48. Subsequent references are given as page numbers in parentheses in the text.
30. Hunt (1995), p. 23.
31. Ibid., pp. 49, 168–9.
32. Darton (1982), p. 157.
33. Sherwood (18 . . .), pp. 6, 7. Subsequent references are given as page numbers in brackets in the text.
34. Kelly (1993), p. 299.

Chapter 5

Wordsworth's Transitions

The topic of blindness figures in some of Wordsworth's most important poems, and is associated with central developments in his thought. The blind man, for instance, appears in a famous passage in 'Tintern Abbey'; the Blind Beggar passage in *Prelude* VII is essential to the understanding of the poem; and Alan Bewell makes a good case for regarding the speaker of the Intimations Ode as 'the blind poet'.[1] And despite Wordsworth's reservations about Macpherson, there are occasional similarities between the self-presentation of the speaker in *The Prelude* and in the *Ossian* poems.[2] There is sometimes an autobiographical element in play: from at least early 1805, Wordsworth suffered a tormenting disease of the eyes, trachoma, in which the insides of the eyelids are afflicted with hard pustules; the disease was spread in these years by soldiers returning from the wars.[3] From 1820 onwards, he often wore a green eye-shade, in and out of doors.[4] Not surprisingly, the disease 'raised the spectre of future blindness'.[5] Some late passages in the 1805 *Prelude* may have been influenced by Wordsworth's reflections on his condition. An interest in blindness and the blind pre-dates this affliction, however. And given the importance to many Enlightenment philosophers of examples drawn from the condition of the blind, and of speculation about their experience, it is scarcely surprising that these things should matter also to a poet who read those philosophers, and who was also concerned with the role of mental images in the development of intellectual and moral life. The topic becomes intertwined with that of inward vision, and thus also with mental images and 'impressions'. When the external promptings of these are evoked, they may be described as 'forms' or 'shapes'; but a 'shape' may also, in eighteenth-century parlance, be an 'apparition' or a 'spectre'.[6] Thus the topics both of blindness and of inward vision may be attended by the same ambiguity one finds in the description of 'second sight' in general: is one seeing a mental image or a ghost? Wordsworth's revision of the Gothic is subtle, but he does exploit this ambiguity. And vision may improve or fade: failing sight is an important metaphor in *The Prelude*.

But blindness also involves questions about intellectual transition or development, and the borders, bounds or barriers which seem to separate one stage of life or thought from another, or even our world from 'the invisible world'. As Jonathan Wordsworth says, 'there are many [. . .] examples in [Wordsworth's] poetry of this preoccupation with border-states'.[7] All this has relevance for Wordsworth's conception of poetic language. He hoped to make poetic language subsist in, and provide hope and comfort for, a world without the benefit of supernatural intervention, at least in any sense in which that had hitherto been understood. At the same time he wished to connect the possibility of poetic sublimity with the capacity of that language to adumbrate transcendence. This poet's treading of a path between two realms makes the Word, as Deanne Westbrook puts it, 'a Borderer'.[8] On a more mundane level, such transitions may include changes of political view. Not just transitions, but also exchanges may occur across borders, as they so memorably do in those ballads of Faery of which Wordsworth was well aware. Questions to do with exchanging bardic vision (in which a fairy might appear) for modernity are present in his work, though his handling of them is, of course, anything but simplistic. And these may involve also questions to do with financial exchange and the exchange of goods in a world infected by the utilitarian calculus of commercial progress.

But the largest exchange which occurs in Wordsworth is that where visionary intensity is renounced in favour of the world of habit and custom. This exchange is prompted by a valuing of familiar associations, and these are understood in terms of the association of ideas. Familiar associations can best be recovered through the poetic use of language, with all its aural resources. The most characteristic structure in Wordsworth's thought is modelled on the idea of compensatory enhancement of aural sensitivity in the blind, which, as we noted in a previous chapter (referring to Katie Trumpener), was a familiar Enlightenment topic. In this light, 'The Blind Highland Boy' can be seen as exemplary for the understanding of Wordsworth's thought, and one can see why it lent its title to a whole sequence, ending with the Immortality Ode.

Yet at the same time, and notwithstanding the 'tyranny of the eye', Wordsworth's poetry never loses touch with the evocation of visual perception. At the simplest level (though it is not all that simple) this is explained by Geoffrey Thurley's point, to which we have already referred, that much writing of the Romantic period 'requires the thing to be itself'. For Galperin, this requirement may issue in a 'return of the visible' through a facticity that is unassimilable to the grand projects of Romantic writers. The persistence of the language of sight alongside that of the aural should remind us that, as David P. Haney says, 'Language is both heard and seen, vocal and written in Wordsworth, and both heard and seen language can be articulate or inarticulate, commonplace or visionary, usurping of experience or continuous with experience, representational or performative'.[9] In particular, the voice of streams may represent the beneficent influence of nature, and 'harmony' the great underlying principle. The power of music and poetry are connected topics, increasingly emphasised in Wordsworth's work from his great period onwards, where they are already involved in the questioning of the superficiality of 'sight' and 'sights'. By the time he writes 'On the Power of Sound' (1828) the divine voice appears to have priority: 'A Voice to Light Gave Being.' But even David Haney, who is patient and convincing in his argument for the general priority of voice in later Wordsworth, admits towards the end of his article that,

> There is, of course, another side to the story. Not only does Wordsworth combine the Augustinian inner word with the Hebrew sense of an ethical command as an antidote to representational visuality, but he also participates in an Enlightenment model of sight even as he invokes an earlier, Platonic notion of vision.[10]

To put it another way, Wordsworth's primary intention is disturbance of 'sight' by the divine voice, but this voice may awaken Platonic vision, which is also positive; and then, to complicate matters, the Platonic vision may be dressed in words which are indebted to Enlightenment philosophical discourses, words which may sound confusingly similar to the superficial language of 'sight'. This seems to me to master some of the complexity of the question. But there is an important omission from the accounting, even though Haney makes a brief initial reference to it: the question of the adequacy of words. At their best, the poet's words may nearly approximate the inner voice of the divine. But the spectre of the 'counter-spirit' is never exorcised: for instance, it is raised in a subtly ambivalent form by the Pastor's oral epitaphs in *The Excursion* – among which that of the Blind Dalesman plays a crucial role. In practice, whatever may have been Wordsworth's notional assent to the priority of voice, he constantly questions the adequacy both of voice and sight, often, as Stuart Allen puts it, 'using the ear to criticize the eye, but equally refusing to allow the ear a positive value'.[11] The result, I would claim, is more border-crossings: crossings, that is, between the more or the less adequate, or between the visual and the aural and back again.

The epitaphs in *The Excursion* are akin to separate poems: at one and the same time they raise the questions of how one might adequately epitomise others, and how others might each speak and write irreducibly unique and individual words. They may serve to remind us of Wordsworth's profoundly textual notion of how to represent persons and aspects of persons. This may express itself in different forms for different aspects of one self – 'Moods of My Own Mind' – or else in the virtuoso display of different forms for different subjects, so that *Poems in Two Volumes* looks like a deliberately various anthology. Even *Lyrical Ballads* may be seen in practice to qualify any simplistic understanding of 'the real language of men': as Thomas Pfau says, Wordsworth seeks 'to achieve community poetically, that is as the effect of interpretive participation elicited by a complex array of rhetorical forms, rather than being postulated conceptually'.[12] As much as this aspect of his work is dictated by the requirement to find fit words, it also derives from the imperative to foster a proper attentiveness in his audience. To elaborate different forms of expression is to facilitate a more successful crossing of the border between author and audience: at the same time, it is to educate readers, as they move from one type of poem to another, in crossing borders between different ways of understanding. This concern is echoed at the thematic level by the various solitaries, not least those in *The Prelude*. Famously, they are liminal characters: the Discharged Soldier, espied at dawn and long away from home; the Blind Beggar, standing still amid the overflowing crowd, 'Beyond the reach of common indication'. In so far as marginal humans possess the quality of spectrality, it may be further illuminated by Bewell's discussion. Referring to the lines about 'the blind man's eye' in 'Tintern Abbey', he asserts that 'their primary purpose is to insert a "blind man" into the poem' so that there may be a 'textual marker' for the poem's shift 'toward philosophical statement'.[13] This remark refers to the salience of discussions of the blind in enlightenment philosophy. Bewell offers another contextualisation of Wordsworth's marginals which has similar implications, in adverting to enlightenment anthropology and the study of early peoples.[14] In other words, the marginals in Wordsworth are akin to data in a philosophical discourse. While their uncanniness has several aspects, one aspect has to do with the way in which they are separate from community: they appear like a familiar quotation taken out of context. In this way, the strangeness of the uncanny connects with the related concept of alienation: the marginals are disturbing witnesses to damaged community. At the same time, they function like the data upon which Wordsworth's 'philosophic mind' can work to develop the ideas which should underpin the recovery of community in the world of modernity and commerce. These ideas are inseparable from the aural qualities of the poetry, since they inhere in his poetic style, and are partly founded on the exploration of association of ideas as embedded in the community where associations themselves are nurtured and anchored.

But to encounter these liminal characters is also to approach the border between self and other. And to find words for that encounter, even if they are not words such as they themselves might have chosen, is to have understood something to which they, as separate beings, were essential. Wordsworth's Blind Beggar possesses the privilege of encompassing at one and the same time questions about the rootedness of individuals in modern society, questions about how to understand them philosophically, and questions about how to describe the other person. Wordsworth begins to think about questions such as these as early as *The Borderers*, and in that work they are framed in terms of blindness and insight, and radiate outwards from the figure of the blind Herbert.

The Borders of Blindness

The Borderers, a play in which the blind Herbert explicitly reminds us of Lear, does not raise many questions about language and association of ideas, but it certainly does raise questions about exchange and transition. It can be seen as the beginning of a search for an adequate and properly instructed philosophical outlook in the aftermath of the disillusionment and trauma occasioned by the course of the French Revolution. Specifically, it raises questions about the roots of compassion and sympathy, and how they might successfully be extended and built upon. The Revolution pretended to offer compassion to society; its behaviour raises the question of what happens when compassion for individuals is relegated in favour of the ruthless pursuit of the General Will. How could knowledge, and what sort of knowledge, enable the valuing of the human? The search for a better mode of perception, which might lead to better-founded knowledge, is figuratively linked to ideas of blindness and insight. The reason which adopts 'One guide, the light of circumstances, flashed / Upon an independent intellect' is criticised as founded in 'the ungrounded liberty of Enlightenment ocularity', as David Haney puts it.[15] There are also many references to sights and 'spectacles'. The associations Herbert might have for a contemporary reader, who would think both of *Lear* and of the philosopher's blind man, are themselves almost allegorical. *Lear* connects him to questions about custom and usurpation, philosophy to what the Enlightenment – sceptical of custom – might discover and propose. As for the central character, Kenneth Johnston remarks that 'The trouble with *The Borderers* is that everybody but Mortimer can see right away that Rivers is evil'.[16] This obvious figurative blindness is part of the general obviousness of the tropes. Furthermore, these tropes are themselves linked to the title. Apart from its most obvious connotations, this refers to the transitions which all the chief characters undergo. Rivers' reference to his passing 'Beyond the visible barriers of the world' (IV.ii.144) is the most overt signal of this, one which increases our ironic awareness of the 'invisible barrier' of his character, as Nicholas Roe points out.[17] The phrase neatly links blindness and barriers.

The temptation to see Herbert as either possessing or gaining a compensatory wisdom should be resisted. His likeness to Lear is partly pathos on a blasted heath, partly blindness figuring spiritual limitation. It is only Mortimer who learns anything. Indeed, we should also resist the temptation to 'sentimentalize' Herbert: not because Rivers' stories are true, but because Herbert's type of naïveté is an ethical stumbling block, and at best represents a stage to move beyond.[18] This insufficiency works at two levels, the political-juridical and that of family ties and affection.

As for the political, the date of the fictional action, in the reign of Henry III, puts us in the feudal period. The fact that Herbert's demesne has been usurped raises the question of the justice of the feudal lord's entitlements, and his claim associates him with a trust in feudal institutions and morality. The assumptions of the characters are wedded to feudalism: Mortimer's abandonment of Herbert, for instance, is a form of justice by ordeal, in which the judgment is left to God. As for Rivers, while his scheming is at odds with feudal values, it is to a significant degree reactive: an individualist rebellion against a communal code. Are we then to see Wordsworth as re-appropriating feudal morality in stark reaction against Godwin and the *philosophes*? This would be a drastic over-simplification. The play is more exploratory than that. It is a representation of a political and ethical problem: granted that morality must respect its roots in sympathy and in custom, how to afford it the wisdom and determination to defend itself against the moral and political opportunism of a character such as Rivers? As Burke had noted in *A Regicide Peace*, there is danger in a state of affairs where 'the moral principles are formed systematically to play into the hand of the passions'.[19] Rivers neatly embodies a pretence of the moral principles and the reality of the worst kind of passions. Of course, though Rivers may precipitate a sad knowledge in Mortimer, he is no tutor for the times. His isolation is arid and Satanic. Wordsworth's note on his character describes his 'morbid state' in tropes of partial blindness: 'He looks at society through an optical glass of a peculiar tint'.[20] So partial is his view, that Wordsworth can describe it in terms of self-deception in language that is strikingly reminiscent of Blake's description of the mutual exclusivity of opposed visions in *The Marriage*: 'He is perpetually imposing upon himself [. . .].'[21] His attitude is congruent with the inhuman calculation symbolised in child-selling, but, like Edmund in *King Lear*, upon whom he is in part modelled, his callousness is an aspect of a passionate if perverted selfishness, and this is confirmed in the speech where he weighs up the relative merits of 'passion' and 'proof' in achieving one's aim, by imagining that they could be tabulated in '[t]wo columns', one for passion and one for proof (III.ii.5–16). In the end, passion wins because it gives us what we want.

The imagery and action of the play support the notion that the figurative aspect of Herbert's blindness refers to a naïveté about the way passion can abuse principle. It is a naïveté which is shared by Mortimer. Yet although the play offers no solution, any more than it offers a resolution, at least by its end Mortimer knows the right questions. They are large ones, and they impose upon him the burden of a solitude which sounds a trifle like a melancholy version of Wordsworth's own quest: 'I will go forth a wanderer on the earth' (V.iii.265). These questions are, in fact, about Nature, Man and Society. But it is equally important that his unsettled seeking should be unlike both the naïve complacency of Herbert and the grossly presumptuous and callous reasoning of Rivers, for both are in fact forms of blindness. Mortimer himself is a precursor of the fundamental Wordsworthian idea of 'something ever more about to be'.

The idea of being a 'wanderer' finds its echo in a certain critique of unreflective custom. The family tie of Herbert and Matilda, being that of father and daughter, should be outgrown, at least in the passionate form in which it is represented. Rivers claims that Herbert practises upon Matilda's emotions: 'To see him thus provoke her tenderness / With tales of symptoms and infirmities' (I.i.215–16). This is not a case of Rivers' discovery of a truth which he misuses (he speaks of 'a flash / Of truth enough to dazzle and to blind'; II.i.10–11), but of his mendacity directing us to a truth that lies close to hand. There is something of Blake's imperfect innocence about Herbert and Matilda, though Matilda's evident love for Mortimer (e.g., III.v.161–650) points the direction in which she should go. Thus Wordsworth compounds a picture of arrested development, both politically and emotionally. This enforces the realisation that Rivers has a point when he tells Mortimer that, 'Enough is done to save you from the curse / Of living without knowledge that you live. / You will be taught to think' (IV.iii.205–7). For Mortimer's virtues had 'as yet' been but 'the spontaneous growth of instinct' (II.i.74–5). The idea that Mortimer should be taught 'to think' can hardly in itself be negative: it sounds exactly like Wordsworth's desideratum for his experimental poetry. This is the point at which questions about the aesthetic thinking behind the work overlap instructively with its themes, and at which the notion of 'wanderer' as alienated from the customary overlaps with that of wanderer as one who thinks independently.

The aesthetic point is characteristically embodied in a subversion of a mode some versions of which would be implicated in passionate lack of principle. *The Borderers*, a play set in the place of origin of the border-ballads, and offering events sensational enough for one of that genre, is rightly seen in relation to the contemporary taste for the Gothic. In his essay on the character of Rivers, Wordsworth draws out the possibilities for moral comment in the delineation of a powerful but vicious being. He speaks of how, 'In processes of vice the effects are more frequently immediate, palpable and extensive. Power is much more easily manifested in destroying than in creating'.[22] Put this with the suggestion that Mortimer's fate henceforth is to wander and 'think', and one can see a suggestion of those highly significant lines from *The Ruined Cottage*, in which Wordsworth avows that his story offers no sensational pleasures, lines which have counterparts in 'Simon Lee' and 'Hart-Leap Well', and of which a theoretical justification is offered in the Preface to *Lyrical Ballads* when it speaks of the feeling giving importance to the action and situation, rather than the other way around:

> 'Tis a common tale,
> By moving accidents uncharactered,
> A tale of silent suffering, hardly clothed
> In bodily form, and to the grosser sense
> But ill adapted, scarcely palpable
> To him who does not think.[23]

Interestingly, in the crucial phrases relating to 'moving accidents', there are echoes of *Othello*, one of the most important intertexts of *The Borderers*.[24] The aesthetic and thematic intentions of the play are at one in rejecting feudal modes as characteristic of an epoch vulnerable to violent irrationality. This is a connection readers had already been taught to perceive, not least by reading *Caleb Williams*, where Falkland's early taste for romance and tales of chivalry, which offer parallels with the Gothic, belongs to the vicious part of his education, and prepares us for his mature addiction to false notions such as 'honour'. As with *Caleb Williams* and with Wordsworth's contributions to *Lyrical*

Ballads we are conscious of two types of text: one that is being subverted and one that looks to very different lights.

But such a connection aligns Wordsworth with Godwin; yet we have been taught that *The Borderers* is anti-Godwinian in its themes and language. There is no doubt about the negativity of many of the echoes of Godwin, for instance in the famous passage where Rivers compliments Mortimer on his supposed murder of Herbert, claiming that he has obeyed 'the immediate law / Flashed from the light of circumstances / Upon an independent intellect' (III.v.31–3), which is clearly indebted to a passage in *Political Justice* about acting according to 'independent and individual impressions of truth upon [the] mind'.[25] But on the other hand Rivers is notoriously lacking in Godwinian benevolence; and at the same time, Mortimer is motivated more by outrage and love than by any kind of 'reason'.[26] It is true that the play is anti-Godwinian in the sense that it reveals the unconsidered weakness of Godwin's argument, by exhibiting the capacity of destructive passion or malevolence to exploit the rhetoric of rationality. But the demonstration might be just as apt, if not more apt, in relation to other reasoning philosophers, such as Destutt de Tracy, whose theory of 'ideology' probably became known at this time to Wordsworth from the pages of the *Monthly Magazine*, as James K. Chandler has shown.[27] In fact, there is good reason for thinking that Wordsworth retained his respect for certain aspects of Godwin's thought, specifically the latter's mistrust of gratitude. As David Bromwich observes of a slightly later work, 'The Old Cumberland Beggar', 'gratitude, or any reciprocal feeling or action, can hardly be what matters in the social exchange that he recounts'.[28] In *The Borderers* we may associate such a point of view with the horror of monetary exchange usurping the natural affections, as symbolised in the false tale of Herbert's buying the infant Matilda. The story evokes a central Shakespearean theme about the obscenity of quantifying love, most famously embodied in *The Merchant of Venice*, with its pound of flesh, but very much present also in *King Lear* where the line, 'There's beggary in the love that can be reckoned', offers a basic critique of Lear's attempt to measure his daughters' love. *The Borderers* again blends reflections on *Lear* and Godwin when Rivers provokes us into asking how far Herbert is imposing upon a daughter's gratitude: he is effectively reminding us of Godwin's question about the morality of children's gratitude to their parents. The occasion of Herbert's blinding, when he saves his daughter from a fire, is a clear reference to Godwin's most notorious moral parable: the one in which he asks whether, if a house were burning down, one would save a beloved person or the philosopher Fénelon, and answers that we should save the latter as being more useful to humanity. That Herbert saved Matilda can hardly be held against him in Wordsworth's estimation, and that marks out one mighty difference with Godwin. That there is something cloying about Matilda's gratitude to Herbert is part of Wordsworth's ethical provocation: what are the proper limits of filial gratitude? As we have seen, Wordsworth's answer is a subtle one, suggesting that it should not be a barrier to individuation.

That indecision is most subtly embodied in one of *The Borderers'* more astute reminders of the potential unsatisfactoriness of unreflective custom: Rivers' deceitful crime with Mortimer and Herbert is a repetition of the manner in which he himself was deceived, in his crusading days, into thinking his ship's captain was conspiring against him, and therefore murdering him by abandoning him on a barren island (IV.ii). In one aspect, this theme addresses the contemporary concern of Wordsworth and Coleridge with the Origin of Evil, an interest which pre-dates the attempted collaboration on 'The Wanderings of Cain' in the autumn of 1797.[29] In context, because of the relationship of *The Borderers* to the French Revolution, the point addressed is as much to do with the poisoning of politics as of personal morality. But it points to a flaw in the human urge to repeat, which itself is present in the politics of custom. It perverts and misdirects the notion of honour by, so to speak, taking revenge on the wrong person. At the same time, it dramatises the link between repetition and association. Although it may not actually explain the origin of evil, the obtrusion of the idea of repetition does attempt to show how things may progress thereafter: by association of ideas. In other words, we have here a dark, proleptic parody of the homing instinct which was to be such a central feature of Wordsworth's poetry.

When he came to offer a more positive prospectus, he sought to suggest, in visual terms, the kind of perception which would assist a 'transition' to a view of life more valid than the blindnesses of the characters in *The Borderers*, and to explore and delineate the ways in which association of ideas and repetition might achieve benignity. But to be a 'wanderer on the earth' is to look for the largest possible framework of understanding in which to place the question of human compassion. In other words, *The Borderers* is an early exploration of the question which was to be fundamental to Wordsworth's greatest poems. And while the style of *The Borderers* may not look like that of the mature, philosophical Wordsworth, and may not offer the same transitions – both subtle and startling – between immediacy and reflection, the play proposes an unfinished dialogue between custom and the deracinated individual which has many successors in the later work. *The Borderers* neither is, nor is not, Godwinian; it neither is, nor is it not, a pointer to some new mode of understanding the world; it neither is nor is it not the rejection of custom. The capacity to become settled in one of these ways of thinking is compared to blindness. It is perhaps not surprising that what Ashton Nichols calls Wordsworth's 'confusing interactions among speakers [. . .] even when the speaking voice belongs to an ostensible "self"' should find their prototype in a play.[30] But this may serve to remind us of the marked differences which may exist between one part of a Wordsworth poem and another, and certainly of the pondered variety of style and genre which may characterise a volume of poems. These different types of text correspond to points of view which may be conceived as possessing borders, and between which transitions may be made.

The title of *The Borderers* refers not only to 'the borders of vision', or to any region where jurisdiction (and thus notions of justice) is contested: it also refers to the border between England and Scotland. That is to say, it makes symbolic use of a boundary between an Anglo-Saxon and a Celtic country, specifically the Celtic country associated with Ossian and 'second sight'. Not that the play exploits this opposition in detail; rather, the title, and thus the play, profits by the association when it suggests that there may be higher modes of perception to which one can make a 'transition' through 'barriers'. In *The Pedlar* and *The Ruined Cottage*, which follow, it is possible to identify a layer of thinking which associates insight with second sight and with the bardic, as I have already suggested elsewhere.[31] Like his successor in *The Excursion*, the pedlar, by 1802, has become a Scot. His name was Patrick Drummond; and this merely reflects the nationality of his real-life inspiration, James Patrick, the 'intellectual pedlar', who was 'by birth and education a Scotchman'.[32] In *The Excursion*, the Scottish wanderer is plainly described as a poet formed by Nature ('Oh many are the Poets that are sown / By Nature': *Excursion* I: 77–8) In all versions of *The Pedlar*, he possesses an exceptional 'eye', and references abound to this, and to 'sight' and 'images'. By the time of the composition of MS M, in 1804, he has 'a peculiar eye' (l. 176; Wordsworth 1979b: 395); but as early as *Ruined Cottage* MS. B (1798) he has 'a luminous eye' and 'His eye / Flash[es] poetic fire' (ll. 49, 71–2; Wordsworth 1979b: 44, 46); and among the famous lines about giving a moral life even to 'the loose stones that cover the highway', we should note that 'In all shapes / He found a secret and mysterious soul', with the result that his expression could look a trifle strange, and 'Some called it madness' (ll. 80–93; Wordsworth 1979b: 46). It is important to note that, when he first conceived the passage describing the pedlar's mental development, Wordsworth laid more stress on his clairvoyance than on the Hartleian explanation for it. Thus in 1798, we are also told that 'he had an eye which evermore / Looked deep into the shades of difference / As they lie hid in all exterior forms' (ll. 94–6; Wordsworth 1979b: 46); but we have to wait until 1803–4 for an account of the way the young pedlar received 'impressions', and for the fine lines about an 'active power to fasten images / Upon his brain' (*Pedlar*, MS E, ll. 139, 143–4; Wordsworth 1979b: 394). Back in 1798 these lines do not occur. When they are added, though, we also learn that the objects 'impressed' on his mind seemed to 'haunt the bodily sense'. He is introduced to us with his eyes shut: he is taking a rest, but in context we may wonder what images are going through his mind (*Ruined Cottage*, MS B, l. 108; Wordsworth 1979b: 48). Soon he announces that 'I see around me [. . .] / Things which you cannot see' (ll. 129–30; Wordsworth 1979b: 48). The things he sees are memories provoked by sights of common things: 'Seest thou that path?' (l. 493; Wordsworth 1979b: 70). And among the memories, like a confirmation of his powers, we find that he always did have a keen interpretive eye while the events he describes were happening, aware of all the little signs that things were still getting worse for Margaret even before he was told. In other words, for all the talk of his 'eye' and of his 'seeing', what is acute about his vision is that it sees so clearly what is not literally there. This is a signal case of what is common enough in Wordsworth: as David Simpson puts it, 'It is the mind that sees, not the eye'.[33] Of course, this is the Gothic and the spectral naturalised; but it is specifically a Gothic with overtones of second sight and the bardic, and specifically an inward vision whose substance is memory rather than fancy. Having accepted the pedlar's keenness of sight at this level, we are being tempted to accept the notorious judgement that Margaret's suffering is softened in the larger pattern of Nature. In other words, we have here an exploration of the relationship between compassion for individuals and an understanding of the cosmos which was central to the subject-matter of *The Borderers*, and is conceived in terms of a mode of sight which goes beyond the immediate.

'Tintern Abbey': Abundant Recompense

The experience of the eye is a central reference point in 'Lines Written a Few Miles above Tintern Abbey', and the experience of the blind man an important theme. But first one should ask what is looked at. I say this in order to lay stress on the title. There have been so many studies in recent years which offer valuable information about attitudes to monasteries, to Gothic ruins, to the Dissolution, or to the contemporary disestablishment of the French church, that it seems worth observing a prior piece of scholarly punctilio: not only does the title refer to a spot a few miles above Tintern Abbey, but the abbey makes no appearance whatsoever in the poem. This is indeed a nature poem, offering a striking reinterpretation of the picturesque and its union with the sublime, in relation to a secluded spot: an attempt of which Wordsworth had a model in Coleridge's conversation poems. Notoriously, the iron-works make no appearance either. To that extent, the poem is at one with the selectively softening impulse of picturesque art. Yet human suffering is there from the start: those 'vagrant dwellers in the houseless woods'. Along with the hermit, they make up a medieval-sounding crew. As Alan Bewell points out, Wordsworth makes a journey to the past of the Abbey.[34] He also makes a journey to the time of its building. In either case, the absence of the actual edifice seems appropriate. The intention is universalising: the 'still, sad music of humanity', like the poor, is always with us: there were vagrants in medieval times, and even before then. Now, with the war and economic conditions in the nineties, there are vagrants again. The peculiar fact is that, in the name of this universal view, we are offered not a sanitisation of poverty as such, but the concealment of specifically contemporary industry. From Wordsworth's point of view, this is an appropriate strategy for the kind of poem he is writing, a poem with strong universalising ambition. Despite this it is not at all an unhistorical poem, as I hope to suggest. These facts may not be to the taste of every modern reader, but in order to go further and convict Wordsworth of aestheticising the social picture, one has to ignore too much of this complex poem. As it happens, one also has to do violence to the context provided by other poems he was writing in this period, poems he conceived of as performing a different kind of task from that which he undertook in 'Tintern Abbey': 'The Old Cumberland Beggar' may end with the wish that almost insentient mendicant continue to live 'in the eye of Nature'. But Wordsworth's eye has been roving over him throughout the poem. And what an unpromising subject he is. Wordsworth goes out of his way to emphasise the way in which his near-blindness can be taken as a metaphor for the lack of any interesting perception, moral or otherwise. It is not just the statesman who might be tempted to find him 'useless'. There can be no return for any generosity afforded him: certainly not material, but nothing of human interest either. We are back in a Shakespearean world of not attempting to quantify the benefits of compassion. Likewise, in 'Tintern Abbey', the vagrants in 'the houseless woods' point us subtly back towards the world of *The Borderers*, and 'The Female Vagrant'. The first line of the latter is 'Hard is the life when naked and unhouzed'; and 'houseless' is a word that occurs twice in the same speech when Lear responds 'for the first time to the nakedness and suffering of his people'.[35] 'How shall your houseless heads and unfed sides / Your loop'd and window'd raggedness, defend you / From seasons such as these?' (III.iv.30–2).

'Tintern Abbey', then, shows that its speaker is attentive to – really does see – both nature and human suffering. In the past he experienced a moment like an enlightenment, an escape from blindness, but it was unreflective. Now he does not see the immediate scene so well, but is able to hear a 'harmony' and 'see into the life of things'. He moves towards something akin to literal blindness, but assumes a more significant seeing. The disavowal of blindness near the beginning of the poem is an important thematic statement, for it immediately suggests that the speaker will not suffer from the egotistical blindness of Lear at the beginning of Shakespeare's play. It also marks one point of divergence from Coleridge's subsequent revision of 'This Lime-Tree Bower My Prison', which starts by suggesting that its speaker is thus blind, and proceeds to show Nature, and his own imagining of the landscape seen by his friends, as liberating him. Wordsworth, on the other hand, starts the poem already released from this kind of blindness, although it is important to note that, as in Coleridge, the decisive images of Nature have occurred to memory and imagination, rather than to immediate sight. The lines in question are these:

> Though absent long
> These forms of beauty have not been to me
> As is a landscape to a blind man's eye [. . .] (23–5)

The 'forms' (a word which itself has connections to 'visual image') have made impressions (to use a philosophers' word), in the way that they cannot on the blind man's mind. The latter's reconstruction of the landscape will always be theoretical, and the best he can do is in the manner of Descartes' blind man, who can build a working model of the universe by means of his stick, which operates as an enhancement of the sense of touch.[36] Of course, he may in this way be able to offer a plausible verbal account, but it will always be marked by its theoretical character. As Wordsworth says in the 'Essay, Supplementary to the Preface', when castigating the way in which Pope wrote about landscape, 'A blind man, in the habit of attending accurately to descriptions casually dropped from the lips of those around him, might easily depict these appearances with more truth'.[37] Better than Pope, but only just. Wordsworth's negative simile in 'Tintern Abbey' thus comprises suggestions of vision and of the immediate, while his handling of the associations of *Lear* prepares us for the idea that his vision will encompass sensitivity to human suffering. Interestingly, though, as in *The Pedlar*, the very immediacy of vision is conveyed in terms of 'haunting': 'The sounding cataract / Haunted me like a passion' (ll. 77–8) sounds very much like the way, for the pedlar, 'impressed [. . .] objects [. . .] seemed / To haunt the bodily sense' (*Pedlar*, ll. 30–4), so that one feels the uncanny presence of second sight in what should be primary. It is as if Wordsworth wants to emphasise the immediacy of vision, but is unhappy with the idea that it should not contain at least a hint of the complex wisdom to which it may some day give rise. But since immediacy must perforce be unreflective, that hint must necessarily be obscure: 'an obscure sense of possible sublimity'. Uncanniness is the right word: the alienated spectral quality of immediate vision cannot be assimilated to a unified sense of self; but if the later mind, which has found a philosophic 'recompence', is founded in loss, then it scarcely bears witness to that unity either. The poem does not pretend to offer stability, except in so far as this can be found in a sanctified process marked by gain and loss.

As in Coleridge's conversation poems (to which the poem alludes, as Lucy Newlyn has shown), that process is roughly modelled on the Christian redemptive schema, with the first visit to Tintern as Edenic, the intervening years as fallen, and the return visit redemptively combining salvation and knowledge.[38] In this connection, it is instructive to note that Nicholas Roe has demonstrated that one influence on the poem is 'the Miltonic picturesque': a mode which suggests the Paradisal, even as it remembers the Fall.[39] Wordsworth gives the schema a characteristically Pauline inflection, with the initial stage corresponding to an access of grace which is also a recovery from blindness associated with 'Flying from something that he dreads', as Saul of Tarsus might be said to have been doing on the road to Damascus. Looking on Nature 'not as in the hour / Of thoughtless youth' (90–1), on the other hand, refers to 1 Corinthians 11, where Paul looks forward to our future knowledge of God: 'when I became a man, I put away childish things'. At the later stage, however, a new form of blindness supervenes. Nature always had the power to induce states of profound meditation where 'we are laid asleep / In body and become a living soul' (ll. 46–7; note that Paul's remarks refer to the state of man after death). In this state, we also experience '*an eye made quiet* by the power / Of harmony and the deep power of joy' (my emphasis). Blinded to immediate sense impressions, we hear the principle of harmony, with its overtones both of the auditory and of a combined principle of pattern and unity which cannot be grasped in the given. In this state, we gain a higher form of vision, an insight whereby 'We see into the life of things'. Are we seeing or hearing, then? We are no longer seeing immediate sense impressions, except in memory. Our seeing is intellectual, and is bound up with language. This process, for which the potential is always present, prefigures and prepares the larger movement in which one no longer 'look[s]' on Nature as in the 'hour' (a temporary stage) of 'thoughtless youth'. In the lines about 'hearing oftentimes / The still, sad music of humanity', the verb, and the idea of music, connote reflection and interiority. These are qualities echoed by the ensuing 'felt / A presence', and contrasted with the earlier 'looking'. Once one realises the extent to which the older Wordsworth experiences, and has experienced, the inward vision of memory, one begins to see that it is an important feature of the poem from the start. Even in the opening lines, the reference to seeing '*these* steep and lofty cliffs' and '*this* dark sycamore' is not just an index of particularity (important though that is) but also of memory: it's the same one again, and the demonstratives work with the phrase 'Once again'. As he continues to contemplate the scene above Tintern Abbey, he notes that 'The picture of the mind revives again'. The memory of the past is exactly superimposed on the landscape, but with the uncanny difference that the superimposition is more intense than the objects onto which it fits. This point can be brought into useful relation with the more familiar one of Wordsworth's concentrating on the essentials of a scene, rather than offering a detailed descriptive analysis.[40] The idea of encroaching blindness provides an important resonance in the poem, and draws on echoes of St Paul, of Lear, of Ossian and of Milton. In this respect, as in others, the poem is a clear precursor of *The Prelude*. In particular, the voluminousness of the poem's syntax, its sententiousness, offers a fullness and authority to the ear which is intended to enact the recompense for loss of immediate vision.

'Tintern Abbey', then, describes a felt change of perception. As Robert Langbaum says, 'there is some change in the perception which the physical sameness of the scene renders unaccountable'.[41] But Wordsworth offers many clues as to the nature of the mature and more profoundly instructed view which now modifies that scene. It is important to reach an adequate estimation of what is involved in it. The philosophic view, though it is in touch with, and instructed by the past, just as it is in touch with and instructed by past sense experience, is a modern one. It is important to keep in mind that the 'sense sublime / Of something far more deeply interfused' has Newtonian connections. Geoffrey Durrant has pointed out that 'Tintern Abbey' has much in common with Addison's Ode, 'The spacious firmament on high [. . .]', and with Thomson's 'To the Memory of Sir Isaac Newton'.[42] This is true despite the immanence essential to Wordsworth's and Coleridge's conceptions of the One Life, for this is as it were added on to the Newtonian conception.[43] In this connection, it is instructive to note the lines of Humphry Davy, soon to become Coleridge's good friend, in his poem 'The Sons of Genius', from the mid-1790s:

> To scan the laws of Nature, to explore
>   The tranquil reign of mild Philosophy,
> Or on Newtonian wings sublime to soar
>   Through the bright regions of the starry sky.[44]

Davy was soon to pen his own thoughts on Tintern Abbey, very much under the influence both of Coleridge and of Wordsworth's poem. Durrant rightly notes that a telling phrase in Wordsworth's poem is 'A motion and a spirit', where motion is 'a term which compels an association with Newton's laws of motion and with the whole picture of the universe as a wonderful machine in which material objects are impelled by eternal law to follow their pre-ordained courses'.[45] Humphry Davy exclaims, contemplating the light of the moon in what his brother calls a 'sketch' of Tintern Abbey which dates from shortly after his arrival in Bristol in October 1798, 'How intimately connected together are life, light, and motion!'[46] In general terms, it would seem that Wordsworth's primitive sensory response to nature has inevitably led up to a conviction of the rightness of the most advanced scientific view. But the implications run deeper than that. It is not possible, in this period, to separate Newton from the Locke tradition, at least in the minds of most educated people; for, as we saw in previous chapters, Locke was held to encourage a Newtonian spirit of experiment, and Lockeian assumptions about ideas and impressions were thought to be broadly validated in the same way as Newton's findings. These are assumptions which have bred the Hartleian view of moral development which plays its part in 'Tintern Abbey'; and the phrase 'the mighty world / Of eye and ear' (ll. 106–7) marks the point at which the instructed Newtonian joins hands with the instructed Hartleian: Newton's *Principia* and *Optics* with Hartley's theories about the nerves and sensory impressions. And Nicholas Roe has shown how the 'something far more deeply interfused' which can have such an effect on the 'corporeal frame' is indebted to Thelwall's materialist conception of 'animal vitality'.[47] Of course, one can make these connections in a different way, and be just as faithful, if not more so, to Wordsworth's intent: tracing the movement of the poem, one can build up the mature life of the mind, following his rather sketchy, but in historical context intelligible, scenario. Thus simple sense impressions of the beautiful and sublime forms of nature impart their associations to the mind and act as the 'anchor' of developed moral and intellectual life. But my purpose in adverting to the history of ideas is to insist that Wordsworth also intends to obtrude the poem's place in that history; nor would the contemporary reader have been capable of ignoring it. In this manner, the poem insists on its embodiment of a mature, enlightened, modern philosophic view, which, among other things, transcends the 'monkish times' (Gilpin's phrase) which produced the abbey, while finding its origins in the Nature that was present long before the abbey was built.[48] In its historiographical implications, it sketches a long view of social evolution to compete with and better the discourses of revolution at home and across the Channel.

The enlightened view must comprise a developed moral sense, and this is evident from the lines about 'hearing [. . .] the still, sad music of humanity', where the verb, and the idea of music, connote reflection and interiority. These are qualities echoed by the ensuing 'felt / A presence', but contrasted with the 'look[ing]' appropriate to 'thoughtless youth' when it contemplates Nature. The stasis of 'still' consolidates the sense of timeless suffering already suggested by the absence of the iron-works. Wordsworth's point is morally serious, and, as Nicholas Roe observes, has its roots in his radicalism of the 1790s.[49] It is also ultimately capable of being assimilated to a view more conservative than that. A schematic account would say that this conservatism will attempt to unite an individualist ideology appropriate to a dynamic middle class with a new, organicist view of society which can make links with the old landed interest.

But such a view is reductionist when put in those bald terms. The poem attempts to synthesise so many different aspects of the experience it records. And one also needs to register alongside this the novelty of the new picture of the individualism it represents. It is registered, in part, by the solitude the poem presumes. While the poem can certainly be read in terms of a certain understanding of the picturesque, it offers a novel interest (as do Coleridge's conversation poems) in the irreducible thisness of the landscape: as we have suggested, this is one way of taking 'these plots' and 'these orchard-tufts'.[50] The coinage 'orchard-tufts', alluding, as Nicholas Roe has shown, to Milton's 'L'Allegro' and to William Crowe's *Lewesdon Hill*, is brilliantly turned into a locution reminiscent of Goethe's coinings in his Frankfurt period, and in its concision conveys particularity.[51] This is another aspect of the poem's modernity. And although we shall later have to address the piquant fact that such passages in Wordsworth are either in the past or state that the past was even more vivid, it is arguable that this sense of a split between the primitive and the reflective consciousness is itself a striking index of modernity. From another point of view, which is entirely connected with this, these locutions emphasise 'the private quality of the experience'.[52] This quality is closely related to the poem's feeling of solitude, and to the solitude, as we have seen, of a remembering subject. Both the privacy and the solitude are markers of the ideology of individualism, and the force with which this quality would have struck a contemporary reader is, I think, conveyed by Humphry Davy's 'sketch' of Tintern Abbey, which is patently influenced by Wordsworth's poem:

> No, my friend, individuality can never cease to exist; that ideal self which exists in dreams and reveries, that ideal self which never slumbers, is the child of immortality, and those deep intense feelings, which man sometimes perceives in the bosom of Nature and Deity, are presentiments of a more sublime and energetic state of existence.[53]

The 'uses of Dorothy' (in John Barrell's phrase) include, above all, the relief of solitude: an earnest that the poet's conception of individuality is not at odds with the social. Indeed, the mere fact of there being an intimate nearby is the first thing to register, even before one thinks of the meaning of its being his sister, or of the kind of experiences imputed to her: her first role is simply to suggest that the poet thinks about other people, as Coleridge does of his 'friends' in 'This Lime-Tree Bower', or of his baby son in 'Frost at Midnight'. The ideas of sympathy and sociality can be concretised in this way. Almost as important is the attempt to show that the kind of 'individuality' Wordsworth describes is a common possession, developing for all in the same way. Barrell says that '[Wordsworth] needs to believe that Dorothy will grow up and sober up, for by doing so she will naturalise and legitimate his own loss of immediate pleasure in nature'.[54] This certainly touches on an important point, but perhaps couches the matter too much in terms of manipulation: Wordsworth wishes to show that the self in process, from the wildness of the senses to the philosophic mind, describes a potentially universal journey.

This idea of the self in process registers the dynamism of a historically new form of the self. This is evoked in the most optimistic fashion in the lines about 'something ever more about to be' in the Simplon Pass passage from *The Prelude*. As we suggested earlier, the self in process is also split, but the at the same time the poem embodies a drive to unify. In effect, it records both division and the attempt to heal division. The commanding style, to which we referred, is, as we saw, a way of compensating aurally for failing vision, but is by the same token associated simultaneously with the loss it would seek to assuage, both tonally and, we discover, thematically, in that the poem records a loss. It finds its correlative in the poem's strong drive to find the universal in what it admits to be the disparate and the differing. There is, of course, the grand difference between earlier and later self, which finds its correlative in the differing languages of early sensibility and later philosophic sublimity, both of which the poem actually embodies in its own words. The poem combines a number of genres – ode, elegy, meditative poem, the picturesque, both Miltonic and more recent – as well as making reference to characteristics of the contemporary sonnet revival, as represented by figures such as William Lisle Bowles and Charlotte Smith.[55] Mention of Smith should remind us, as indeed should Dorothy's presence, that the difference between the languages of sensibility and of the sublime has gender implications, in that sensibility is seen as a predominantly feminine mode, and when Wordsworth sees what once he was in her, he sees himself as having once operated only in that mode, as he still fitfully does. If in a sense he patronises that mode, there is another sense in which the regret he offers seems undeniably authentic, so that what we are really presented with is another nuance of self-division, rather than the malign figure presented by suspicionist criticism.

Wordsworth's relationship to the picturesque is similarly both ambiguous and unifying, for even as the poem offers a perspective which at least recalls the prospect view, and records the unification of particulars (the woods and copses 'lose themselves'), it also reminds one of Uvedale Price's opinion that the picturesque was characterised by 'wildness and irregularity'.[56] The relationship to the prospect view is also troubled: the sense of 'seclusion', along with the displacement of the Gothic subject, suggest (scarcely surprisingly) that this is not a poem which is a simple descendant of art-works allowing one to 'appropriate the scenery of [one's] own land', as Linda Colley puts it.[57] The poem also foregrounds a number of qualifications of its initial descriptions or syntheses: the 'hedge-rows' which are 'hardly hedge-rows, little lines of sportive wood run wild', or the remark 'if this be but a vain belief'.[58] Indeed, it is probable that Wordsworth is actively soliciting a comparison with those oil sketches which it was fashionable to undertake on visiting a picturesque scene: this would be a way of achieving something comparable to the immediacy, the sense of presentness, achieved by Coleridge in his conversation poems. 'Tintern Abbey', then, not only foregrounds difference, it also enacts a tentative manner and a sense of faith triumphing over uncertainty. These qualities help to emphasise the realistic and time-bound character of the experience. It is a complex and allusive tissue of meanings created in the struggles of the world, able to apprehend a possible transcendence as the principle of that world, but only imperfectly.

A consideration of the figure of Dorothy may help to elucidate several of these points. One of the things Wordsworth's poetry requires in order to unfold itself, he informs us, is Dorothy, or what she represents. The phrase 'genial spirits' (l. 113) is an allusion to *Samson Agonistes* (l. 594), where the blind Samson feels them 'droop'. The 'shooting lights' of Dorothy's 'wild eyes', on the other hand, evidence an 'animal' *élan vital*, or 'animal vitality', and an intensity of sight which Wordsworth is at pains to stress that he cannot recover. Dorothy both is and is not the principle of writing. She is the principle of writing, to the extent that, like the Child in the Intimations Ode, she is only thus moved because she is not merely subdued to visual data: she has an instinctive sense of the presentness of the 'something far more deeply' interfused. On the other hand, she is not the principle of writing to the extent that, with experience, that 'something' detaches itself from its paradoxical inherence in the immediate, and we are left with the 'philosophic mind' which reconstructs its role. She cannot understand that something in this way, whereas Wordsworth has to work between the barriers to vision which erect themselves before the now separated realms of the (possibly) transcendent and the immediate. What is so striking about his poetry is the way that his own apprehension of it as founded in different types of perception and different discourses becomes part of the poem: it is as if, being shown our blindness both to the immediate and to the transcendent we are asked, in the intervening space between, to make subordinate transitions from one way of seeing (which is also one way of writing) to another – as a way of enacting a continuous process of seeing differently. At the same time, the poetry also apprehends a necessary contradiction in its representation of the principle that lies behind writing: is it immediacy, or transcendence? It is both, and yet logically this is impossible. As we shall see, Wordsworth addresses these concepts again in 'I am not One who much or oft delight' (from *Poems in Two Volumes*), where the wonder of children's existence lies in the fact that their world lies 'partly at their feet' and 'part far from them'.

The idea of the self presented in this poem is a profoundly historicised one. We are shown the value of the primitive past and the manner in which it is lost in a way that could only be known in Wordsworth's own historical period. The conception of the self is a modern philososphical one, but that philosophy itself is historically placed. In a parallel manoeuvre, the poem places the self and its own knowledge of the past in a contemporary history, by alluding to historical crisis, and by placing that crisis in a long perspective. Moving wider, it places the movement of history in the largest possible, scientifically-based cosmological perspective. None of this knowledge would have been possible at an earlier time. Finally, the poem insinuates that the historically contemporary has the opportunity to engage in a process of constant discovery, characterised by movements between different discourses and literary genres, which ideally it should seek to unify without attempting to impose artificial unity. The poem also hints, through the idea of a transition in the self, through the partial unknowability of the 'something far more deeply interfused', and through the figure of Dorothy, who has not made the poet's transition, at the possibility of barriers to knowledge. But these are not necessarily to be accepted. One may have glimpses beyond barriers. All of these topics can be referred to the statement that the remembered scene has not been 'As is a landscape to a blind man's eye'. This notion introduces the contrast between two modes of perception, and the poem implies that the vitality of the landscape and the vitality of the self are consequent on a willingness to make transitions from one mode of perception to another.

'Home at Grasmere': Within Barriers

One who wishes to see beyond barriers nevertheless recognises their existence: recognises that there are some states to which we must be blind. We have already referred to a wider context in Wordsworth's work supplied by the imagery of borders and liminal states. 'Tintern Abbey' shows how the poem exists on the borders of vision. It is illuminated by a brief but undoubted light cast from the 'something far more deeply interfused', a light which is both attained and threatened by natural processes. This conception of the poem has a clear thematic correlative in 'Home at Grasmere'. The last lines of MS A, though written down in 1806, probably represent a reworking of material dating from 1800.[59] Referring to the encircling mountains, they describe 'lofty barriers' which offer partial protection.

> And as these lofty barriers break the force
> Of winds this deep vale as it doth in part
> Conceal us from the storm so here there is
> Or seems to be for it befits it yet
> Newcomer as I am to speak in doubt.
> (ll. 455–9; Wordsworth 1977: 137)

The opening of MS D, which dates from between 1812 and 1814, replaces an earlier formulation about the 'brow' of a hill, with lines yet again referring to the 'barrier' around Grasmere: 'Once to the verge of yon steep barrier came / A roving School-boy.' (ll. 1–2; Wordsworth 1977: 39). Within the 'barriers' surrounding Grasmere one may find the nearest thing to Paradise, which one finds in this 'green earth', which surpasses 'the most fair ideal Forms' (MS B, ll. 991–2; Wordsworth 1977: 102):

> Paradise and groves
> Elysian, fortunate islands, fields like those of old
> In the deep ocean – wherefore should they be
> A History, or but a dream, when minds
> Once wedded to this outward frame of things
> In love, find these the growth of common day?
> (ll. 996–1001; Wordsworth 1977: 102)

The 'outward frame' denotes not merely the facticity of this world, but its potential to be apprehended as limitation, a sense which chimes with the word 'barriers'. For nothing in Wordsworth's poetry suggests that we can live as if we were timeless and constantly ecstatic spirits: the Paradisal is the 'growth' of 'common day' – the world of habit – not its undifferentiated mode. When it does thus grow, not only does it offer salve and recompense, it makes tolerable the suffering and loss which are bound to occur. Unrelieved by the vision Nature makes possible, the barriers become oppressive: 'Sorrow, *barricadoed* evermore / Within the walls of cities' (my emphasis ll. 1022–3; Wordsworth 1977: 104). But barriers there will always be. In the pursuit of this high argument, which also found a place in the Prospectus for *The Recluse*, it may be significant that Wordsworth dons the mantle of Milton: 'fit audience let me find though few! [. . .] thus prayed the Bard / Holiest of Men' (ll. 972–4; Wordsworth 1977: 100). For one of the purposes of 'Home at Grasmere' is to offer a visionary treatment of a domestication of vision, of the acquisition of partial blindness.

'The Blind Highland Boy' and 'the Eye among the blind'

Finding the paradisal in the world of habit is the theme of the Intimations Ode, and the point is expounded with greater concision and force than critics have realised. We have seen in Chapter 2 that this poem was the last in a section of *Poems in Two Volumes* (1807) called 'The Blind Highland Boy; with Other Poems', the first poem being 'The Blind Highland Boy' itself.[60] The choice of title, and this particular way of framing the section, is significant. Both the Blind Highland Boy and the Child in the Ode possess resources of inner vision, and it is in this sense that the latter is an 'Eye among the blind'. How does the poem demonstrate the child's visionary inheritance? Only in those passages where he imitates 'his dream of human life'. The whole strophe beginning 'Behold the Child among his new-born blisses' (l. 85) shows the youthful 'imitation' of life.[61] He imitates the whole of life, for the 'little Actor' plays all the parts, 'down to palsied Age' (ll. 102, 104). These lines are couched in terms of artistry and imagination: 'newly-learned art', 'song', 'dialogues' and acting (ll. 92–102). The ensuing strophe gives no hint of anything amiss, but proceeds, as if in consequence of the artistry described, to apostrophise the Child as 'best Philosopher', 'Eye among the blind', 'Mighty Prophet! Seer blest!' (ll. 110–14). The first melancholy note in the 'Child' strophes is only struck when we reach the claim that 'we are toiling all our lives to find' the truths which already 'rest' upon the Child (ll. 115–16), who did not have to seek or discover them. It is this which prepares us for the lines in which the Child is asked why he provokes the years to bring the weight of custom upon him. Until we reach this point, there is nothing to suggest that the Child's genius does not lie precisely in being a great artist, albeit a mimetic one. The artist Child does *the same things* as the adult. The problem does not lie at all in performing repetitively the tasks and roles of life – and in any case, there is no escaping that – but in the spirit of the repetition. That is the true meaning of Wordsworth's disavowal of any but a figurative role for the Platonic myth of pre-existence. What he really seeks is startlingly close to Kierkegaard's concept of repetition:

> One never grows weary of the old, and when one has that, one is happy. He alone is truly happy who is not deluded into thinking that the repetition should be something new, for then one grows weary of it.[62]

The question is, though, when does one *have* the old? For one does not possess it merely by repeating: one has 'to will repetition'.[63] One has to realise the delusive character of trusting or hoping in the new. The child in Wordsworth's poem, who has no close counterpart in Kierkegaard, has not yet had to learn the true lesson of the loss of intensity which propels the adult into a hopeless quest for the new. (This quest is recounted with the appropriate melancholy cynicism by Byron and Baudelaire.) The adult should learn this lesson, and by repeating can keep in distant touch with the visionary intensity that first so joyfully imbued action and role-play. This is understood by the speaker of Wordsworth's poem, whom Bewell refers to as 'the blind poet': that is, the poet who has learnt to live in reconcilement with his stinted powers. Stinted, but not extinguished; for the 'celestial light' which the youth perceives at the beginning of the Ode remains as the 'fountain light' and 'master light' of this blind poet. Unlike in Milton, these inward lights come not from heaven, but from the child's experiences, the 'first affections' and 'shadowy recollections'.[64] The conception of repetition or custom in the Ode thus has a notably static quality. The great forms of life's rituals and tasks repeat and repeat from childhood onwards: the shadows gather around them, but their outlines are unchanging. It is appropriate therefore that Wordsworth's great

Ode should embody the universalising style of Romantic neoclassicism, as Marjorie Levinson observes. Romantic neoclassicism, a style both pristine and ancient, redolent of the revolutionary and the timeless, is the very manner for the kind of redeemed repetition which in this poem provides such a memorable development of Wordsworth's theme of the redemption of the customary.

In respect of this style, though, it is alone. As much as any series Wordsworth ever composed (including *Lyrical Ballads*, which was a model), 'The Blind Highland Boy; with Other Poems' is various in genre and tone: sonnets, ballads (of various tone, including the 'namby-pamby' to which Byron referred), quiet meditations ('I am not One who much or oft delight'), the sombre inconsolability of the 'Elegiac Stanzas'.[65] At the same time, all its variety conduces to the same broad end. We have noted the connections between the first poem and the last; but the 'Elegiac Stanzas' are designedly placed just before the great Ode so that the statement in the former that 'A power is gone, which nothing can restore' may be balanced by the recompense offered in the latter. That balance has already been suggested in the reaction to the death of Fox in 'Lines, Composed at Grasmere', the poem just preceding 'Elegiac Stanzas': always, man returns to God, 'Then wherefore should we mourn?' There are other connections which support the idea that this volume emerges from a period of serious meditation on the relationship of childhood and vision. In 'I am not One', Wordsworth notes that

> Children are blest, and powerful; their world lies
> More justly balanced; partly at their feet,
> And part far from them: – sweetest melodies
> Are those that are by distance made more sweet;
> Whose mind is but the mind of his own eyes
> He is a Slave; the meanest we can meet![66]

These are lines which connect backwards to 'The Blind Highland Boy' and forward to the Intimations Ode. They sketch a proleptic relationship between the child's imagination and the auditory sensitivity which to a large degree takes its place for the adult, and which had already perforce done so for the highland boy himself. Children live between two intensities: the immediate ('at their feet') and imagination ('far from them'). In maturity, we may hope to fill the ever-widening gap between these two intensities, to which we become blind, with a music which recalls them both. They are beyond the 'barriers' to vision, to recall the language of 'Home at Grasmere'. We cannot recover them by succumbing to the 'tyranny of the eye'. As for the child, its way of inhabiting the space between these two intensities is a strange mystery: it is also uncanny, for both child and adult inhabit this in-betweenness. The child

even does the same things as adults by imitating adults. These considerations prompt the exclamatory wonder of the Ode's apostrophe to
the Child.

We are induced to connect such passages in a reflective process of
reading and re-reading. It is an educative process, and not just because
of the general rule adduced by Alan Richardson, that 'In its wider sense
of mental growth, education might be taken as defining the Romantic
ethos'.[67] The Ode's passages on the child, as Richardson points out,
themselves satirise 'the new rational approach to education'.[68] The fact
that the ballads were seen by many reviewers as childish ironically con-
firms Wordsworth's intention to draw his readers into a state of mind
where they could at least approximate some of the qualities of the
unspoilt child. But these qualities were to be linked by the reading
process to maturer reflections upon that very state of mind. The difference involves genre. But it also involves class, for the Sonnet and the Ode
were not to be seen in the same light as ballads. Jon P. Klancher has
emphasised Wordsworth's consciousness of his potential readerships,
and it is clear that he later drew satisfaction from the fact that a grocer
might appreciate the simpler poems better than the polite reviewers
could.[69] This educative process, then, is an attempt to transcend the
boundaries set by different types of education in reading: partially to
overcome the blindness that they might involve; to make 'transitions'.
This working on his readers is much more interesting and novel than a
reductionist account might offer, in terms, let us say, of attempting to
bolster the organic unity of the nation. So central is this kind of effort
to Wordsworth's intention that it is even illuminating about parts of *The
Prelude* to think in terms of an anthology of different poems.

Seeing and Describing the Other: The Blind Beggar and the blind man in *The Excursion*

The Blind Beggar in Book VII of *The Prelude* recalls the context of the
blind bard and second sight. When the crowd becomes 'a second-sight
procession, such as glides / Over still mountains, or appears in dreams',
not only is it spectral, it is also described in terms of a particular genre
of the spectral; for 'procession' is not an uninstructed usage, but a startling reference to the phenomenon which so often, as we saw in Chapter
2, presented itself to the 'seer': a host of the dead. '[D]reams' refers to
visions; but 'mountains' identifies the characteristic location of the
visions which were granted to Ossian and other Celtic seers. The proximity to the Blind Beggar of lines about second sight evokes connections

between blindness and bardic vision which would have been automatic for a contemporary reader (if *The Prelude* had possessed one). They raise, though in no mechanical fashion, the possibility that the Beggar is as capable of sublime imagination as the blind poet in Burke's *Enquiry*. This does not have to be more than a possibility: indeed, it must not be. The point is to induce speculation about the beggar's mental experience, a speculation which leads to the giddy impasse of sublimity. This spec-ulation is only the striking form of what the speaker has already been induced to by the uninterpretable faces of the crowd, in a passage which, like Blake's 'London', is an early example of the 'big city' poem Benjamin found in Baudelaire: compare Blake's speaker, 'marking' the faces of those he encounters, with Wordsworth's speaker exclaiming:

> 'The face of every one
> That passes by me is a mystery!'
> Thus have I looked, nor ceased to look, oppressed
> By thoughts of what and whither, when and how [. . .]
>   (1805; ll. 596–9)

The true origin and identity of the beggar are famously mocked by the pitiful label on his chest, which he himself could not have written, explaining 'The story of the man, and who he was'. They are also mocked by the currency of the story of the Blind Beggar of Bethnal Green, a figure from a popular ballad such as might have been sold or sung at Bartholomew Fair, or any number of other places: 'Here files of ballads dangle from dead walls' (l. 209). Wordsworth asks us what might lie behind such tales. Might the beggar once, perhaps, have been 'The pride and pleasure of all lookers-on', like the prostitute's 'rosy babe'? Who knows to what infernal destinies the city may lead a promis-ing innocent? So that in the end the 'babe' may come to envy the hapless child of Mary of Buttermere, in his stony rustic grave, with his own epi-taphic label; which fate, if it came to pass, would prove the city a living death, as we may fancy it has become for the beggar. The Beggar, the Maid of Buttermere, Jack the Giant Killer, are ballad figures who are given rewritten ballads as part of another educative process for the reader prepared to make 'transitions'.

But there are other textual references. Like the Discharged Soldier, the Beggar is one of those figures who solicits echoes of Dante's *Inferno*. And that is not the only thing these damaged solitaries share. For the multi-tudes of blind beggars to be found in London were often casualties of war. The Blind Beggar is an overdetermined hieroglyph of social damage, and before we entertain questions about the sublime and the signifier, relevant though these are, we need to register that fact, and the fact that he is begging: that is, urgently soliciting help. The 'admonish[ment]' of which the speaker feels the force, is an example of that ethical tendency Kant identified in the sublime, and least of all can it be denied this description when it comes as if from 'another world', and when the speaker's mind has turned round, in a phrase redolent of the sublime of the Bible, 'As with the might of waters'. But the more proximate echo, as Mary Jacobus has stressed, is that of *Samson Agonistes*.[70] When Wordsworth's eyes are 'smitten with the view' of the beggar, we may be reminded of Samson's boast that his blind man's strength 'with amaze shall strike all who behold' (l. 1645). And when Samson attacks the pillars he does so 'As with the force of winds and waters pent' (l. 1647). The city of London, busy and hard-hearted centre of commerce, is threatened both in its moral and literal foundations by the condition of its poor. As Blake was to say, 'The harlot's cry from street to street / Shall weave old England's winding sheet'. The moralism of the passage links up with the more generalised disapproval of London, and especially perhaps, with the suggestion that Bartholomew Fair, a type of the city itself, is akin to Vanity Fair. In one aspect, then, the passage lives up to its overt hint of admonishment. But it also probes a deeper level of ethical speculation. If we bring together the themes of obscure identity and the ethical call to compassion, we can see how the passage intensifies to the highest pitch questions about human relationship: what are the limits to compassion? How far is compassion best accompanied by knowledge? And, as in *The Borderers* and *The Ruined Cottage*, how can ethical concern be accommodated within the wider understanding of the cosmos; how can those two different perspectives be brought into focus with each other?

By a kind of paradox, given the absence of any obvious sign of Nature, the blind beggar episode is one of Wordsworth's most successful examples of the union of the sublime with human ethical concern, and one of the most powerful self-reflexive passages on his own high calling to encompass such a union in his work. The mere fact of the beggar's being blind widens the question about knowledge, in that the sighted can merely speculate about the experience of the blind. But there is the added point that the figure of the blind man often appears in philosophical discussions about the bases of knowledge, so that there is something eloquently self-conscious about the blind beggar appearing here alongside the phrase 'the utmost that we know / Both of ourselves and of the universe'. The poem is saying, 'I am a philosophical poem'. The label's inadequacy stands for the inadequate word, the *reductio ad absurdum* of language as counter-spirit; it is also the inadequate poem, and the limit case of the potential for inadequacy in an autobiographical poem such as *The Prelude*, since it is akin to a pitiful epitaph which colludes in the city's attempt to consign the beggar to a living death. There have been inadequate words aplenty in Book VII: advertisements, 'ballads hanging from dead walls', the 'written characters' beside the crippled sailor (ll. 220–3). Yet these apparently inadequate signs are deeply involved with the many 'spectacles' we are shown. As Neil Hertz has written, there is a 'confusion' between the expected roles of 'seeing and reading'.[71] But when we are confronted by the beggar, the relationship between these roles is once again in tension. The 'spectacle' of the beggar overpowers the patent sense of the words on his chest, and indicates their inadequacy; and for the speaker, this gap becomes wide enough to include his own dim sense of vast questions about the universe and human identity. The label operates like the words under the gibbet mast in the 'spots of time' incident, or like the phrase *'that we had crossed the Alps'* in the Simplon Pass passage (italicised in 1850): having lost his way, as he does in each case (in London he strays 'beyond the reach of common indications', or signs), he is shaken out of the stock response and his mind rushes on past the barrier of reduced definition, apprehending large questions and possibilities which he cannot formulate, although he is able to sketch their awful affect in sublime terms.

Another way of considering the question of language is to realise that, because he is blind, the beggar raises in an extreme form the question of how to write or speak about a separate person in a way that recognises their separateness and uniqueness. This is a point which Wordsworth recurs to, again making use of the figure of a blind man, in *The Excursion*, Book VII. The dead blind man, of whom the Pastor offers one of his impromptu epitaphs, is a very paragon of those compensatory acccomplishments of hearing, touch, and indeed smell, with which the Enlightenment was so fascinated. Approaching a precipice, he would not fall, because it was as if he was 'Protected, say enlightened, by his ear' (VII: 495). He could find flowers by smell, and of these there was 'none whose figure did not live / Upon his touch' (VII: 501–2). Furthermore, he is well stocked with knowledge supplied by a wide curiosity, and 'by science led, / His genius mounted to the plains of heaven' (VII: 505–6). The Wanderer draws a number of conclusions: first, that 'transfer' of sense is permitted as a 'recompense' and out of 'love and charity', but also that it gives our imagination a reminder that spiritual darkness will be vanquished. He proceeds to evoke the power of blind prophets and poets. But the context of the poem offers a further perspective: the preceding character-sketch had been that of the Deaf Dalesman. We are thus reminded of the great difference that may be required in the tale we tell of one person, compared with that which we offer of another. And in principle, this may be a matter of language. These are difficult cases: no less than the blind, the deaf raise questions about how to speak and write of another. This is what I mean by claiming that even *The Prelude* or, indeed, *The Excursion*, may evoke the idea of a collection of poems. To pursue the point, the presence of the deaf and the blind man, placed together with such very obvious deliberation, is intended to raise the question of the adequacy of epitaph or biography not just in their case, but in relation to the whole series of tales offered by the Pastor. The fact of their disabilities underlines the potential difficulty, and their juxtaposition further emphasises the point. And the correct phrase is indeed 'raise the question'. Critics have been undecided as to whether the Pastor's cameos are examples of the dead letter or the living. Susan Wolfson, for instance, refers to 'the rigid prescriptions of the exemplum'; and Galperin thinks that they fail, that they are 'negations'. Kenneth Johnston, on the other hand, thinks that they are aligned with 'naturalistic communities', and are characteristic of Wordsworth's 'best poetry' in this respect.[72] This uncertainty should surely alert us to the possibility that Wordsworth is suggesting that the tales can be looked at in both ways.

To return to *The Prelude* VII in the spirit of this suggestion, there is a palpable awareness of the degree to which the experience has indeed been formulated. That awareness is conveyed by the lines which follow, and which create a curiously chilling distance between the self-conscious writer and the sense of ethical concern evoked by the beggar. 'Though reared upon the base of outward things', notes Wordsworth, 'These, chiefly, are such structures as the mind / Builds for itself' (ll. 624–6). At one moment, then, the beggar is soliciting in the reader a multi-faceted combination of concern and speculation; at the next moment, he is being treated as a piece of data in the description of a mental structure. The modernity of that idea is striking; but the point is that the use of the word 'structure' also reveals the extent to which Wordsworth is aware of the multi-faceted character of this passage as writing. It is true, of course, as Nicholas Roe points out, that, starting with the words 'Far travelled in such mood', the passage opens 'the border between outer and inner spaces'.[73] But if it is a structure, and built up of anything, it is substantially built up of textual references – to the Old Testament, to blind bards such as Ossian, to Milton, to ballads of the Blind Beggar of Bethnal Green, to philosophical treatises in which the blind man is the subject of thought experiments. So revealing, indeed, is that word 'structure' that it should be treated as part of the Blind Beggar passage, from which it is only separated in the original draft by being written on its verso.[74]

A structure more malign can be found in the vision of the wicker-man – a method of human sacrifice practised, according to Caesar, by the druids:

> I called upon the darkness, and it took –
> A midnight darkness seemed to come and take –
> All objects from my sight; and lo, again
> The desart visible by dismal flames!
> It is the sacrificial altar, fed
> With living men – how deep the groans! – the voice
> Of those in the gigantic wicker thrills
> Throughout the region far and near, pervades
> The monumental hillocks, and the pomp
> Is for both worlds, the living and the dead.
>
> (XII: 327–36)

Mary Jacobus has detailed the connections of this passage with eighteenth-century antiquarianism and its beliefs about the druids, but she also deftly details the connections Wordsworth is making between these human sacrifices and the suffering individuals he treats of elsewhere in *The Prelude*.[75] In this light, the initial phrase, 'I called upon the darkness', sounds like a darkly sublime parody of the invocation of the muse. It recalls Milton, but the druidical context recalls again the blind bard, especially as bards were understood to be associated with the druids.[76] This bard of Albion sees the wicker man as a metaphor for the Hobbesian Leviathan, as depicted in Abraham Bosse's famous and much-reproduced engraving for the 1651 title-page. He is thus seeing modernity as a place of sacrifice. But the passage begins with an invocation, depends on the kinship of druid and bard, recalls that other blind visionary, Milton, and cannot erase Wordsworth's dependence on a tradition of philosophical speculation and political economy at the beginning of which lies Hobbes. The passage is a dark apprehension of what may be unassimilable to a consoling view of humanity, but may still be inextricable from the modernity of his own discourse. It therefore offers a parody of those verbal structures in which Wordsworth seeks to build a counterpart to the mental structures of response to another human being. While it is not an epitaph, it is a passage evoking the counter-spirit, in that it is a kind of summation of the death of humanity as encompassed by a reductionist philosophy.

Associations

Such passages in Wordsworth are couched in terms of altered vision. In Book XI (1805) the encounter with the letters under the gibbet mast is followed by the inexpressible 'visionary dreariness', to describe which the speaker would require 'Colours and words that are unknown to man'. There is an undeniable quality of the supernatural here. The blind beggar and Simplon Pass passages are explicit in emphasising the border between visible and invisible worlds: in the Simplon Pass 'the light of sense / Goes out in flashes that have shown to us / The invisible world' (VI: 534–6). And the admonishment from 'another world' in the face of the blind beggar is accompanied by looking. The suggestion of the 'invisible world' in Book VII has already been prepared by the passage about Jack the Giant-Killer, which offers a figure self-consciously anti-thetical to the beggar: sighted but wearing a sign on his chest saying '*Invisible*', Jack is a grotesque parody of the sublime. Yet despite all this we can discount the notion that the truthful poem has much to do with access of visibility. It has to do with the sounds and associations of words.

Not, of course, that vision and visual experiences are anything other than pervasive topics for 'the Eye and progress' of Wordsworth's song. His labour at the verisimilitude of things seen is often startling, as is the constant sense, which we have already observed in 'Tintern Abbey', of interrogating appearances. This is important, for rather than some imperial eye of transcendence, or some subtly dominative sophistication of the prospect view, Wordsworth traces a path of visual exploration. It is true, as Alan Liu points out, that in Book VII (1805; ll. 256–79) we are shown panoptic panoramas of the city, and by implication offered an alternative.[77] Indeed, in order to see a panorama, we are to be planted by a power 'Like that of angels or commissioned spirits [. . .] upon some lofty pinnacle' (259–61), which sounds like surrendering to the tempter in the Gospel story of Christ in the wilderness. But the alternative is not a rival power and control: Wordsworth tries to take seriously the idea of depicting an opposite to the abstract and controlling connotations of the panorama. And although at times his eye dares to verge on transcendence, it is at this point that the light of sense goes out.

Yet, to revert to the topic of association, the unprecedented realisation of things seen to be found in *The Prelude* is entirely subject to the law of 'two consciousnesses': it is all in the past. Much of the power of the poem derives from the way in which a present consciousness elaborates the associations which radiate from these past intensities, a process which began in the past itself, and which persists into a present where the visual has faded and a sort of blindness is setting in. The topic of association is raised by the examples of labels in the spots of time in *The Prelude*. When the mind runs on beyond the bare words, it apprehends the wider field of association to which the words are so pitifully inadequate, even though those words acted as the prompt. It is true that there are aspects of these experiences which Wordsworth avows he could never put into words: 'colours and words that are unknown to man'. But it is equally true that the 'visionary dreariness' which 'invests' the 'ordinary sight' of the girl with the pitcher and the surrounding scene is a product of the displaced affect of terrifying associations to do with the gibbet mast, to which the characters beneath it have acted as a prompt. A similar process is at work with the blind beggar.

Now Wordsworth's poetry, as we have said, does not pretend to recover everything for language: the glimpses of the 'invisible world' cannot be recovered, and have to be referred to as what cannot be spoken. Yet it does seek to recover and to be faithful to those chains of association which form around and extend from many an 'ordinary sight' – or which have their roots in ordinary sights seen long ago. But these associations should not be explained in purely mimetic terms as the realistic recovery of forgotten memories and sights. They should be understood as the recovery of affective words. The process can be exemplified from 'The Thorn' and Wordsworth's Note upon it. The speaker's obsessional recurrence to the spot of the supposed grave is also an obsessional recurrence to certain phrases which are constantly repeated. In this way, 'The Thorn' demonstrates the inherence of association in language, and in language conceived as the locus of affect and the vehicle of passion. Wordsworth makes this clear in his Note, when he offers reasons for the beauty of 'repetition and apparent tautology'.[78] His reasons, however, go beyond these phenomena to a characterisation of the power of words: 'Among the chief of these reasons is the interest which the mind attaches to words, not only as symbols of the passion, but as *things*, active and efficient, which are of themselves part of the passion'.[79] That last phrase, in particular, makes the point about the indivisibility of language and association. It is a view which is implicit in associationism in any case, and is put succinctly by Archibald Alison, in his *Essays on the Nature and Principles of Taste*, whose tenets are a logical development of associationism, and whom in any case Wordsworth may have read, where he demonstrates that language imbues experience with its own socio-historical deposit of associations:[80] 'Language itself is another very important cause of the extent of such Associations [between qualities of matter and mind. . . .] the use of Language gives, to every individual who employs it the possession of all the analogies which so many ages have observed, between material qualities and qualities capable of producing Emotion'.[81] Interestingly, Alison subsequently (Essay II, Chapter ii) provides a lengthy analysis, with many subdivisions, of the aesthetic and associative qualities of sounds, including music and the sound of the human voice.[82]

The view of language as active in terms of both semantic and phonic associations is congruent with the Dream of the Arab in *Prelude* V, where poetry, being figured as a shell, is the ear containing 'voices more than all the winds'. Yet it, like the whole of time, is threatened by an apocalypse when it will be submerged by 'the waters of the deep': an end to time in which 'the might of waters' will destroy the different voices and the 'many gods' of poetry. Again, we see the limit of association where it touches the invisible world beyond time.

Association is potentially conservative and patriotic. As Samuel Rogers puts it, in the 'Analysis' of the first part of *The Pleasures of Memory*:

> When ideas have any relation whatever, they are attractive of each other in the mind; and the conception of any object naturally leads to the idea of another which was connected with it either in time or place, or which can be compared or contrasted with it. Hence arises our attachment to inanimate objects; hence also, in some degree, the love of our country.[83]

Historical associations, Archibald Alison observes, may enhance sublimity: 'The majesty of the Alps themselves is increased by the remembrance of Hannibal's march over them' and it is therefore scarcely surprising that 'National associations have a similar effect in increasing the emotions of sublimity and beauty'[84] The constant return to the beloved place or landscape is for Wordsworth a good in itself: it is the natural bent of those who do not give a reason for their love, or calculate a benefit from it; of those who understand why a little boy would love the only place he knew and had played in ('Anecdote for Fathers') or who might be capable of loving a Lucy for herself, even though she counted for nothing in the world's eyes ('Lucy Gray'). It was a logical step to extend such conservative affection to one's own nation ('I travell'd among unknown men'); but, as we have seen, it was also a step which was already part of the logic of associationism. Poetry is the place for the most cogent, adequate and authentic embodiment of a conservative ideology of custom, for poetry is the verbal science of faithfully reconstructing beloved association. There is then a link between encroaching blindness, the aurality of poetry, and the conservative ideology of custom.

The Note to 'The Thorn' illustrates the delight in verbal repetition from the Old Testament, almost certainly with the encouragement of Bishop Lowth's *On the Sacred Poetry of the Hebrews*.[85] The point might serve as a reminder (if one be needed) that Wordsworth's sense of his literary indebtedness was scarcely naïve, and that the echoes of the Bible, Milton and Shakespeare to be found in his work are deployed in a highly complex and self-conscious game of allusion, such as his readers would expect and appreciate in poetry. Of course, he is also the poet whose assault on 'poetic diction' in the Preface to *Lyrical Ballads* reminds one that he is engaged in a remaking of poetic language, though one which is self-consciously seeking better models.

A poem of 1816, 'To Dora', brings together the themes of blindness, patriotism, diction and poetry in a way that is not only instructive about Wordsworth post-Waterloo, but also sheds a retrospective light. It begins with a quotation from *Samson Agonistes*, '*A little onward lend thy guiding hand / To these dark steps, a little further on!*'[86] Such echoes, however moderated by wry humour, suggest an heroic potential in the speaker, so that one can almost imagine him vieing with 'Time / The Conqueror', who significantly has so far failed to enrol him among the truly blind.[87] Despite the contrasting youth of his daughter, his message, at least, will outlast time, as it has successfully challenged (at least figuratively) the warlike tyranny of Napoleon (Simon Bainbridge refers to Wordsworth's 'contest' with the Emperor[88]). Napoleon is himself described by Wordsworth as 'Conqueror', and is transparently figured as the Conqueror Canute in 'A Fact, and an Imagination; or, Canute and Alfred', also written in 1816.[89] Yet the overtones of Oedipus being led by Antigone are not so auspicious, any more than are the references to *Hamlet* ('nymph in thy orisons'). Both allusions bear some relation to incest, though admittedly that of *Hamlet* is less direct. The poem seeks to lead us in the direction of purity, taking the sting out of the imputation: Dora will not get her to a nunnery, but the light in the forest will remind them of nuns: Nature is the guardian of moral purity. Yet the suspicion that some crisis has occurred is reinforced by the statement that 'the page of classic lore' and 'the book of Holy writ' will '*again / Lie open*' (my emphasis) to 'these glad eyes from bondage freed'. Literally, this may be a reference to those remissions in his eye disease which procured such a striking improvement to Wordsworth's mood when they occurred. Figuratively it is, so to speak, Samson released simultaneously from blindness and from bondage, Napoleon having been defeated. But since there are also suggestions of transgression in the Oedipal associations, it seems that this defeat must also be a farewell to transgression, to impurity. The epoch which included the affair with Annette Vallon and the birth of Caroline, as well as sympathy with the French Revolution and a remaking of poetic language, is suddenly, as they say, history. In retrospect it takes on an ambivalent aspect: Wordsworth fought the tyrant, but he was also figuratively blinded to the true nature of purity. While he has always understood the sanctity of custom, and that there is no culturally unmediated understanding of Nature, he now feels the need to emphasise this. The Romantic topos of forest as Gothic cathedral, which goes back at least to Warburton, here seems to look both ways:[90] Nature may be the 'Original', but the forest unavoidably looks like a cathedral. It is significant, therefore, that it is not only the Bible that Wordsworth will now read again, but also 'the page of classic lore'. This points self-reflexively to the presence of Oedipus, as other echoes do to the Bible and Milton, so that, in the first place, the poem foregrounds its own intertextuality as an example of the mediations of culture. But the reference is to the classics, not just to Oedipus, and the poem provides a clue to the understanding of this in its very diction: the ravens, for instance, are said to 'spread their plumy vans', and there is a 'brink precipitous'. Whatever Wordsworth may have learnt from Coleridge about poetic diction, we only need a certain way of developing the theory of associations to see how a more conservative approach to diction finds its parallel in the ideology of custom. But we only need to remember such traits as the personification of Nature in Book I of *The Prelude* to see how such an approach is not really a radical break.

The visuality Wordsworth records in his poetry is of an unprecedented modernity. Further, it is the experience of an eye which is very much connected to the body, as Wordsworth's stress on physical experience, for instance in 'Tintern Abbey', makes clear. While one can see a relationship between such visuality and the aestheticising tendencies of the picturesque, it is insensitive not to be struck most of all by Wordsworth's deliberate emphasis on poverty and suffering which could not be countenanced in that mode, and by the disturbing instability of the gaze implied in his poetry, something which sets it substantially at odds with the prospect view of the picturesque. The intensity and strangeness of this embodied viewer are striking; but they are usually properties of a past self. Wordsworth labours to explain that self and its subsequent development in terms which draw heavily on the role of association, both in the original experiences, and in the subsequent interpretations of them; those associations can only be known in language, which itself helped to form them. The mature self subsists largely on these verbal associations. Almost blind to any recurrence of visual intensity, it seeks comfort and wholeness in a sonorous, verbal recreation of the past. Doing so, it finds the essentially human in such an activity. Finding this, Wordsworth increasingly admits the value of hallowed association. But it must be remembered that such a morality is appropriate to one who nevertheless, as Tim Fulford observes, continues to set art at odds with *laissez-faire* and commercial ideologies.[91] While conservative tendencies may have been present as early as the 1790s, even in his later work, as Nicholas Roe points out, they consort, as in the revisions of *The Prelude*, with a scrutiny of 'quotidian strangeness' which links back to earlier democratic aspirations.[92] This is the large picture within which one may begin to reach an understanding of the unstable transitions between one perspective and another to be found in Wordsworth's poetry.

Notes

1. Bewell (1989), p. 225.
2. Stafford (1991), pp. 49–72, esp. p. 54; Moore (1925), pp. 362–78.
3. Moorman (1965), p. 255; Gill (1990), pp. 287, 350, 358, 368.
4. Moorman (1965), p. 256.
5. Gill (1995), p. 287.
6. Clarke (1962), pp. 2–3.
7. J. Wordsworth (1982), p. 3.
8. Westbrook (2001), pp. 27–78.
9. Haney (1997), pp. 173–99, esp. p. 176.
10. Ibid., p. 196.
11. Allen (2003), pp. 37–54, esp. p. 37.
12. Pfau (1993), pp. 125–46, esp. p. 143.
13. Ibid., p. 285, n.38.
14. Ibid., pp. 20–2, 29–46.
15. Haney (1997), p. 180.
16. Johnston (1998), p. 496.
17. Wordsworth (1982), p. 238; Roe (1988), p. 134.
18. Compare Parker (1987), pp. 229–31. Parker asks us to consider the cogency of Rivers' view of Herbert and Matilda.
19. Burke (1796), p. 67.
20. Wordsworth (1982), p. 65.
21. Ibid., p. 64.
22. '[On the Character of Rivers]', ibid., p. 63.
23. MS B, 290–5; MS D, 231–6, Wordsworth (1979b), p. 58.
24. Bate (1989), p. 93.
25. Welsford (1966), p. 146.
26. Wordsworth (1982), p. 31: Rivers' lack of benevolence; and Newlyn (1986), p. 11: Mortimer's true motivation.
27. Chandler (1984), pp. 227–8.
28. Bromwich (1998), p. 41.
29. Holmes (1989), p. 139: letter from Lamb to Coleridge.
30. Nichols (1998), p. xi.
31. Larrissy (1999), p. 52.
32. Wordsworth (1979b), p. 26.
33. Simpson (1982), p. xi.
34. Bewell (1989), p. 36.
35. Bate (1989), p. 97.
36. Descartes (1965), p. 67. Levinson (1986) offers a slightly fuller discussion of this influence on 'Tintern Abbey' pp. 44–5.

37. Wordsworth (1936), p. 747.
38. Newlyn (1986), pp. 53–6.
39. Roe (2002), pp. 162–6.
40. Pottle (1970), pp. 273–87.
41. Langbaum (1957), pp. 36–7.
42. Durrant (1970), p. 98.
43. Piper (1962), p. 11, on immanence in Wordsworth and Coleridge.
44. Davy (1839–40), I, p. 26.
45. Durrant (1970), p. 98.
46. Davy (1839–40), p. 65.
47. Roe (2002), pp. 87–95.
48. Gilpin (1789), p. 47.
49. Roe (1988), p. 274.
50. Hartman (1954), p. 4.
51. Roe (2002), p. 163.
52. Watson (1970), p. 86.
53. Davy (1839–40), p. 66.
54. Barrell (1988), p. 162.
55. See Cox (1996), pp. 42–4, for a discussion of the possible influence of the contemporary sonnet on 'Tintern Abbey'.
56. Labbe (1998), pp. 57–8.
57. Colley (1992), p. 174. These remarks extend to observations on 'the primacy of polite vision' in the fine arts, something with which Wordsworth was not in sympathy. See also Fulford (1996), p. 158, who claims that Wordsworth rejects the prospect view.
58. Bialostosky (1992), p. 75. Bialostosky speaks of a 'hidden dialogue' with 'other voices' which are not at one with the speaker's desires. Theoretical support is offered from Bakhtin, though it has to be said that, valuable as Bialostosky's point is, his book does not offer much evidence for the discursive heterogeneity which would make it a specifically Bakhtinian analysis.
59. Wordsworth (1977), p. 16.
60. See Wordsworth (1983). A reading text of the sub-section, *The Blind Highland Boy, with Other Poems*, is to be found on pages 219–77.
61. Ibid., p. 273.
62. Kierkegaard (1983), p. 132.
63. Ibid.
64. Trott (1994), p. 117.
65. See the excellent introduction to Wordsworth (1987), pp.vii–xxvii, on the gestation and reception of the work: the relationship to *Lyrical Ballads* is addressed at pp. ix–xi.
66. Wordsworth (1983), p. 254.
67. Richardson (1994), p. 6.
68. Ibid., p. 4.
69. Wordsworth (1987), p. xxiii; Wordsworth and Wordsworth (1970); Klancher (1987): see pp. 25–6 on Wordsworth's consciousness of the affiliations of periodicals and their role in creating readerships.
70. Jacobus (1995), p. 217.
71. Hertz (1985), p. 59.

72. Galperin (1989), pp. 51, 52; Johnston (1984), p. 294.
73. Roe (1992), p. 89.
74. Wordsworth (1991), p. 348.
75. Jacobus (1995), pp. 84–6.
76. Owen (1962), pp. 196–210.
77. Liu (1989), p. 113.
78. Wordsworth (1936), p. 701.
79. Ibid.
80. Hayden (1984), pp. 94–118.
81. Alison (1810), p. 29. This does not differ from the first edition (1790) except in the addition of observations on the human countenance and form, not discussed here.
82. Ibid., pp. 29–43.
83. Rogers (1792), p. vi.
84. Alison (1810), pp. 4, 6.
85. Wu (1993), p. 89.
86. A reading text of the earliest complete version is to be found in Wordsworth (1989), pp. 223–4.
87. This poem, and the allusions to be found in it, is discussed in 'Words, Wish, Worth' and 'Diction and Defense', in Hartman (1987), pp. 90–119, 120–8, and in Bate (1989), pp. 104–5.
88. Bainbridge (1995), p. 169.
89. Wordsworth (1989), pp. 210–12.
90. See Leatherbarrow (1985), p. 57.
91. Fulford (1996), p. 211.
92. Roe (1992), p. 91.

Coleridge, Keats and a Full Perception

The lines about aged blindness added to 'This Lime-Tree Bower My Prison' by 1800 evoke the idea of egotistical blindness. The full perception ultimately attained by the speaker transcends, however, the 'despotism' of the eye and comprehends responses of hearing, and even touch. Even before 1800, then, Coleridge is attempting to adumbrate a unified creative power – granted that, in this period, the Platonic overtones cannot be separated from the continued influence of empiricism. Nevertheless, the purport of this poem is broadly consonant with that of the later 'Limbo', in which I shall claim (contrary to some readers) that the blind man possesses a creative joy which precedes the experience of the senses. This creative joy, which finds expression through all the senses, is only found under historically determined modes: in the 1790s the small community in which it may be nurtured is a kind of recovered Eden, but it incorporates the recognition of its own modernity and makes a virtue out of the loss of the society of the ancient bard.

In 'Epistle to J. H. Reynolds', Keats's 'material sublime' goes beyond 'purgatory blind' (a negative blindness, unable to integrate reality and imaginative ardour) in such a way that one finds the 'triple sight in blindness keen' (from 'To Homer'); a fruitful point where the ardour of imagination encounters the real. This fruitful point is suggested by a reading of *Lamia, The Eve of St Agnes* (the unseeing sleep of Madeline is taken as a strong playing on the trope of blindness), and 'Ode on Melancholy', and is the origin of and prompt to the richly evocative use of words in Keats. However, Keats can also be shown to feel a more straightforward desire to make present to vision, and this can be seen in relation to the tradition of *ut pictura poesis*, since he is also indebted to the contemporary critical tendencies which were dissatisfied with that tradition and emphasised the associations of words. Keats, in wishing to load every rift with ore, wishes (in no pejorative sense) to have it both ways: to make things visually present, and to exploit the associations of words.

Just as Keats obeys his own injunction to load every rift with ore, so Coleridge unites the senses. For both poets, this fullness of perception exists in a modern form which remembers, but cannot recover, the visionary intensity of the bard. The fullness is defined in relation to the idea of blindness: it is specifically contrasted with blindness as limitation of perception, but at the same time specifically elaborated in relation to the discovery of the compensatory powers of the blind. In this complex way, the overcoming of blindness and the transformation of the world of commerce constitute parallel tales of compensatory salvation.

The Conversation Poems and the Union of the Senses

The published version of 'This Lime-Tree Bower My Prison' introduces a subtle reworking of the topos of the blind bard by means of an Ossianic echo. But the first version of this poem, contained in a letter to Southey, did not mention blindness, though it did refer, in lines which were excised, to the accident which had stopped Coleridge going for a walk with his friends, leaving him at home in the bower: his wife had spilt boiling milk on his foot. This is described in the letter as his being 'Lam'd by the scathe of fire', a phrase redolent both of heaven's punishment, and of the crippled but creative god of fire and the forge, Hephaestus (or Vulcan).[1] Both major versions of the poem transform this dual aspect into the figuring of loss followed by redemption, a movement which is typical of the conversation poems.

A version of the canonical 'This Lime-Tree Bower My Prison' first appeared in 1800 in Southey's *Annual Anthology*.[2] It represents the soliloquising of the speaker complaining that, because he cannot go for a walk with his friends, he has

> lost
> Beauties and feelings, such as would have been
> Most sweet to my remembrance even when age
> Had dimmed mine eyes to blindness!

The lines introduce, in a notably oblique way, Coleridge's reflections later in the poem on the recent experiences of his visiting friend Charles Lamb, who had had to cope with the trauma of his wife's deranged murder of his own mother. This meditation is a component in the poem's wider reflections on the potentially providential uses of suffering and loss. Lamb's *A Tale of Rosamund Gray and Old Blind Margaret* had been published in 1798, after the first version of 'This Lime-Tree Bower', but in good time for the revised version with their lines about 'blindness'. An intervening estrangement between the two friends had been mended long before 1800. Old Margaret's affliction was simply a result of age, and the *Tale* is a meditation on the patient and good-hearted tolerance of suffering and misfortune. This way of talking about blindness in terms of the dimming brought on by age is also specifically reminiscent of Ossian. This is especially so for one of a group of poems which includes 'The Eolian Harp', since by far the most celebrated example of the wind-harp in this period was that of Ossian himself – or, to be precise, the example of Ossian's harp hung in a tree and making music there. ('My harp hangs on a blasted branch; the sound of its strings is mournful. Does the wind touch thee, oh harp! or is it some passing ghost?'). As for 'This Lime-Tree Bower', the first version pre-dates the Ossian-influenced prose-poem, 'The Wanderings of Cain' (probably 1798) by not many months. ('Wanderings' contains phrases such as 'Pallid, as the reflection of the sheeted lightning on the heavy-sailing night-cloud, became the face of Cain'.[3]) Coleridge's admiration for Ossian was at its height in this period.[4] The echo of Ossian is congruent with the idea of lost intensity and the requirement for its recovery. 'Wanderings' was, of course, the first failed fruit of the project for a poem on the Origin of Evil, a project which may well have been suggested by Charles Lamb. There would be nothing incongruous to Coleridge about bringing together retired domesticity and echoes of the bardic. This is precisely what he had done in *Sonnets from Various Authors* (1796). David Fairer has shown how Coleridge associated the sonnet form with the pleasing confinement of domestic retirement, and that this association is itself one of the things referred to in Coleridge's contributions to the series.[5] But he also notes that Coleridge ends the sequence with an apostrophe to Schiller ('Ah! Bard tremendous in sublimity!') which 'almost bursts the bounds of the sonnet and reaches for the loftier ode'.[6]

Soliloquising is the right word for these opening lines: the present-tense expostulation, in the vehicle of 'conversational' blank verse, deliberately evokes the manner of Elizabethan and Jacobean soliloquy, and especially, in view of some of the references in the poem, the style of Shakespeare.[7] Soliloquies may be used to demonstrate a character's lack of self-knowledge to an audience, and this is the case here. Furthermore, the disparity between the Shakespearean allusion and the humble subject is deliberately employed in the satirical depiction of the speaker's inflated and obtuse self-dramatisation, a point underlined by the slightly hysterical exaggeration of 'Friends whom I never more may meet again'. Broadly speaking, the rest of the poem offers an intense delight in the visual experience of finely realised natural phenomena: thus, the reference to blindness ironises the figurative blindness of the speaker at the beginning of the poem, and introduces the theme of his learning to see during the period of time implied by the poem's representation of present-tense utterance. The question is, what type of figurative blindness is described, and what exactly is the true seeing which is discovered, or rediscovered, in the course of the poem? The added lines suggest that the landscape has become 'as is a landscape to a blind man's eye' – an allusion to Wordsworth which is now possible in the revised version of the poem.

The tone of the first few lines combines melancholy with self-dramatisation, and they may reflect Coleridge's knowledge of Burton's association of blindness and melancholy. This blindness, in Coleridge's treatment, is a matter of egotistical self-regard. It is customary to note the probable influence of Wordsworth's 'Lines left upon a Seat in a Yew-Tree' – a seat, that is, in a kind of natural bower, and one that is occupied by another victim of self-regard. It will be worth briefly rehearsing the points in this comparison which have to do with this kind of blindness. The self-indulgent melancholy of Coleridge's speaker is paralleled by the 'morbid pleasure' with which Wordsworth's solitary traces the 'emblem of his own unfruitful life' with his 'downward eye'. In a characteristically admonitory passage, Wordsworth castigates the 'man, whose eye / Is ever on himself'. Yet the comparison is by no means straightforward, and neither is Wordsworth's poem. For the solitary lifts up his head and gazes on the 'lovely' scene, as the speaker does in 'This Lime-Tree'. Wordsworth's character, however, gazes until 'it became / Far lovelier', and the poem proceeds to imply that it becomes far lovelier than it really is or should be, first by a near-repetition of the phrase ('still more beauteous') and then by referring to the 'visionary views' on which his 'fancy fed' when recalling those sociable people who engaged in 'labours of benevolence' and felt the loveliness of 'The world, and man himself'. The tears which stream from his eyes distinguish him from these happy beings, for they are tears shed for himself.

Wordsworth's solitary, like Coleridge's speaker, moves away from inadvertence towards the surrounding beauty, but only to impose on it a kind of unreal excess created by his hungry solitude. Coleridge, by contrast, appears to have set himself the task of showing how such a movement towards attentiveness could avoid excess by stopping at a just and true registering of visual experience, while enjoying an ecstacy consequent upon the fact that these scenes were nothing less than the 'cloth[ing]' or 'veil' of the Almighty Spirit. Coleridge, then, moves swiftly away from the self-absorption of the opening lines towards the memory of intense looking, although the whole poem makes it clear that the initial self-absorption must have comprised a superficiality in seeing.

This gives crucial importance to the visual phenomena recorded in the poem. Once again, we see the visual being offered in such a way as to emphasise its pure, recalcitrant visuality. That is to say, although the thing may become such an emblem through the poet's discoveries, it must not start out by looking like one. For this reason, the delightful detailed description of the 'roaring dell', into which he knows his friends will descend, offers its riches 'far in excess of the requirements of any thesis', as I have put it elsewhere.[8] Not that the passage lacks symbolic intent. Their descent into the dell, the discovery of pleasure there, followed by their emergence mirrors, and indeed introduces, the poem's overall pattern of redemptive descent and rise. But the descriptions are not neatly folded into this purpose: they go beyond it, offering themselves as a record of the pleasure of the eye. The same goes for the subsequent descriptions of the speaker's own pleasure in the lime-tree bower and its surroundings.

Such importance given to the visual requires a commensurate seriousness and thoroughness in the representation of what visual experience is: thus, there is an attempt to offer a simulacrum of its depth, and of the different perspectives it may contain. Clearly there is a contrast between the 'roaring dell' and the wide view of the 'magnificent' tract of land his friends perceive when they emerge, and clearly the movement from one to another possesses a symbolic purpose. But the contrast itself is characteristic of the richness of visual experience, a richness that comprises the minute as well as the grand, and which requires adjustment to the muscles of the eye to procure the right focal length.

There is an obvious painterly convention supporting these various pleasures: the picturesque. The implied movement of the eye through the lovingly realised detail of a variegated natural scene is easy to understand in these terms. It is true, of course, that Coleridge's poem arguably participates in that concealment of the reality of rural life which was almost constitutive of the mode.[9] Ignoring rather than concealment may be the better word, however. As we shall see, the whole drift of the poem is to validate the single poetic self, even as it criticises a certain mode of solitude. It would not serve Coleridge's purpose to be distracted from this task, even though a sense of guilt about the contemporary fate of nature and of rural communities may be part of the matter out of which all the conversation poems arose.[10] But it is surely pertinent to observe that this is something the poem is attempting to palliate in its implied social values to do with retirement and the small community.

Coleridge has a liberal approach to the picturesque, however. He is happy to include in his poem a moment of sublimity, when the Almighty Spirit is divined behind the wide view. Such a moment is fully in accord with his observation that the style of the conversation poems was 'capable of sublimity.' Furthermore, he seeks to enrich from his philosophical speculations our sense of what is involved in the appreciation of these scenes. For the poem attempts to enact and demonstrate that perception is active rather than passive, and this intention modifies the way in which we must regard its use of description. Kathleen Wheeler shows how the fact that Coleridge draws on 'remembered beauties' in imagining his friends' progress 'stimulate[s] his imagination', and enacts a change from passive to active perception. This change is analogous to a change from what he would call 'single' to 'two-fold' vision, though passivity and 'singleness' are not co-extensive concepts.[11] Jennifer Ford explains how when seeing 'is considered as part of complex relational processes within the material act of seeing – questions of magnitude, space, and consciousness of the other senses – Coleridge describes the vision as double'.[12] Clearly this is the mode of vision represented in 'This Lime-Tree Bower'. The poem elaborates different perspectives in depth. Seamus Perry makes a very cogent point when he observes, of the passing of the rook, that 'The effect is almost dimensional, as though adding a new space or angle within the poem's structure, like brackets in a chemical formula'.[13] To questions of magnitude and space we should add the introduction of the twittering swallow, singing 'humble-bee' and 'creek[ing]' rook, which mingle auditory with visual response. There is an analogy here with the fluttering flame and the sound of the baby breathing in 'Frost at Midnight'; the general point is addressed by the lines added to 'The Eolian Harp' about a 'light in sound, a sound-like power in light'. The point about sound touches on a major theme of the conversation poems: the Berkeleyan equation of the appearances of the natural world with the language of God, the 'Almighty Spirit'. These are poems in which the aural and the visual mingle in order to represent the apprehension of that language.

Yet matters are more complicated even than this. It is not sufficient to say that the visual response is simply a full engagement with the world in the context of a full engagement of all the senses. For the truth is that, by an apparent paradox, the attentive joy that characterises the speaker's renewed vision borrows something from the world of dreams. The paradox looks more acute when one recalls Coleridge's definition of dreaming: 'to dream is to allow the eyes to "make pictures when they are shut"'.[14] Yet this remark is made in the course of a meditation on daydreams which evinces the similarities between this and dreaming proper. This is a clue to the significance of the intense combination of memory and imagination which includes the description of the 'roaring dell', a passage which finds some parallels in the speaker's memories of school in 'Frost at Midnight', but also in the daydreaming which he remembers engaging in when he was there. Another clue lies in the way in which these passages are precursors to the movement away from ego towards a full appreciation of nature. For while it is true that in the imaginings of 'This Lime-Tree Bower' this is partly a result of the intuiting of the presence of the 'Almighty Spirit', it is also true that the very state of mind represented by such imaginings may be a prompt to 'double vision'. At a symbolic level, this is suggested by the broad analogy with the passage in 'The Ancient Mariner' where the Mariner blesses the water-snakes 'unaware' and the albatross falls from his neck: in 'This Lime-Tree Bower', a delight 'comes sudden' on the speaker's 'heart'. But it is also partly suggested by the analogy with 'Frost at Midnight' (where the Almighty Spirit does not appear in the reverie), and partly by the 'systolic' structure of the conversation poems: for this means that the reverie passages, which provide the second moment of a tripartite development, are essential to the whole – and essential in their very character, as a temporary movement away from the immediate which presages a return: a fortunate and fully-responsive return to the immediate. These realisations suggest that, furthermore, a full and adequate response to nature has more in common with dream, and thus with pictures the eyes make when they are shut, than a common-sense view would predict. The later remarks in *Biographia Literaria* about 'the despotism of the eye', or in *Philosophical Lectures* about 'that Slavery of the Mind to the Eye', are congruent with the meaning of the central event of 'This Lime-Tree Bower'. So the initial reference to blindness is informed by a richer irony than at first appears; for the insentience of that initial response is balanced by a transfiguration which, on another plane of imagery, is like a different kind of blindness: that which is possessed by the bard or prophet.

The partial screen constructed by the lime-tree bower itself figures the privation of sight which is involved in the poem's theme. This is paralleled by the darkness in 'Frost at Midnight' and 'The Nightingale'. In 'This Lime-Tree Bower' and 'Frost at Midnight', darkness also figures the isolation of the self. The version of 'Frost at Midnight' which first appeared in *Fears in Solitude* is clearer in associating the position of the speaker at the outset of the poem with an arid state of mind, in some ways comparable with that evoked in the first lines of 'This Lime-Tree Bower'. The lines on the 'film' hint at self-pitying dissatisfaction with solitude: it offers 'dim sympathies with me who live, / Making it a

companionable form / With which I can hold commune. Idle thought!'
(ll. 18–20). The poem will suggest that this is not in fact an idle thought
because of the livingness of nature. But this is not a perception which is
at first available to the speaker, and we are soon informed that this is
one of the 'toys / Of the self-watching subtilizing mind' (ll. 26–7).

The 'film' is the central image in this earlier version of the poem: the
word 'flutter' is deliberately repeated in the last lines (subsequently
excised) about little Hartley's excitement at seeing the icicles which
will 'make thee shout / And stretch and *flutter*' (my emphasis).
Although this beautifully captures the excited movement of a baby's
limbs, most of the developments of the 'film' image are to do with
sound. In the first instance, it is the sole 'unquiet thing' in the 'hush of
nature'. Of course, the poem undoubtedly proceeds in a Coleridgean
arc of controlled association: myself and babe with the film; the same
film in my own childhood, in fact in my schooldays; the different education my own child will receive at the hands of nature; the child will
learn from its experience to perceive the beauty of every aspect of
nature, including winter. The schoolboy had dreamt – or daydreamed
with 'unclosed lids' – about his sweet birthplace, but in doing so, what
he remembers is the sound of the church-bells, which 'stirred and
haunted' him with 'a wild pleasure'. When his thoughts return to his
child, it is first of all to notice his 'gentle breathings heard in this dead
calm'. The ministry of nature means that he will 'see and hear / The
lovely shapes and sounds intelligible' of the 'eternal language which
thy God / Utters', and the phrase 'see and hear', so far from being
casual, is a grand, simple underlining of the poem's deliberate concentration on sound as well as sight. It is therefore fitting that the evocation of winter's beauties should include 'the eave-drops' which are
'Heard only in the trances of the blast'. In fact, while the poem emphasises the totality of experience, it might be more accurate to say that it
makes use of the relative salience of sound when sight is diminished in
order to develop from this the topic of combined sight and sound, and
further, from that, the unity of creative imagination, which mirrors the
unity of nature.

One of the main conceits of 'The Nightingale; A Conversational
Poem' is the subversion of conventional responses to nature. The traditional figuring of the nightingale as the bird of melancholy is presented as the anthropomorphism of the 'night-wandering' egotist who
fills 'all things with himself' (l. 19). Thus the poem alludes yet again to
the association of egotism and privation of sight. However, the melancholy nightingale is an unrealistic invention, and the feminine
Philomela of ignorant tradition becomes a male bird, in recognition of

the fact of nature that only male birds sing. As in the other conversation poems, much brilliant effort is expended on procuring the effect of reality:

> They answer and provoke each other's songs
> With skirmish and capricious passagings,
> And murmurs musical and swift jug jug
> And one low piping sound more sweet than all [. . .]
> (ll. 58–61)

This realism is tendentiously made to subserve the thesis promoted by all the conversation poems, that 'In Nature there is nothing melancholy' (l. 15). The explicit rejection of Milton's nightingale in *Il Penseroso* (' "Most musical, most melancholy" bird!' (*Il Penseroso*, l. 62; 'The Nightingale', l. 13)) half conceals the implication that any reasons Milton might have had for melancholy are in fact invalid. But in order to understand what content this implication might have had for Coleridge, it is helpful to look at Miltonic allusion in the two conversation poems we have already discussed, for both 'This Lime-Tree Bower' and 'Frost at Midnight' allude to the same lines in *Paradise Lost* IX, where Satan, slithering in serpent form through Eden, and seeking Eve 'In Bowre and Field' (l. 417) glimpses her, half-hidden by roses in a 'spot' described as 'delicious' (l. 439):

> Much hee the Place admir'd, the Person more.
> As one who long in populous City pent,
> Where Houses thick and Sewers annoy the Aire,
> Forth issuing on a Summers Morn to breathe
> Among the pleasant Villages and Farmes
> Adjoyn'd, from each thing met conceaves delight [. . .]
> (ll. 444–9)

Eve is to fail the ensuing test of temptation, so the passage reminds us of the cost of the fall, as well as the beauty of Eden. Coleridge picks up the line about being 'in populous City pent'. In 'This Lime-Tree Bower' (recalling Milton's 'Bowre'), Charles Lamb is said to have been 'In the great City pent', though 'winning' his way through 'evil and pain'. In 'Frost at Midnight', Coleridge recalls how he was 'reared / In the great city, pent 'mid cloisters dim' – site of his uncreative education. The city, home of commerce, is the hell to the recovered paradise embodied in the conclusions of the poems: a paradise which is dependent on a contrasting form of society. It may be that this point is clearest from 'The Nightingale', and Kelvin Everest gives a persuasive reading of the poem in these terms:

> Coleridge has brought together here all the central values of the conversation poems. The voice is serene, self-possessed, optimistic; it is confident in

the values that are shared with a small and intimate group in nature, 'my friends', 'my dear babe', a group that belongs to its environment, finding their 'dear homes' in retirement.[15]

A similar point, though, is easily discernible in 'This Lime-Tree Bower', with its imagining of the pleasures of 'friends'. The point is also conveyed by the lines about the castle in 'The Nightingale'. As with the abbey in 'Tintern Abbey', composed a few months later, one of the purposes of this castle is to be shown to belong to an outmoded social form. It is symbolically significant that the great lord is absent and that the grounds are beautifully overgrown. Neither the modern city, nor the aristocratic and feudal social organisation, are the *tertium quid*: that is provided by the small community which still makes covert allusion to the ideals of Pantisocracy. Of course, the element of 'Gothic titillation' in the story of the 'castle' and the 'maid' is very much present.[16] But as in Wordsworth's uses of the Gothic, it is only there to be subtly subverted. The maid's experience of nature makes her 'like' a lady 'vowed and dedicate / To something more than nature in the grove', but she is also unlike that lady. As for that 'something more', again: it is like the something more which the lady might have been dedicated to, and also unlike it.

Coleridge's Natural Supernaturalism

In these poems in which the speaker is decidedly not blind in the literal sense, the shadowy presence of tropes on blindness serves to remind us that the 'despotism of the eye' and 'single vision' are deficient, and that the positive concept with which Coleridge wishes to replace these has to do with evolving 'all the five senses [. . .] from *one* sense'.[17] David Miall, noting that for Coleridge the sense of touch is primordial, and that 'The Will' is 'itself a mighty Touching', concludes that 'the "one sense" appears to be feeling, in terms of touch or other "bodily feelings" '.[18] This seems a reasonable conclusion, and one that makes good sense of the conversation poems.

'Feeling' is entirely open to those who are literally blind. This precise point is emphasised in the late poem 'Limbo' (MS draft 1811), which derives from what Morton D. Paley calls 'the Limbo Constellation': namely, 'a longer piece of prose and verse in Coleridge's Notebook 18'.[19] Here, the figure of a blind man plays a central role. Referring to the poems 'Hope and Time', 'Fancy in Nubibus', 'The Blossoming of a Solitary Date Tree' and 'Love's Apparition and Evanishment', Paley points out that 'The blindness of a solitary figure is an image that deeply engaged Coleridge over a long period of time'.[20] But none of these examples is much developed. In 'Fancy in Nubibus' we encounter Homer 'the blind bard' being given 'inward light' by the sounds of the sea, with the result that he 'Beheld the Iliad and the Odyssee [*sic*]'. The misspelling underscores the notion of inner light. The blind Arabs of 'The Blossoming' and 'Love's Apparition' are melancholy depictions of deracination and emotional privation.

The blind man in 'Limbo', however, offers some complexity to interpretation. He is not depicted in terms of 'inward vision', but nor is he by any means melancholy. He is contrasted with the state of Limbo itself, which represents the world unredeemed by feeling. This allegory becomes clearer when one puts together the associations of the opening lines with those towards the end of the poem. At the beginning it is affirmed that Limbo is still a locus of 'Time and weary Space', while in later lines it is said to be 'made a spirit-jail secure / By the mere horror of blank Naught-at-all'. This sounds like a Coleridgean characterisation of dead materialism. But if this is not enough to make the point about allegory, it is established beyond doubt by Coleridge's explanation of some lines which form part of the same Notebook entry, but which ended up as a separate poem called 'Moles'. These creatures, who 'Creep back from light', were equated with 'the partizans of a crass and sensual materialism' when the poem was first published in *The Friend* (1818). By contrast, the old blind man in 'Limbo' looks towards the skies 'with a steady look sublime' and his 'whole face seemeth to rejoice in light!' In this way, he himself becomes a 'sweet sight' and, significantly, he 'looks like human Time' – that is, time as redeemed by the fullness of humanity. His representation of ecstatic looking is not an empty parody at all. Rather, by a brilliant paradox, Coleridge is using the blind man to represent the essence of all ecstatic looking: feeling. This is not a conclusion with which all would concur. Specifically, Paley is persuaded by Stephen Prickett's emphasis on the idea of 'seeming' in the poem: 'His whole face seemeth to rejoice in light! / [. . .] / He seems to gaze at that which seems to gaze on him!'[21] There is a basic problem with such an approach, and it is this: if Coleridge is to write a poem about a blind man's joy, he might still need to refer to 'seeming' to see, rather than to actual seeing. On this evidence alone, Prickett's point is unverifiable. Second, there is internal evidence, to which I have already referred, that the blind man is not himself in Limbo. The line in question is clearly intended to set off a contrasting train of thought: referring back to the blind man, it states that 'No such sweet sights does Limbo den immure'. Whether or not, as Prickett claims, Coleridge came to feel the 'limitations' of Kant's doctrine of the thing-in-itself, this is not the poem in which he does so.[22]

In fact, 'Limbo' is best read alongside Coleridge's nearly contemporaneous (1812) contribution to *Omniana*, 'The Soul and Its Organs of Sense'. The very title of this piece is telling, since reflections on the blind take up some third of the essay. Ostensibly, we find the rehearsal of the familiar topic of transference to other senses: 'when the organ is obliterated, or totally suspended, then the mind applies some other organ to a double use'.[23] Among the examples given is none other than John Gough of Kendal, the Blind Man of Wordsworth's *Excursion*. His sense of touch is particularly acute and accurate. But the most notable thing is the way his delight in sensory experience expresses itself in his face:

> Good heavens! it needs only to look at him [. . .]! Why, his face sees all over! It is all one eye! I almost envied him, never broken in upon by those evil looks (or features, which are looks become fixtures) with which low cunning, habitual cupidity, presumptuous sciolism, and heart-hardening vanity *caledonianize* the human face. It is the mere stamp, the undisturbed *ectypon*, of his own soul![24]

The passage possesses striking similarities to 'Limbo'. It makes it clear that the point lies in the animation of the face, not in whether or not the eyes can really see. The last sentence, about the stamp of the 'soul', reveals the essential point, and the reason that the essay has the title that it does. Looking back on Coleridge's treatment of sensory transference, one notes that it is 'the mind' that applies another organ to double use. At the heart of this essay lies wonder at the potential independence of creative mind from the senses, not least from the despotism of the eye. As Coleridge says in another *Omniana* piece, 'Inward Blindness', blind men know they lack sight, but 'there are certain internal senses, which a man may want, and yet be wholly ignorant that he wants them'.[25]

Of course 'Limbo', being a late poem, post-dates Coleridge's decisive repudiation of Hartley and the Locke tradition. But with respect to 'This Lime-Tree Bower' it needs to be shown how Coleridge related bardic vision, or the creative powers of a Vulcan, to the empiricist philosophies in which he was still interested, and how far that interest needs to be qualified. In the letter to Southey which contains the first known version of the poem, Coleridge observes 'You remember, I am a *Berklian*'. The influence of Berkeley seems most evident in the lines which speak of the hues which 'cloathe the Almighty Spirit' (in all versions except the final, where they 'veil' Him), for as John Gutteridge has noted, they recall the lines in *Siris*: 'clothes the mind of the universe'.[26] The attraction of such a concept is that it allows Coleridge to explain how the divine can act upon and through the senses, an endeavour for which there are obvious parallels in Wordsworth. It is acceptable to say that the interest in Berkeley is consonant with a probing of the limitations of empiricism,

This raises an obvious question about Shelley's *The Triumph of Life*. We take the point about the philosophers. But are the conceptions of poets also identified with transient figures on the bubble? After all, *A Defence of Poetry* and many other passages in Shelley would align them rather with a dim perception of eternity. In *The Triumph*, there is a candidate for a figure representing this perception in our world, namely the 'shape all light' (l. 352). The idea of light implies both the radiance of something akin to the beautiful and true, and the perception of it by a mind, its susceptibility of being intellectually 'seen'. The shape is not, as some have thought, malign: the reason why this might be so is that, when his lips touch her cup, Rousseau's brain becomes as sand and he follows the dreadful chariot. It is a powerful potion. Rousseau is like some figure from romance: like one who is not worthy to drink from the Grail cup, or to pluck the sword from the stone, or to sit in the Siege Perilous, which destroys any unworthy knight. This is the answer to Rousseau's question regarding 'whence I came, and where I am, and why' (l. 398). Shelley's poem has already established that Rousseau's will is flawed. It is from this flaw that his enslavement to the car derives, not vice versa. The flaw is a mental flaw, and this is emphasised by the way in which his vision superimposes upon the first, as if he were entering a different dimension. The fair shape does not disappear when the vision of the chariot appears, but 'wane[s] in the coming light' (l. 412). This is an echo of the way in which the scene of vision is superimposed upon the actual scene for the speaker at the beginning of the poem.

Such a reading does not concur with the idea that Shelley has reduced the poet's most sublime figurings to shapes on the 'bubble'. On the contrary, although the poem may (not untypically) raise this question, there is nothing to demonstrate that he is not showing what he describes in *A Defence of Poetry*, namely the malign triumph of a combination of 'analytical reasoning' and the lust for dominion. Of course, the sheer numbers of those who are deluded do support a pessimistic thought: how easy is it to avoid this combination? Rousseau and Plato and the others are among the luminaries of humanity; and 'analytical reasoning' is a natural aptitude. It is from some such thought that Shelley has indeed imparted to the 'shape all light' something of the immemorial ambivalence of the fairy enchantress. How are we to regard the way in which her feet seem 'to blot / The thoughts of him who gazed on them' (ll. 383–4)? We are not supposed to have this tonal ambivalence smoothed over until we have assessed the whole poem – which we do not have. So although Michael O'Neill is right to remember 'the contradictions and uncertainties that constitute experience', there is nothing to show that Shelley would not, as so often, have asserted his commitment to the cause of ultimate hope.[22] We have, if we respect the context of Shelley's thoughts, ample evidence of the allegorical thinking behind the poem. The blindness in *The Triumph of Life* is indeed the blindness of those who do not know themselves, which is as much as to say the most damaging blindness of humanity. The blindness of the old man in the Coliseum, by contrast, is an ironic way of underlining the mental nature of the perception of harmony in things. Shelley fears a compound malaise of the ethical and the scientific, but remains, despite discouragement and a proper sense of difficulty, loyal to the hope that imagination can intuit the emanations of the deep truth. The blindness of reason in Shelley is blindness to what should guide reason, both ethically and scientifically. Byron's development of the idea of Milton's blindness reveals, by contrast, that life will always have more to discover than any scheme can comprehend. A good portion of Mary Shelley's disturbing power lies in her combination of a wide-ranging scepticism reminiscent of Byron with an instructed concentration on doubts about the well-foundedness of those scientific and ethical systems in which she shared an interest with her husband. Yet again, the figure of the blind man provides a means of bringing together the central topics.

Notes

1. Baxandall and Morawski (1974), p. 97.
2. All quotations from Byron's poetry are from Byron (1980–93). *Don Juan* is in Volume 5 (1986).
3. McGann (1976), p. 35.
4. Byron (1980–93), Volume 3 (1981), p. 225.
5. Ibid.
6. Ibid., p. 145.
7. Ibid., p. 146.
8. Ibid., p. 147.
9. Cox (1996), pp. 124–6.
10. Kristeva (1982), p. 4.
11. Stabler (2002), p. 148.
12. Robinson (1976), p. 78. The lines from *Childe Harold* IV are from stanza 128.
13. Shelley (1954), p. 224. The spelling of 'The Coliseum' is corrected by the editor to 'The Colosseum' (pp. 224–8). Future references are in the form of page numbers in parentheses in the text.
14. Shelley (2000), p. 521.
15. Leighton (1984), p. 16.
16. Maxwell (2001), p. 30.

17. Keach (1984), pp. 123–4.
18. Ibid., p. 124.
19. Quotations taken from Shelley (2002), pp. 483–500.
20. Bloom (1969), pp. 232–47.
21. Shelley (2002), p. 530.
22. Neill (1989), p. 201.

Chapter 8

Mary Shelley: Blind Fathers and the Magnetic Globe: *Frankenstein* with *Valperga* and *The Last Man*

While the figure of the blind man may not be central to Mary Shelley's work, it is salient enough. The episode where Frankenstein's creature hides in the house of the blind De Lacey and his family is highly significant for the meaning of the book, as is the ensuing one in which he makes himself known to the old man, whose blindness means that he cannot react with prejudice to the creature's hideousness. In the second chapter of the first volume of *Valperga* (1823), we learn of the blindness of Euthanasia's father, Adimari, which prompts her to read to him and thus acquire learning.[1] And not far from the end of *The Last Man* (1826), we encounter the blind old man, who remains ignorant of the fate of humanity, listening to his daughter playing Haydn's 'New Created World' (that is, music from his oratorio *Creation*): an event heavy with an irony which is central to Mary Shelley's intention.[2] These episodes are intellectually and symbolically related. Both De Lacey and the blind father in *The Last Man* suffer from ignorance about a central element in the plot; and both love and enjoy a special sensitivity to music, in line with Enlightenment theories about the compensatory powers of blind people. De Lacey shares with Adimari the experience of listening to the reading aloud of educative literary and historical texts, even though, in the case of the former, it is the escaped Turkish girl Safie who is the intended auditor. Ignoring specificities, all could roughly be termed benevolent optimists. And all are fathers.

Equally important, of course, is the way in which the literal blindness of these old men brings the figurative blindness of others into sharper relief and opens up a play of meanings: in *Frankenstein*, these include large symbolic implications connected to Prometheus and Oedipus. A related point is the way in which they encourage the reader to interpret incidental language about blindness and seeing, as well as references to eyes and eyesight. Especially bold, though, is the way in which, again in *Frankenstein*, Mary Shelley brings scientific questions about animal magnetism and electricity into relationship with her exploration of ironic tropes about blindness and insight.

The Blindness of Reason's Presumption

In *Frankenstein*, one of the first things we notice about De Lacey is his playing a musical instrument, which we later discover to be a guitar. While not much stress is laid on this, as compared with his apparent benevolence, or the fact of the 'godlike science' of language possessed by the whole family, it is clearly something we should note, prompted by the contemporary acceptance of the musical facility of the blind. Considered alongside his benevolent and enlightened character, and with the help of the episode in *The Last Man* involving Haydn's *Creation*, we can see that music figures a harmony that transcends mere sounds, and suggests an order in the universe. It thus consorts with those questions regarding the possibility of a harmonious human order which are raised by the reading of out of Volney's *Ruins*. Furthermore, it alludes to a poetic – a musical – dimension in language, itself an auditory phenomenon which follows close upon music in the apprehension of the learning creature: thus, the communication permitted by language goes far beyond the codifying of information.

De Lacey's blindness also raises questions about how far humanity understands the message of Volney. This is not so much because De Lacey or his family must be assumed to ignore the lesson of cruelty and domination to be found in his work (probably the reverse), but rather because the subsequent response of Felix and Agatha shows that it has not been learned with genuine thoroughness by these enlightened children, who show no trace of prejudice towards a Mahometan. This fact reinforces the idea of the ironic blindness of those who imagine they can see, as is the case with Victor Frankenstein; and indeed, as is also the case with him, the ironic blindness of those who on the face of it are sensitive and well-meaning. De Lacey's blindness figures theirs, and we may as well assume that, could he see the creature, his benevolence would soon find its limitations. In these respects, the episode is clearly a critique of Godwinian ethics, or to be precise, those of the *Political Justice* phase, for it could be said that this work is blind to the depth of the human capacity for prejudice.

But the most obvious direction in which to pursue this theme is towards Victor Frankenstein himself. In so far as he is 'The Modern Prometheus', he is also, according to the Greek meaning of that name, the modern possessor of *forethought*. It is scarcely acute to note that this play on words is ironically apt. But it is worth remembering, in view of the deliberation with which Shelley uses tropes of blindness and insight, that the meaning is close enough to *foresight*. This ironic limitation, as we have already noted, belongs to a man of knowledge and sensitivity and one who aspires to benevolence. Yet the undoubted flaws in his ambitious pursuit of knowledge lend even wider implications to his blindness. Critics will point, and rightly, to the probability of a critique of enlightenment optimism of various kinds, or suggest that it is in fact Shelleyan 'Romanticism' (as we now term it) which is at fault. In so far as these are made to seem like alternatives, though, this is to be befuddled by terms, since Shelleyan 'Romanticism' is not some kind of essence to be separated from the Enlightenment. (Such a divorce would be as sterile as the attempt, made by some critics, to separate 'the Gothic' from 'Romanticism'.) Those aspects of Victor Frankenstein – and of Walton – which remind one of Shelley's *Alastor* need to be remembered, of course, as does the former's early interest in alchemy and occult philosophy. Still, there are differences of emphasis within the series of comparisons the novel asks us to make between the different characters: of the two inquiring natural philosophers, it is Walton, not Frankenstein, who has an early interest in poetry. We learn, from Victor's account of his upbringing, that Elizabeth and Clerval, not he, are interested in poetry, while his passion is to discover the secrets of nature. The contrast is laid out quite deliberately for us in Chapter I: 'I delighted in investigating the facts relative to the actual world; [Elizabeth] busied herself with following the aërial creations of the poets. The world was to me a secret which I desired to discover.'[3] Although Victor and Clerval used to act together in romantic plays, it was the latter who composed them (21). The contrast becomes starker in the 1831 version: '[Clerval] composed heroic songs and began to write many a tale of enchantment and knightly adventure' while 'It was the secrets of heaven and earth that I desired to learn' (208, 209). Nor, unlike Percy Shelley, is Victor interested in politics, history or languages, as we are informed at the same point. None of this is sufficient for us to say that Victor's ideas are to be distinguished from something we would call Romanticism: a passion for natural philosophy is, in any case, part of what we have learned to include in the Shelleyan version. But we are being asked to observe a difference within a similarity: of the various aspiring minds we encounter, Victor's is the least touched by the sympathies nurtured by poetry, notwithstanding the fact that poetry itself may have its dangers, as is suggested by the hint of overreaching in Walton's poetic visions and aspirations. This limitation, as well as the language of ambition, casts a shadow over Victor's profession of philanthropic motives and questions their true depth and substance.

Nevertheless, as Gary Kelly points out, Victor's 'passions of curiosity, desire for fame, and philanthropy are those recognized by major Enlightenment philosophers as causes of social progress'.[4] This supports the idea that Mary Shelley is especially concerned with the limitations of the philosophic mind, and we are given a symbolic reminder of this in the fact that Ingolstadt is the town where the Illuminati were founded.[5] (It is also where Mesmer attended university.) The point about social progress illustrates the high stakes involved in Mary Shelley's questioning. Victor's concentration on knowledge-power separates itself from a true engagement with human sympathy and is uninterested in the human sciences. In this connection, his figurative blindness gives symbolic form to what Alan Rauch calls a 'critique of knowledge'.[6] Victor's conception of the goal of knowledge is, as Fred Botting puts it, the 'desire to reduce all life to one principle, one secret', and this in itself is a procedure characteristic of much Enlightenment philosophy.[7] But, for the reasons already adduced, this does not mean that Shelleyan Romanticism is absolved of criticism or seen as free of danger.

Victor's blindness in the pursuit of his bent is pointed out to us early in the 1831 text: 'My father was not scientific, and I was left to struggle with a child's blindness, added to a student's thirst for knowledge' (210). We note the desirability of paternal guidance, but it is surely right to wonder if this is really another critique of patriarchal negligence: it seems more like a statement of temperamental difference. It is also right to wonder if the phrase 'a child's blindness' does not remain apt for some time.

The critique of knowledge extends to the roots of knowledge. Questions about the nature and origins of the life Frankenstein claims to have created are certainly raised by the ghastly scene of his labours, which evoke echoes of Rousseau's *Reveries*, where he imagines the horror of dissection:[8] a passage which also influenced Wordsworth's famous line, 'We murder to dissect.' The description of Frankenstein's labours is accompanied by references to his eyes. As he goes about his work, 'my eye-balls were starting from their sockets in attending to the details of my employment' (36–7): a phrase which, with its anatomical flavour, suggests a similitude both between the creator and the created, and between the creator and the process he operates. Significantly, while engaged in this unnatural task, his 'eyes were insensible to the charms of nature' (37).

Perhaps the most resonant questioning of the nature of Victor's enterprise is largely symbolic: namely, the episode in which, returning to the environs of Geneva, he witnesses a vigorous thunderstorm in the mountains, and then espies the creature lurching onto the scene. The episode begins with a highly significant observation: 'I saw the lightnings playing on the summit of Mont Blanc in the most beautiful figures' (55). Given both the context established by the novel, and Percy Shelley's own use of Mont Blanc as an emblem of the source of things, we are entitled to interpret this symbolically. The lightnings are another emblem of the unknown power: a more conventional one, derived from a familiar iconography of patriarchal deities. They write upon the blank surface of Mont Blanc's snows, for Mary Shelley, like her husband, exploits the inscrutable suggestions of whiteness, another example being the arctic setting of the framing episodes recounted in Walton's letters. The writing is constituted by 'figurings', which are mysterious and uninterpretable hieroglyphs. The scene thus offers sublimity with a content: what are the ultimate origins of the universe and of life?

The ensuing events constitute a strikingly unusual essay in the sublime. At first the elements are quite conventional: the tempest is 'so beautiful yet terrific'; it elevates Victor's spirits. But when the 'filthy daemon' appears against this backdrop, we realise that Shelley is among those who would go beyond the Burkean categories: this is a sublime which can encompass the grotesque. However, such a description may do a disservice to the disturbing dissonance of the scene, by offering a convenient label: the grotesqueness of the monster redefines the sublime, but at the same time the scene is discordant: as if a Gillray cartoon of a monstrous member of the French mob should be pasted onto a Turner painting of a storm in the Alps. But this is precisely the kind of effect that Mary Shelley is seeking to achieve, French mob included. It is well understood that the creature – the new man, so to speak – symbolises the new kind of humanity projected by the ideologues of the revolution. The painterly construction of the natural sublime is interrupted by allusion to another graphic source: the grotesque representation of the monstrous revolution in contemporary cartoons, as documented by Ronald Paulson in his *Representations of Revolution*.[9] In spreading so widely the implications of her myth, she has, like her husband, or like Blake, developed a symbol which conflates questions about cosmic and human origins with questions about the nature and development of human society.

There is another way of thinking about this combination of questioning with a symbolism which makes creative use of references to the visual arts: namely, that it is a correlative of what Anne K. Mellor calls 'the basic problem of perception in the novel: how are we to *see* the innate being of the creature?'[10] There is an increasing appreciation among critics of the fact that there is no clear answer to this question, and that this problematic character is mirrored in the structure and strategies of the novel. The 'concentric structure', for instance, which seems to enact the existence of a kernel of truth, is understood to be undermined by the parallels between its layers.[11] In reality, the effect is to enact 'the impossibility of a transcendent position'.[12] I'm not sure the situation is as clear cut as that: when we are offered the outline of a concentric structure, we continue to respond to its cogency even as we are reminded of what deconstructs it. As we shall see, there is a symbolism related to the idea of that structure; but there is no reason to dispute the fact that its solidity is also undermined.

Whatever uncertainties Mary Shelley creates, obviously Victor's enterprise stands convicted of certain identifiable flaws. But if an appreciation of the 'domestic affections' is the great omission from Victor's temperament – the main thing to which he is blind – they themselves are seen, in the words of Gary Kelly, as 'fragile'.[13] Not only do the depredations of chance inevitably undermine them, but they are not sufficient to ensure the unprejudiced benevolence of the De Lacey family. Shelley's scepticism includes, but goes wider than, a philosophical 'critique of knowledge'. Domesticity, of a kind, is precisely one of the institutions of which the creature gains something approaching direct experience through the chink in the wall of the De Lacey abode. The creature's eye is one that sees and ponders what is domestic, in a way that Victor Frankenstein's does not. In a figurative respect, it is relevant that there is nothing maladjusted about the creature's eye in terms of how he has learnt to perceive with it: thus, in his earliest experiences, he has 'learned to distinguish between the operations of my various senses' (80) in a way which seems normal according to empiricist theories. On the basis of this, he develops in a way which, as Alan Richardson puts it, is 'instinctively social', so one may feel that he possesses the sensibility with which to judge what he sees.[14]

The image of the invisible eye figures both distance and intimacy, a union of experience and judgement, which he has at least the potential to attain in relation to the bourgeois family. This potential union is also figured in the very nature of what he observes: he both watches living relationships and hears (and reads) the words of books which he may use to explain human society and behaviour. It is suggested that the creature's learned anger at humanity, while at first moderated by a residual trust in the blind father, is soundly based on adequate knowledge. His eye at the chink figures the attainment of insight, while De Lacey's blindness figures its absence.

The union of intimacy and distance is to some extent paralleled in the book's methods: the epistolary mode, and first-person narrative, foster immediacy, while the constant literary allusions offer a range of ideas for interpreting the course of events. These are characteristics, as Gary Kelly has pointed out, which identify *Frankenstein* as an example of 'the coterie novel.' As he observes,

> Many novels from the Godwin and Shelley coteries are written in first-person narrative, specifically the confessional or autobiographical mode, with explicit reflection on the relation between the narrator's experience and the prevailing social and political order. This was intended to be the appropriate form for authoritative representation of systemic oppression experienced at the personal level, by both narrator-protagonist and implied author.[15]

This strategy was intended to show how 'reflection on experience produces political awareness'.[16] That awareness could be fostered and theorised by a group such as the coterie, a fact which is symbolised by the reference to the Illuminati, or to the followers of Beatrice in *Valperga*. At the same time, the coterie novel made use of 'reference and allusion', as *Frankenstein* does with Volney, Plutarch and Milton, and, characteristically, with the works of members of the coterie itself: Percy Shelley and Byron.[17] In this connection, then, the creature's own learning process mirrors the strategy of the book with its recourse both to experience and to literature and history. This fact underlines the piquancy of what Mary Shelley attempted: a corrosive intimate questioning of the assumptions of her own coterie by means of the coterie's own intimate methods. It is in this almost perverse manner that the book is itself ambitious of an educative role. That role can be conceived as the discovery of a better, if disillusioned, way of seeing.

The blind De Lacey does not possess this way of seeing, and consequently it appears that, contrary to a strong contemporary tendency, his blindness does not figure insight but its reverse. The same is true of Adimari in *Valperga* and the blind father in *The Last Man*. However, in an interesting twist, all of these figures do allude, with subtle irony, to the Romantic topos of the inspired blind man. De Lacey has his guitar, and his household contains a copy of *Paradise Lost*. Adimari, in an allusion to that poem, is said to see nothing but 'an universal and impenetrable blank'; like Milton, he is read to by his daughter.[18] The blind father in *The Last Man* enjoys an appreciation of music so keen that it appears to approach ecstasy.[19] He is also an ironic comment on the blind old man (also accompanied by a daughter) in Percy Shelley's 'The Coliseum', who is so apt to interpret the sounds he hears there. Such figures assist in the critique 'of what might simplistically be termed the Romantic ethos'.[20] These remarks of Morton Paley apply to the whole of *The Last Man*; but it is easy to see, in the almost heavy-handed irony of the blind man's appreciation of Haydn's *Creation*, a critique of any view which obscures the incomprehensible indifference of nature to human imaginings and ethics. There are limited similarities here with Camus's use of an allegory of plague in *La Peste*. This is not to deny that Enlightenment optimism about human progress is implicitly found wanting: the reverse movement of starving Americans returning to Europe from their ravaged continent to fight for food with the Irish, of all people, mirrors the narrator's movement back to the Middle East, 'cradle of civilization'.[21] But the fundamental character of Shelley's pessimism, underscored by references to the *Vanitas* theme, is memorably symbolised in another essay in the dark sublime: the reputed appearance of 'a black sun' – not the sun eclipsed, but another, darker orb.[22] The symbol has obvious connotations of death and ill-omen; but it also evokes blindness – the occlusion of 'the eye of day'. Yet despite this parallel, the blindness evoked here is obviously not fulfilling the same function as the image of the naïve old man. Rather, it is a multivalent symbol, suggesting the potential for danger which cannot be known, predicted or comprehended, both in nature and humanity.

And since the sun has associations of great date with the godhead, there are thematic parallels between this symbol and Beatrice's postulating the idea of an evil creator in *Valperga*.[23] An evil creator, symbolically speaking, is a black sun. This 'evil spirit' bears strong similarities to figures in Percy Shelley's work, like Jupiter, who represent both the dangerous imperfection of the created world and that in human nature which worships cruelty, whether under the guise of holiness or not. Clearly, this is a way of conceiving the universe which is not to be perceived by the blind Adimari, in reading to whom Euthanasia first learns to cherish hopes of 'virtue and independence'.[24]

So many blind fathers, even where they are not the obvious perpetrators of patriarchal transgression, raise questions about the influence of the Oedipus story. There is the intriguing proximity of the *Mathilda* story, with its gloomy tale of a self-pitying, self-regarding and literally incestuous father. Furthermore, Tillotama Rajan claims that 'Mathilda returns as Beatrice, who is also raped by patriarchy', and while this seems like a very definite way of putting it, it does point to a real tonal connection.[25] Oedipus was in the air at the Villa Diodati when Mary Shelley's tale was conceived: Polidori's contribution to the ghost-story competition was finally written up as *Ernestus Berchtold; or, The Modern Oedipus* (1819). Within *Frankenstein*, the circumvention of the mother, combined with the other symbolisations of unnaturalness in the fashioning of the creature, can be seen as connoting the infringement of taboo. Most significantly, there is an oedipal dream: immediately after the daemon's creation, Frankenstein's tormented sleep is disturbed by a dream in which his fiancée and childhood sweetheart, Elizabeth, is found to be his dead mother, in a passage which, as Mary Jacobus points out, 'mingl[es] eroticism and the horror of corruption':[26]

> I thought I saw Elizabeth, in the bloom of health, walking in the streets of Ingolstadt. Delighted and surprised, I embraced her; but as I imprinted the first kiss on her lips, they became livid with the hue of death; her features appeared to change, and I thought that I held the corpse of my dead mother in my arms; a shroud enveloped her form, and I saw the grave-worms crawling in the folds of the flannel. (39)

Jacobus goes on to point out that, '[i]n Mary Shelley's novel, intense identification with an oedipal conflict exists at the expense of identification with women'.[27] The benevolent blind fathers, who appear to be attuned to the harmony of the universe, are in a different category from the oedipal agonists to be found elsewhere, though it is important to note that Frankenstein suffers from the delusion of his own benevolence. But the blind fathers are perhaps the more foolish for being ignorant of the irrational power that motivates those others, and perhaps just as culpable. Their blindness also figures some deficiency in a quality that comes out of the eyes. We might call it 'electricity'.

Ambiguous Magnetism

Mary Shelley, like her husband, was interested in mesmerism, the belief that hypnotic trances could be induced by the gestures, manipulations and, occasionally, the stares of the 'operator', as the hypnotist was called.[28] The modern conception of hypnotism, however, can convey little of the strange materialist basis of the beliefs of Mesmer and his followers. Mesmer's own practice initially involved the massage of affected parts of the body and the proximity of magnets in order to affect the disordered flow of the 'magnetic fluid' in this sick patient. Later, however, 'Mesmer realised that the physician need not touch the patient to establish the mental *rapport* and to transmit his magnetic fluid to him'.[29] This development did not mean that the material basis of the technique had been abandoned. Although (like Newton's gravity) the magnetic fluid might exert its action 'at a distance, without the aid of an intermediate body', it had properties not unlike those of light, for 'It is intensified and reflected by mirrors, just like light'.[30] The shift away from palpation and massage was adopted by those who came after Mesmer, particularly by De Mainauduc, who declared that for diagnosis and treatment, 'direction and distance are in every sense of the word immaterial, provided the Attention is properly fixed on the object'.[31]

Notwithstanding the point about direction, 'de Mainauduc and the new generation of magnetic healers believed that the body could be influenced simply by the magnetizer fixing his gaze on the patient, staring intensely into his or her eyes'.[32] As De Mainauduc said, 'A single look will often prove sufficient'.[33] Barbara Stafford claims that the stares of the operator were thought to be effective because of animal magnetism; in other words, they created magnetic effluvia which flowed from the eyes of the operator into the eyes of the subject.[34] This appears to be true of De Mainauduc but not of Mesmer, of whose practice Percy Shelley's poem 'The Magnetic Lady to Her Patient' (1822) is more suggestive, with its emphasis on touch: the patient is in a trance: 'My hand is on thy brow / And from my fingers flow / The powers of life'. As for De Mainauduc, he believed that 'the auditory and optic nerves of one man are the auditory and optic nerves of every animated being in the universe, because all are branches sent off from the same great tree in the parent earth and atmosphere'.[35] Such effluvia were not regarded as necessarily distinct in kind from whatever it was that might flow along the nerves, although of course all of these subjects were topics of debate and controversy: debate and controversy of which both the Shelleys were well aware, and not by any means only from discussions with Polidori, whose Edinburgh thesis was on somnambulism. Whatever may have been Mary Shelley's true opinion about some of these matters, *Frankenstein* makes a connection, which would have been patent in her own time, between whatever goes to make a compelling stare, or indeed other states of the eye, and the very force that galvanises the creature. For while there was some debate as to the relationship between magnetic and wider electrical phenomena, they were recognised as intimately related and often treated together. Thus, Thomas Medwin noted that Percy Shelley's sensitivity was such that, when excited, he felt 'a tremendous shivering of the nerves pass over him, an electric shock, a magnetism of the imagination'.[36] A good example of the treatment of the two forces together derives from the pen of the very same man who devised a form of relief printing for the blind to which we have already referred: the Abbé Haüy's *Exposition raisonnée de la théorie de l'Électricité et du magnétisme* (1787). In this connection, it is interesting to note that the celebrated Giovanni Aldini, who electrically induced twitching in the limbs of executed felons, attempted to cure certain types of blindness by means of galvanism.[37]

Alan Richardson has noted how the 'spirit of animation' might in the Romantic period be registered in the eyes of both animals and humans, and quotes a striking comparison made by Keats in his Letters, where he spies a fieldmouse with 'a purpose and its eyes are bright with it';

he then encounters a man hurrying along with a purpose 'and his eyes are bright with it'.[38] *Frankenstein* is, in fact, very interested in eyes. According to Walton, Frankenstein's eyes 'have generally an expression of wildness and even madness' (14). We have already seen that, as the 'filthy creation' progresses, his 'eye-balls were starting from their sockets in attending to the details of my employment'. When he encounters the creature for the second time in the Alps, he is troubled, and 'a mist came over my eyes' (76). The creature's own eyes are appalling: at the moment of creation, Victor 'saw the dull yellow eye of the creature open [. . .] his watery eyes [. . .] seemed almost of the same colour as the dun white sockets in which they were set' (38–9). When the creature notices his creator, 'His eyes, if eyes they may be called, were fixed on me' (40). The eyes of the creator figure the dangerous dynamism which informs his project; those of his creature suggest some sickness in the very energies which give him life. No wonder that, in the final pages, after all that happens, he avows that he 'shall quit your vessel on the ice-raft which brought me hither, and shall seek the most northern extremity of the globe' (190). He means the North Pole, of course; but since this is magnetic north, he is seeking sustenance for those very magnetic energies which first animated him. For another thing we have to bear in mind is that, in the lucubrations of this period about animal magnetism, no essential difference is assumed between this and 'terrestrial magnetism'. Hazlitt says, in his essay on 'Genius and Common Sense', that 'The imagination gives out what it has first absorbed by congeniality of temperament, what it has attracted and moulded to itself by elective affinity, as the loadstone draws and impregnates iron.'[39] This is no reductionist recourse to contemporary science; but it draws on that background, as Goethe's novel, *Elective Affinities*, does at several points. On the other hand, as late as 1866 we find an account of hypnotism as 'a subtile emanation or fluid being supposed to be transmitted from the magnetiser to the magnetised, like that from the loadstone to the iron which it attracts.'[40] Frankenstein's creature is drawn to magnetic north as to a loadstone. He is also drawn to a point one might call the summit of the earth, analogous to Mont Blanc, and like that, covered in snow. By Mary Shelley's time, magnetism is seen as a property to be found at the very centre of the earth: as Haüy puts it, 'L'action du magnétisme [. . .] émane sans cesse, quoique sourdement, du sein de notre globe'.[41] It is also worth bearing in mind, especially in view of her reference to the experiment with catching lightning, that Benjamin Franklin deduced from his experiments that the earth carried an electrical charge.[42] Indeed, as Jessica Riskin points out, he speculated that the magnetic fluid existed 'in all space; so that there is a magnetical North and South of the universe'.[43] The pole symbolises the nearest point to the mystery of the unstable property which motivates the entire tragic history of the creature's relationship with his creator.

This is the disturbing property to which the blind fathers are insentient, and out of which come good and evil. Magnetism did not in itself possess any particular ethical associations, but it would be involved, as the fluid that passed along the nerves, with any emotion whatsoever. Furthermore, its manipulation might have decidedly progressive political implications. As Nigel Leask has pointed out, mesmerism was seen as having the potential to be an intimate, domestic medical practice, bringing the family together by means of touch and gaze, and challenging 'the hegemony of a centralized medical police'.[44] There is, then, another pessimistic tinge in Mary Shelley's involving matters relevant to mesmerism in her critique of Frankenstein's project. In any case, it might seem in some degree positive that he renounces his enthusiasm for those occult philosophers such as Cornelius Agrippa, Albertus Magnus and Paracelsus, who were reputed to be acquainted with the black arts, even if doubts are raised about his motivation and character by these early predilections. But we need to be reminded that in Mary Shelley's period no clear division had yet been drawn – at least, not one to which all the learned felt they should adhere – between a belief in what many occult philosophers called 'animal spirits' and a belief in 'animal magnetism'. Students of occult arts and philosophy, including neoplatonists such as Henry More, one of Coleridge's favourites, had not in every case been immaterialist in their understanding of all spirits. Barbara Stafford quotes More describing how good or evil spirits emanate from within, or from the 'Eye of the Soul', and then become contagious, taking the form of 'subtle streams and aporrhea's of minute particles, which pass from one body to another'.[45] As late as the time of Yeats, who was a Rosicrucian, like Shelley's St Irvine, 'Daemons' and ghosts might be composed of 'animal spirits' and thus of a subtle material body, as he explains in *Per Amica Silentia Lunae*, quoting More in his support.[46]

The unstable property which is symbolised by magnetism goes beyond any easy categorisation, as does Mary Shelley's judgement on life. At the same time, the novel does offer provisional judgements: for example, as we have seen, cultivation of the domestic affections is far preferable to the alternative. The trouble is, though, that even they can be an uncertain nurse. Again, notoriously, the women in the novel are marginalised, and appear as passive victims, and these facts are bound up with the dangerous relegation of the domestic affections and the dangerous dynamism of heroic masculine aspiration. Partly for these reasons Gilbert and Gubar claim that the creature represents woman.[47] There are good reasons for learning from this view: one of the most convincing, I think, is the nature of the creature's education – stolen, half-autodidact, picked up from listening mutely to others: in this period, such might be a woman's education. In view of the relegation of woman, then, it might be tempting to view the North Pole as symbolising the mother: the natal energy to which the creature is drawn. Yet just as the creature cannot be only woman, but also the despised other in general, so the energy that is present at the North Pole, and around which the whole earth turns, is not in the end distinctively gendered. Indeed, why should it be? If, as Lorenz Oken argued in his *Lehrbuch der Naturphilosophie* (1809–10), 'polarity is the first and only force in the world; [. . .] galvanism or electrical polarity is therefore the principle of life; and [. . .] organic life is galvanism in a state of homogeneous mass', it is an easy step, at least in figurative terms, to see masculine and feminine as a related kind of polarity.[48]

The whole world, at the heart of which is magnetism, is symbolised in the very structure of the book. It is well known that this offers a concentric Chinese box structure: we start with Walton's letters, which then give us Frankenstein's narrative, in the middle of which he recounts the creature's story. We go out, so to speak, via Frankenstein's remaining narrative and end up with Walton writing about the final events in the story. But this also means that the setting of the North Pole frames the novel, rather as poles might be said to contain the world.

It should also be noted, and a few critics have, that there is another narrative to be included in the box, the orientalist story of Safie, the Turkish girl, related in the third person by the creature. In Chris Baldick's redaction,

> the De Laceys are exiles from France, punished for contriving the escape from prison of a Turkish merchant (Safie's father) who has been persecuted by the French government. Felix and Safie have fallen in love, and her father has at first promised to allow the marriage, but has then treacherously planned to take her off to Turkey instead. Safie, however, inspired by the ideals of feminine independence instilled in her by her deceased Christian mother, has escaped him to return to Felix.[49]

This story represents about as positive a turn of events as one can find in the book, and is meant to profit by the supposedly oriental associations of warmth, passion and vivacity, even as it offers a reassuring orientalist narrative of a young woman escaping from eastern despotism and paternal oppression. It functions as an opposite to the desolate cold world of the arctic; and, as in *The Last Man*, the Middle East is there because it is the cradle of civilisation. But warm and passionate as it may be, it is obvious that it is also the locus of despotism, and of the epitome of patriarchal oppression. And, as we have seen, in the end this story links up to the hypocrisy even of Felix. In this way, Mary Shelley is able to bring the popularity of the oriental tale or parable in the Enlightenment within the ambit of her more general scepticism, exhibiting a shrewd point made by Mary Jacobus: 'Romanticism can be read not only as the outcome of the Enlightenment, but as a form of resistance to the imperialism of enlightenment thinking. Women, in turn, come to figure that resistance [. . .]'.[50]

There is, in fact, a more general similarity between *The Last Man* and *Frankenstein*: they both offer, so to speak, *a picture of the world* – the former almost literally, in the form of the world stricken by plague, the latter figuratively, in terms of the polar frame and the oriental centre. In this respect, Mary Shelley's imagery shows the influence of her husband, whose most ambitious philosophising often has a global reach, as in the passage on 'the winter of the world' from Canto IX (stanzas 20–8) of *Laon and Cythna* (1817) which was later developed into the lines about the 'pestilence-stricken' races of humanity in 'Ode to the West Wind'. In Percy Shelley's figurings, these negative images of the world display the plague of human corruption; in his wife's they suggest both the limits of human knowledge, and the limits of human recognition of these limits: a blindness about blindness. The irony is compounded, in *Frankenstein*, by the role given to electricity, a force which informs vision and around which, in a broad but accurate sense, the world literally turns. In this way, Mary Shelley brings the most modern findings of science in aid of her subversive questioning of the limits of human understanding. As with other writers who employ the trope of blindness in this period, the idea of an exchange of innocence for corruption certainly does operate in her work, but with the pessimistic twist added by the suggestion that there are dangers in planning for the protection of innocence, and that the task can never be perfected in any case. The blind fathers in her fiction suggest not only a flaw in what founds life – in its paternity – but also subtly hint at the possible complacency of images of the rediscovery of innocence, by alluding, among other things, to the primitivist topos of the blind bard with his affinity to music and poetry. But if the book has traditionally been conceived as a picture of the world, Mary Shelley's depiction of the magnetic globe is as self-reflexive about the art of writing as are her many allusions to other writers and discourses. They suggest the difficulty of seeing sufficiently clearly beyond pre-established modes of understanding even in modernity.

Notes

1. See M. Shelley (1996b).
2. See Shelley (1996a).
3. Shelley (1994), p. 21. Future references to this work in this chapter are given in the text as numbers in parentheses.
4. Kelly (1989), p. 188.
5. Scott (1979), p. 176.
6. Rauch (1995), esp. pp. 227–53, p. 229.
7. Botting (1991), p. 3.
8. Kilgour (1995), p. 195.
9. Paulson (1983), pp. 171, 244.
10. Mellor (1988), p. 130.
11. Botting (1991), p. 42.
12. Ibid., p. 45.
13. Kelly (1989), p. 189; and compare Howard (1994), p. 282: 'Godwin's ideal of domestic affection leading to public benevolence is again thrown radically into question.'
14. Richardson (1994), p. 25. The remark is made in the context of a discussion of the contrast between Rousseau's natural man, who is 'essentially solitary', and Mary Shelley's creature.
15. Kelly (2000), pp. 147–59, esp. p. 154.
16. Ibid.
17. Ibid., p. 158.
18. Shelley (1996b), p. 18.
19. Shelley (1996a), p. 326.
20. Paley (1993), pp. 107–23, esp. p. 111. Paley's remarks apply to the whole of *The Last Man*.
21. The point about the Middle East is made in Kelly (1997), pp. 198–208, esp. p. 206.
22. Shelley (1996a), p. 177.
23. Shelley (1996b), pp. 242 ff.
24. Ibid., p. 18.
25. Shelley (1998), p. 15.
26. Jacobus (1986), p. 101.
27. Ibid.
28. See Shelley (1987), entry for 15 Dec. (1820), I, 342, and note.
29. Goldsmith (1934), pp. 62–3.
30. Mesmer (1948), Propositions 14 and 15.
31. Mainauduc (1798), p. 182.
32. Rix (2002): 37 pars, 20 <http://users.ox.ac.uk/~scat0385/25rix.html>
33. Mainauduc (1798), p. 107. See the discussion in Fulford (2004), pp. 57–78, esp. pp. 67–9.
34. Stafford (1991), pp. 450–62.
35. Southey (1951), p. 307.
36. Medwin (1847), II, p. 191.
37. Aldini (1803), pp. 104–6.
38. Discussion and quotation in Richardson (2001a), p. 162.
39. Hazlitt (1930–4), VIII (1931), p. 47.

40. Lee (1866), p. 38.
41. Haüy (1787), p. 191. For a discussion of terrestrial magnetism, see Fulford, Lee and Kitson (2004), pp. 149–75.
42. Franklin (1744), p. 128.
43. Riskin (2002), p. 196.
44. Leask (1992), pp. 53–78, esp. p. 63.
45. B. Stafford (1991), p. 456.
46. Yeats (1994), p. 20.
47. Gilbert and Gubar (1979), pp. 213–47.
48. The summary is in Mellor (1998), p. 106.
49. Baldick (1987), p. 202.
50. Jacobus (1998), pp. 240–69, esp. p. 266.

Chapter 9

Conclusion

The idea of blindness – as trope, as image, or exemplified in a character – is central to to some of the most important texts of British Romanticism. The blind, and developed figures of blindness, offer ways of exploring an individual consciousness which conceives itself as, so to speak, lost in history. This consciousness is nostalgic for an innocence and immediacy of vision which it knows cannot be recovered in modern society, and which, moreover, have been thoroughly analysed by modern philosophy and political economy, with the result that even the fleeting glimpses of vision now vouchsafed have to be understood in terms of these discourses. This is even the case, in my estimation, with one who seems as anti-Lockeian as Blake. Yet even as the blind can be shown to be capable, so the modern world will find that it can live, to borrow a phrase of Wordsworth's, 'in reconcilement with its stinted powers'. Not only does Romantic writing figure the capability of disability, but it makes such conditional capability the very emblem of knowledge in the modern world, and even of knowledge in general. We inherit from the Romantic period the hesitation between direct experience and laborious historical understanding which is at the root of the symbolic uses to which blindness was then put; and we also inherit an epistemological version of the capability of disability to which we give names such as *Blindness and Insight*, or the 'prosthesis' of the blind man's stick in Derrida's *Memoirs of the Blind*, which is a version of his 'supplement', and thus not really 'compensatory' at all, but rather an apt image of expression and interpretation in general. When we look back to investigate the root of this important nexus of ideas, we find it explored not only in subtle and scarcely apprehensible tropes, but as a direct result of a meditation on the condition of the blind which preoccupied the thinkers of the eighteenth century.

Bibliography

Editions and Primary Sources

Addison, Joseph (1854), *The Works of the Right Honourable Joseph Addison*, ed. Richard Hurd, vol. 3, London: Bell.

Aldini, John [Giovanni] (1803), *An Account of the Late Improvements in Galvanism, with a Series of Curious and Interesting Experiments*, London: Cuthell and Martin and J. Murray.

Alison, Archibald [1790] (1810), *Essays on the Nature and Principles of Taste*, 2nd edn, Edinburgh.

Anon. (c. 1800?), *Anecdotes of the Deaf, Dumb, and Blind*, Leeds.

Anon. (1814), 'Anecdotes of Carolan, the Irish Bard' *The Gentleman's Magazine* 84:2, [part 1], pp. 29–31, [part 2], pp. 121–3.

Anon. (1814), *The Life of John Metcalf, commonly called Blind Jack of Knaresborough; with many entertaining Anecdotes of his Exploits in Hunting, Card Playing, &c. some Particulars relating to the Expedition against the Rebels, in 1745. In which He bore a Personal Share; And also a succinct Account of his various Contracts for making Roads, erecting Bridges, and other Undertakings*, Leeds: G. Wilson.

Ashfield Andrew (ed.) (1997), *Romantic Women Poets 1770–1838*, vol. 1, 2nd rev. edn, Manchester: Manchester University Press.

Baron, Robert (1650), *Pocula Castalia*, London: W. H. for Thomas Dring.

Barry, James (1831), *Lectures Delivered in the Royal Academy*, London.

Berkeley, George (1948–57), *The Works of George Berkeley, Bishop of Cloyne*, ed. A. A. Luce and T. E. Jessop, 9 vols, London: Thomas Nelson, vol. I: *Philosophical Commentaries, Essay Towards a New Theory of Vision, Theory of Vision Vindicated* (1948).

Blacklock, Thomas (1793), *Poems by the late Reverend Dr. Thomas Blacklock, Together with an Essay on the Education of the Blind*, Edinburgh: W. Creech; London: T. Cadell.

Blackwell, Thomas (1735), *An Enquiry into the Life and Writings of Homer*, London.

Blake, William (1970a), *Drawings of William Blake: 92 Pencil Studies*, ed. Geoffrey Keynes, New York: Dover.

Blake, William [1794] (1970b), *Songs of Innocence and of Experience*, ed. Geoffrey Keynes, London: Oxford University Press.

Blake, William (1974), *The Illuminated Blake*, ed. David V. Erdman, New York: Doubleday.

Blake, William (1977), *The Notebook of William Blake*, ed. David V. Erdman, 2nd rev. edn, Naples, FL: Readex Books.

Blake, William (1988), *The Complete Poetry and Prose of William Blake*, ed. David V. Erdman, newly rev. ed., New York: Anchor Doubleday.

Blake, William (1995), *The Urizen Books: William Blake*, ed. David Worrall, Princeton, NJ: Princeton University Press; London: William Blake Trust/Tate Gallery.

Brooke, Charlotte (1789), *Reliques of Ancient Irish Poetry*, Dublin.

Burke, Edmund [1757] (1759), *A Philosophical Enquiry into the Origin of our Ideas of the Sublime and the Beautiful*, 2nd edn, London: R. and J. Dodsley.

Burke, Edmund (1796), *Thoughts on the Prospect of a Regicide Peace, in a Series of Letters*, London: J. Owen.

Byron, George Gordon, Lord (1980–93), *The Complete Poetical Works*, ed. Jerome J. McGann, 7 vols, Oxford: Clarendon Press.

Campbell, J. F. (ed.) (1862), *Popular Tales of the West Highlands*, 4 vols, Edinburgh.

Coleridge, Samuel Taylor (1956–71), *Collected Letters of Samuel Taylor Coleridge*, ed. E. L. Griggs, 2 vols Oxford: Oxford University Press.

Coleridge, Samuel Taylor (1978), *The Collected Works of Samuel Taylor Coleridge III: Essays on his Times*, ed. David V. Erdman, 3 vols, Princeton, NJ: Princeton University Press.

Coleridge, Samuel Taylor (1990), *The Notebooks of Samuel Taylor Coleridge, IV (1819–1826), Text*, London: Routledge.

Coleridge, Samuel Taylor (2001a), *The Collected Works of Samuel Taylor Coleridge 16: Poetical Works II: Poems (Variorum Text): Part I*, ed. J. C. C. Mays, Princeton, NJ: Princeton University Press.

Coleridge, Samuel Taylor (2001b), *The Collected Works of Samuel Taylor Coleridge: Poetical Works I: Poems (Reading Text): Part I*, ed. J. C. C. Mays, Princeton, NJ: Princeton University Press.

Cooper, Anthony Ashley, Third Earl of Shaftesbury (1999), *Characteristics of Men, Manners, Opinions, Times*, ed. Lawrence B. Klein, Cambridge: Cambridge University Press.

Culpeper's Complete Herbal To Which is Now Added Upwards of One Hundred Additional Herbs (1816), London: Richard Evans,

Davis, Thomas (*c.*1911), *Thomas Davis: Selections from his Prose and Poetry*, ed. T. W. Rolleston, Dublin: Talbot.

Davy, Sir Humphry (1839–40), *The Collected Works*, ed. John Davy, MD, FRS, 9 vols, London: Smith, Elder and Co.

Descartes, René [1637] (1965) *Discourse on Method, Optics, Geometry, and Meteorology*, trans., and intro. Paul J. Olscamp, Indianapolis, IN: Bobbs-Merrill.

Diderot, Denis (1966), *Diderot's Selected Writings*, ed. Lester G. Crocker, trans. Derek Coltman, New York: Macmillan; London: Collier-Macmillan.

Dodsley, Robert (1741), *The Blind Beggar of Bethnal Green*, London: R. Dodsley.

Edgeworth, Maria [1812] (1988), *The Absentee*, ed. W. J. McCormack and Kim Walker, Oxford: Oxford University Press.

Encyclopaedia Britannica: Or, A Dictionary of the Arts, Sciences, &c. on a Plan entirely new (1778–83), 10 vols, Edinburgh: J. Balfour [etc.]

Ferguson, Adam (1767), *An Essay on the History of Civil Society*, Edinburgh: A. Millar, T. Cadell, A. Kinnaird, J. Bell.

Fontenelle, Bernard le Bovier de [1686] (1777), *A Conversation on the Plurality of Worlds*, trans. W. Gardiner, London.

Franklin, Benjamin (1744), *Experiments and Observations on Electricity made at Philadelphia in America*, 5th edn, London: F. Newbery.

Genlis, Stéphanie de [1779–80] (1787), *The Theatre of Education*, 4 vols, London: J. Walter.

Genlis, Stéphanie de [1789] (*c.*1820), 'The Blind Girl', in Robert Southey, *Mary, the Maid of the Inn*, London: Dean and Munday.

Gilpin, William (1789), *Observations on the River Wye, and Several Parts of South Wales, &c. Relative Chiefly to Picturesque Beauty; Made in the Summer of the Year 1770*, 2nd edn, London: R. Blamire.

Goldsmith, Oliver (1966), *The Collected Works of Oliver Goldsmith*, ed. Arthur Friedman, 4 vols, Oxford: Clarendon Press.

Gunn, John (1807), *An Historical Enquiry Respecting the Performance of the Harp in the Highlands of Scotland*, Edinburgh.

Haüy, Abbé (1787), *Exposition raisonnée de la théorie de l'Électricité et du magnétisme*, Paris: Desaint.

Haüy, Valentin [1789], 'An Essay on the Education of the Blind', trans. Thomas Blacklock, in Blacklock (1793), pp. 217–62.

Hazlitt, William (1930–4), *The Complete Works of William Hazlitt*, ed. P. P. Howe, 21 vols, London: J. M. Dent.

Hemans, Felicia (1849), *The Poems of Felicia Hemans*, Edinburgh and London: Blackwood and Sons.

Heron, Robert (1793), *Observations Made in a Journey through the Western Counties of Scotland, in the Autumn of M,DCC,XCII*, 2 vols, Perth, Scotland.

Hofland, Barbara (1816), *The Blind Farmer and His Children*, London: J. Harris.

Hume, David (1932), *The Letters of David Hume*, ed. J. Y. T. Greig, 2 vols, Oxford: Oxford University Press.

Hume, David [1739–40] (1978), *A Treatise of Human Nature*, ed. L.A. Selby-Bigge, 2nd edn, ed. P. H. Nidditch, Oxford: Clarendon Press.

James, Robert (1743–5), *A Medicinal Dictionary*, 3 vols, London.

Johnson, Samuel [1775] (1985), *A Journey to the Western Islands of Scotland (1775)*, ed. J. D. Fleeman, Oxford: Clarendon Press.

Keats, John (1958), *The Letters of John Keats*, ed. Hyder Edward Rollins, 2 vols, Cambridge, MA: Harvard University Press.

Keats, John (1970), *Letters of John Keats: A Selection*, ed. Robert Gittings, Oxford: Oxford University Press.

Keats, John (1982), *Complete Poems*, ed. Jack Stillinger, 2nd edn, Cambridge, MA: Belknap Press of Harvard University Press.

Kenney, James (1808), *The Blind Boy: A Melo-Drama, in Two Acts*, London.

Lamb, Charles (1895), *Poems, Plays and Miscellaneous Essays of Charles Lamb*, ed. Alfred Ainger, London and New York: Macmillan.

Lamb, Charles (1924), *The Life, Letters and Writings of Charles Lamb*, ed. Percy. Fitzgerald, 6 vols, London: Navarre Society.

Lee, John (1780), *Favourite Collection of the So Much Admired Irish Tunes, the Original and Genuine Compositions of Carolan, the Celebrated Irish Bard*, London.

Locke, John (1894), *An Essay Concerning Human Understanding*, ed. Alexander Campbell Fraser, 2 vols, Oxford: Clarendon Press.

Lonsdale, Roger (ed.) (1969), *The Poems of Thomas Gray, William Collins, Oliver Goldsmith*, Harlow, Essex: Longman.

Macpherson, James [1760–3] (1996), *The Poems of Ossian and Related Works*, ed. Howard Gaskill, intro. Fiona Stafford, Edinburgh: Edinburgh University Press.

Mainauduc J. B. de (1798), *The Lectures of J. B. de Mainauduc, Part the First*, London: For the Executrix.

Mallet, David, and James Thomson (1740), *Alfred: A Masque*, London: A. Millar.

Mandeville, Bernard [1705] (1924), *The Fable of the Bees: or, Private Vices, Publick Benefits*, ed. F. B. Kaye, 2 vols, Oxford: Clarendon Press.

Martin, Martin (1703), *A Description of the Western Islands of Scotland*, London.

Mason, William [1759] (1796), *Caractacus: A Dramatic Poem*, London.

Mesmer, Franz Anton [1779] (1948), *Mesmerism*, trans. V. R. Myers, ed. Gilbert Frankau, London: Macdonald.

Montgomery, James (1856), *Memoirs of the Life and Writings of James Montgomery*, ed. John Howard and James Everett, 7 vols, London: Longman, Brown, Green & Longmans.

Moore, Thomas (18??), *Oft in the Stilly Night: Poetry by Thomas Moore*, ed. Sir John Stevenson, London: C. Sheard.

Moore, Thomas (1835–46), *The History of Ireland from the Earliest Kings of that Realm, Down to its Last Chief*, 4 vols, London: Longman, Brown, Green & Longmans, and John Taylor.

Moore, Thomas (1872), *The Poetical Works of Thomas Moore*, ed. David Herbert, Edinburgh: William P. Nimmo.

Moxon, Joseph [1683–84] (1962), *Mechanick Exercises on the whole Art of Printing (1683–4)*, ed. Herbert Davis and Harry Carter, 2nd edn, London: Oxford University Press.

Owenson, Sydney, Lady Morgan [1806] (1999), *The Wild Irish Girl: A National Tale*, ed. Kathryn Kirkpatrick, Oxford: Oxford University Press.

Park, Andrew (1839), *Blindness; or, The Second Sense Restored and Lost. A Poem, in Three Parts*, London: Smith, Elder and Co.

Pennant, Thomas [1772] (1774), *A Tour in Scotland 1769*, 3rd edn, Warrington.

The Penny Cyclopaedia of the Society for the Diffusion of Useful Knowledge (1833–6), 27 vols, London: Society for the Diffusion of Useful Knowledge.

Phillips, Michael and Robin Hamlyn (eds) (2000), *William Blake*, London: Tate Publishing.

Pinchard, Elizabeth [1791] (1793), *The Blind Child, or Anecdotes of the Wyndham Family. Written for the Use of Young People, By a Lady*, 2nd edn, London: E. Newbery.

Prestwich, John (1775), *Prestwich's Dissertation on Mineral, Animal, & Vegetable Poisons*, London: F. Newbery.

Reid, Thomas [1764] (1997), *An Inquiry into the Human Mind on the Principles of Common Sense*, ed. Derek R. Brookes, Edinburgh: Edinburgh University Press.

Roberts, Samuel (1813), *Tales of the Poor, or Infant Sufferings*, London: Longman, Darton and W. Phillips.

Roberts, Samuel (1816), *The Blind Man and His Son: A Tale for Young People. The Four Friends: A Fable and a Word for the Gipsies*, London: Taylor and Hessey.

Roberts, Samuel (1839), *Vital Christianity Opposed to the Reformation Society*, Sheffield: A. Whitaker.

Roberts, Samuel (1849), *Autobiography and Select Remains of the late Samuel Roberts*, London: Longman, Brown, Green and Longmans.

Rogers, Samuel (1792), *The Pleasures of Memory, A Poem in Two Parts*, London: T. Cadell.

Scott, Walter [1819] (1991), *The Bride of Lammermoor*, ed. Fiona Robertson, Oxford: Oxford University Press.

Scott, Walter [1824] (1985), *Redgauntlet*, ed. Kathryn Sutherland, Oxford: Oxford University Press.

Seward, Anna (1806), *Blindness, A Poem, Written at the Request of an Artist who lost his Sight by the Gutta Serena, and who was therefore obliged to change his Profession for that of Music*, Sheffield: William Platt.

Shelley, Mary (1987), *The Journals of Mary Shelley*, ed. Paula R. Feldman and Diana Scott-Kilvert, 2 vols, Oxford: Clarendon Press.

Shelley, Mary [1818] (1994), *Frankenstein, or The Modern Prometheus: The 1818 Text*, ed. Marilyn Butler, Oxford: Oxford University Press.

Shelley, Mary [1826] (1996a), *The Last Man*, ed. Jane Blumberg with Nora Crook, vol. 4 of *The Novels and Selected Works of Mary Shelley*, gen. ed. Nora Crook, 8 vols, London: Pickering.

Shelley, Mary [1823] (1996b), *Valperga: or, The Life and Adventures of Castruccio, Prince of Lucca*, ed. Nora Crook, vol. 3 of *The Novels and Selected Works of Mary Shelley*, gen. ed. Nora Crook, 8 vols, London: Pickering.

Shelley, Mary [1823] (1998), *Valperga or, The Life and Adventures of Castruccio, Prince of Lucca*, ed. Tillotama Rajan, Peterborough, Ontario: Broadview Press.

Shelley, Percy Bysshe (1954), *Shelley's Prose or The Trumpet of a Prophecy*, ed. David Lee Clark, Albuquerque: University of New Mexico Press.

Shelley, Percy Bysshe (1989), *The Poems of Shelley: Volume I, 1804–1817*, ed. Geoffrey Matthews and Kelvin Everest, London and New York: Longman.

Shelley, Percy Bysshe (2000), *The Poems of Shelley: Volume II, 1817–1819*, ed. Kelvin Everest and Geoffrey Matthews, Harlow, Essex: Longman.

Shelley, Percy Bysshe (2002), *Shelley's Poetry and Prose*, ed. Donald H. Reiman and Neil Fraistat, 2nd edn, 1st edn co-edited by Sharon B. Powers, New York: Norton.

Sherwood, Mary Martha (18??), *The Blind Man and Little George*, 3rd edn, London: W. Whittemore.

Smith, Adam (1980), *Essays on Philosophical Subjects*, ed. W. P. D. Wightman and J. C. Bryce, Oxford: Clarendon Press (vol. 3 of *The Glasgow Edition of the Works and Correspondence of Adam Smith*, 6 vols, Oxford: Clarendon Press, 1976–87).

Smith, J. T. (1828), *Nollekens and his Times*, 2 vols, London.

Southey, Robert [1807] (1951), *Letters from England; by Don Manuel Alvarez Espriella. Translated from the Spanish*, ed. J. Simmons, London: Cresset Press.

Southey, Robert (1909), *Poems of Robert Southey*, ed. Maurice H. Fitzgerald, London: Oxford University Press.

Southey, Robert (1965), *New Letters of Robert Southey*, ed. Kenneth Curry, 2 vols, New York and London: Columbia University Press.

Southey, Robert, and S. T. Coleridge (1969), *Omniana or Horae Otiosiores*, ed. Robert Gittings, Fontwell: Centaur Press.

Spence, Joseph (1754), *An Account of the Life, Character, and Poems of Mr Blacklock*, London: R. and J. Dodsley.

Thomson, James (1787) *The Poetical Works of James Thomson*, 2 vols, London: [John Bell].

Voltaire, François Marie Arouet de [1766] (1767), *The Ignorant Philosopher*, London: S. Bladon.

Voltaire, François Marie Arouet de (1799–81), *The Works of the late M. de Voltaire*, ed. D. Williams *et al.*, 14 vols, London: Fielding and Walker.

Warburton, W. [1736] (1748), *The Alliance between Church and State: or, the Necessity and Equity of an Established Religion and a Test Law Demonstrated in Three Books*, London.

Watson, William J. (ed.) (1937), *Scottish Verse from the Book of the Dean of Lismore*, Edinburgh.

Wilkie, David (1868), *The Great Works of Sir David Wilkie*, ed. Mrs Charles Heaton, London.

Wordsworth, William (1936), *Wordsworth: Poetical Works*, ed. Thomas Hutchinson, rev. Ernest de Selincourt, London: Oxford University Press.

Wordsworth, William (1977), *Home at Grasmere: Part First, Book First of* The Recluse, ed. Beth Darlington, Ithaca, NY: Cornell University Press; Hassocks, Sussex: Harvester Press.

Wordsworth, William (1979a), *The Prelude 1799, 1805, 1850*, ed. Jonathan Wordsworth, M. H. Abrams and Stephen Gill, New York: W. W. Norton.

Wordsworth, William (1979b), *The Ruined Cottage and The Pedlar*, ed. James Butler, Ithaca, NY: Cornell University Press; Hassocks, Sussex: Harvester Press.

Wordsworth, William (1982), *The Borderers*, ed. Robert Osborn, Ithaca, NY, and London: Cornell University Press.

Wordsworth, William [1807] (1983), *Poems, in Two Volumes, and Other Poems, 1800–1807*, ed. Jared Curtis, Ithaca, NY: Cornell University Press.

Wordsworth, William (1987), *Wordsworth's Poems of 1807*, ed. Alun R. Jones, Basingstoke: Macmillan.

Wordsworth, William [1807–20] (1989), *Shorter Poems, 1807–1820*, ed. Carl H. Ketcham, Ithaca, NY: Cornell University Press.

Wordsworth, William (1991), *The Thirteen-Book Prelude*, ed. Mark L. Reed, Ithaca, NY, and London: Cornell University Press.

Wordsworth, William, and Dorothy Wordsworth (1939), *Letters of William and Dorothy Wordsworth, The Later Years*, ed. E. de Selincourt, 2 vols, Oxford: Clarendon Press.

Wordsworth, William, and Dorothy Wordsworth (1970), *The Letters of William and Dorothy Wordsworth: The Middle Years*, II, 1812–1820, ed. Mary Moorman and Alan G. Hill, 2nd rev. edn, Oxford: Clarendon Press.

Wordsworth, William, and Dorothy Wordsworth (1979), *The Letters of William and Dorothy Wordsworth*, ed. Alan G. Hill, 2nd edn, vol. 5, *The Later Years*, II: 1829–1834, rev. and from the first edn of Ernest de Selincourt, Oxford: Clarendon Press.

Wu, Duncan (ed.) (1997), *Romantic Women Poets: An Anthology*, Oxford: Blackwell.

Wu, Duncan (ed.) (1998), *Romanticism: An Anthology*, 2nd edn, Oxford: Blackwell.

Secondary Sources

Aaron, Jane (1991), *A Double Singleness: Gender and the Writings of Charles and Mary Lamb*, Oxford: Clarendon Press.

Abrams, M. H. (1953), *The Mirror and the Lamp: Romantic Theory and the Critical Tradition*, New York: Oxford University Press.

Ackroyd, Peter (1995), *Blake*, London: Sinclair-Stevenson.

Allen, Stuart (2003), 'Wordsworth's Ear and the Politics of Aesthetic Autonomy', *Romanticism*, 9, pp. 37–54.

Almeida, Hermione de (1991), *Romantic Medicine and John Keats*, New York: Oxford University Press.

Bainbridge, Simon (1995), *Napoleon and English Romanticism*, Cambridge: Cambridge University Press.

Baldick, Chris (1987), *In Frankenstein's Shadow: Myth, Monstrosity, and Nineteenth-century Writing*, Oxford: Clarendon Press.

Barasch, Moshe (2001), *Blindness: The History of a Mental Image in Western Thought*, New York and London: Routledge.

Barnard, John (1987), *John Keats*, Cambridge: Cambridge University Press.

Barnard, John (2001), 'Keats's Letters: "Remembrancing and enchaining"', *The Cambridge Companion to Keats*, ed. Susan J. Wolfson, Cambridge: Cambridge University Press.

Barrell, John (1988), *Poetry, Language and Politics*, Manchester: Manchester University Press.

Bate, Jonathan (1989), *Shakespeare and the English Romantic Imagination*, Oxford: Clarendon Press.

Bates, Kathleen (1998), 'A Social History of Blindness'. Unpublished doctoral dissertation, University of Loughborough.

Batten, Guinn (1998), *The Orphaned Imagination: Melancholy and Commodity Culture in English Romanticism*, Durham, NC: Duke University Press.

Baxandall, Lee, and Stefan Morawski (eds) (1973), *Karl Marx and Frederick Engels on Literature and Art*, St Louis, MO: Telos Press.

Beer, John (1977), *Coleridge's Poetic Intelligence*, London and Basingstoke: Macmillan.

Beer, John (1978), 'Influence and Independence', in Michael Phillips (ed.), *Interpreting Blake*, Cambridge: Cambridge University Press, pp. 196–261.

Bennett, Andrew (1994), *Keats, Narrative and Audience: The Posthumous Life of Writing*, Cambridge: Cambridge University Press.

Berry, Christopher J. (1997), *Social Theory of the Scottish Enlightenment*, Edinburgh: Edinburgh University Press.

Bewell, Alan (1989), *Wordsworth and the Enlightenment: Nature, Man and Society in the Experimental Poetry*, New Haven, CT, and London: Yale University Press.

Bialostosky, Don H. (1992), *Wordsworth, Dialogics, and the Practice of Criticism*, Cambridge: Cambridge University Press.

Bloom, Harold (1969), *Shelley's Mythmaking*, 2nd edn, Ithaca, NY: Cornell University Press.

Bogel, Fredric V. (1984), *Literature and Insubstantiality in Later Eighteenth-Century England*, Princeton, NJ: Princeton University Press.

Bogen, Nancy (1970), 'A New Look at Blake's *Tiriel*', *Bulletin of the New York Public Library*, 74:3, pp. 153–65.

Bolla, Peter de (1994), 'The charm'd eye', in Veronica Kelly and Dorothea von Mücke, *Body and Text in the Eighteenth Century*, Stanford, CA: Stanford University Press, pp. 89–111.

Botting, Fred (1991), *Making Monstrous:* Frankenstein, *Criticism, Theory*, Manchester: Manchester University Press.

Bromwich, David (1998), *Disowned by Memory: Wordsworth's Poetry of the 1790s*, Chicago and London: University of Chicago Press.

Butler, Marilyn (1983), *Romantics, Rebels and Reactionaries: English Literature and Its Background 1760–1830*, Oxford: Oxford University Press.

Butler, Marilyn (1985), 'Druids, Bards and Twice-Born Bacchus: Peacock's Engagement with Primitive Mythology', *Keats–Shelley Review*, 36, pp. 57–76.

Bygrave, Stephen (1986), *Coleridge and the Self: Romantic Egotism*, Basingstoke: Macmillan.

Campbell, Colin (1983), 'Romanticism and the Consumer Ethic: Intimations of a Weber-style Thesis', *Sociological Analysis*, 44, pp. 279–95.

Carr, Stephen Leo (1986), 'Illuminated Printing: Toward a Logic of Difference', in Hilton and Vogler, pp. 177–96.

Cassirer, Ernst [1932] (1951), *The Philosophy of the Enlightenment*, trans. F. C. A. Koelln and J. P. Pettegrove, Princeton, NJ: Princeton University Press.

Castle, Terry (1995), *The Female Thermometer: Eighteenth-Century Culture and the Invention of the Uncanny*, New York and Oxford: Oxford University Press.

Caudwell, Christopher (1946), *Illusion and Reality: A Study of the Sources of Poetry*, 2nd edn, London: Lawrence and Wishart.

Céitinn, Seathrún (1902), *Foras Feasa Ar Éirinn*, in Geoffrey Keating, *The History of Ireland: Irish Texts Society*, IV, ed. and trans., David Comyn, London: Irish Texts Society.

Chandler, James K. (1984), *Wordsworth's Second Nature: A Study of the Poetry and Politics*, Chicago and London: University of Chicago Press.

Chandler, James (1998), *England in 1819: The Politics of Literary Culture and the Case of Romantic Historicism*, Chicago and London: University of Chicago Press.

Clarke, C. C. (1962), *Romantic Paradox: An Essay on the Poetry of Wordsworth*, London: Routledge and Kegan Paul.

Coburn, Kathleen (1974), 'A Bridge Between Science and Philosophy', in *Coleridge's Variety: Bicentenary Essays*, ed. John Beer, Basingstoke: Macmillan, pp. 81–100.

Colley, Linda (1992), *Britons: Forging the Nation 1707–1837*, New Haven, CT: Yale University Press.

Connell, Philip (2002), *Romanticism, Economics and the Question of Culture*, Oxford: Oxford University Press.

Cox, Philip (1996), *Gender, Genre and the Romantic Poets*, Manchester: Manchester University Press.

Darton, F. J. Harvey (1982), *Children's Books in England: Five Centuries of Social Life*, 3rd edn, rev. Brian Alderson, Cambridge: Cambridge University Press.

Davidson, Hilda Ellis (ed.) (1989), *The Seer in Celtic and Other Traditions*, Edinburgh: John Donald.

Davies, Keri, and Martha Keith Schuchard (2004), 'Recovering the Lost Moravian History of William Blake's Family', *Blake/An Illustrated Quarterly*, 38, pp. 36–43.

De Luca, Vincent Arthur (1991), *Words of Eternity: Blake and the Poetics of the Sublime*, Princeton, NJ: Princeton University Press.

Durrant, Geoffrey (1970), *Wordsworth and the Great System: A Study of Wordsworth's Poetic Universe*, Cambridge: Cambridge University Press.

Eagleton, Terry (1998), 'The Masochism of Thomas Moore', in *Crazy John and the Bishop, and Other Essays on Irish Culture*, Cork: Cork University Press in association with Field Day, pp. 140–57.

Ende, Stuart A. (1976), *Keats and the Sublime*, New Haven, CT, and London: Yale University Press.

Essick, Robert N. (1980), *William Blake: Printmaker*, Princeton, NJ: Princeton University Press.

Essick, Robert N. (1986), 'How Blake's Body Means', in Hilton and Vogler, pp. 197–217.

Essick, Robert N. (1989), *William Blake and the Language of Adam*, Oxford: Clarendon Press.

Everest, Kelvin (1979), *Coleridge's Secret Ministry: The Context of the Conversation Poems 1795–1798*, Hassocks, Sussex: Harvester Press.

Fairer, David (2002), 'Coleridge's *Sonnets from Various Authors* (1796): A Lost Conversation Poem?', *Studies in Romanticism*, 41, pp. 585–604.

Fairer, David (2005), 'The Sonnet', in *Romanticism: An Oxford Guide*, ed. Nicholas Roe, Oxford: Oxford University Press, pp. 292–309.

Farrell, Gabriel (1956), *The Story of Blindness*, Cambridge, MA: Harvard University Press.

Ferry, Anne Davidson (1962), 'The Bird, The Blind Bard, and the Fortunate Fall', in *Reason and Imagination: Studies in the History of Ideas 1600–1800*, ed. J. A. Mazzeo, New York: Columbia University Press; London: Routledge Kegan Paul, pp. 183–200.

Flannery, James W. (1997), *Dear Harp of My Country: The Irish Melodies of Thomas Moore*, with two CDs, Nashville, TN: J. S. Sanders & Company.

Ford, Jennifer (1998), *Coleridge and Dreaming: Romanticism, Dreams and the Medical Imagination*, Cambridge: Cambridge University Press.

Fruman, Norman (1972), *Coleridge: The Damaged Archangel*, London: Allen and Unwin.

Fulford, Tim (1996), *Landscape, Liberty and Authority: Poetry, Criticism and Politics*, Cambridge: Cambridge University Press.

Fulford, Tim (2004) 'Conducting the Vital Fluid: The Politics and Poetics of Mesmerism', *Studies in Romanticism*, 43, pp. 57–78.

Fulford, Tim, Debbie Lee and Peter J. Kitson (2004), 'Magnetism and the Search for the Poes', in *Literature, Science and Exploration in the Romantic Era: Bodies of Knowledge*, Cambridge: Cambridge University Press, pp. 149–75

Galperin, William H. (1989), *Revision and Authority in Wordsworth: The Interpretation of a Career*, Philadelphia: University of Pennsylvania Press.

Gerard, Albert (1960), 'The Systolic Rhythm: The Structure of Coleridge's Conversation Poems', *Essays in Criticism*, 10, pp. 307–19.

Gilbert, Sandra M., and Susan Gubar (1979), *The Madwoman in the Attic: The Woman Writer and the Nineteenth-Century Literary Imagination*, New Haven, CT: Yale University Press.

Gill, Stephen (1990), *William Wordsworth: A Life*, Oxford: Oxford University Press.

Goldsmith, Margaret (1934), *Franz Anton Mesmer: The History of an Idea*, London: Arthur Barker.

Green, Matthew J. A. (2005), *Visionary Materialism in the Early Works of William Blake: The Intersection of Enthusiasm and Empiricism*, Basingstoke: Palgrave Macmillan.

Griffiths, Antony, Timothy Clifford and Martin Royalton-Kisch (1978), *Gainsborough and Reynolds*, London: British Museum.

Gutteridge, John (1981), 'Scenery and Ecstasy: Three of Coleridge's Blank Verse Poems', in *New Approaches to Coleridge: Biographical and Critical Essays*, London and Totowa, NJ: Vision Press and Barnes and Noble, pp. 151–71.

Hall, Mary S. (1970), 'Blake's *Tiriel*: A Visionary Form Pedantic', *Bulletin of the New York Public Library*, 74, pp. 166–76.

Hamilton, Paul (1983), *Coleridge's Poetics*, Oxford: Blackwell.

Haney, David P. (1997), ' "Rents and Openings in the Ideal World": Eye and Ear in Wordsworth', *Studies in Romanticism*, 36, pp. 173–99.

Hartman, Geoffrey (1954), *The Unmediated Vision*, New Haven, CT: Yale University Press.

Hartman, Geoffrey (1987), *The Unremarkable Wordsworth*, London: Methuen.

Hayden, John (1984), 'Wordsworth, Hartley and the Revisionists', *Studies in Philology*, 81, pp. 94–118.

Hertz, Neil (1985), *The End of the Line: Essays on Psychoanalysis and the Sublime*, New York: Columbia University Press.

Hilton, Nelson (1983), *Literal Imagination: Blake's Vision of Words*, Berkeley, Los Angeles and London: University of California Press.

Hilton, Nelson, and Thomas Vogler (eds) (1986), *Unnam'd Forms: Blake and Textuality*, Berkeley and Los Angeles: University of California Press.

Holmes, Richard (1989), *Coleridge: Early Visions*, London: Hodder and Stoughton.

Honour, Hugh (1968), *Neo-classicism*, Harmondsworth: Penguin.

Howard, Jacqueline (1994), *Reading Gothic Fiction: A Bakhtinian Approach*, Oxford: Clarendon Press.

Hunt, Peter (ed.) (1995), *Children's Literature: An Illustrated History*, Oxford and New York: Oxford University Press.

Hunter, Michael (ed.) (2001), *The Occult Laboratory: Magic, Science and Second Sight in Late Seventeenth-Century Scotland*, Woodbridge, Surrey: Boydell Press.

Illingworth, W. H. (1910), *The History of the Education of the Blind*, London: Sampson Low, Master & Co.

Jacobus, Mary (1986), *Reading Woman: Essays in Feminist Criticism*, London: Methuen.

Jacobus, Mary (1995), *Romanticism, Writing and Sexual Difference: Essays on* The Prelude, Oxford: Clarendon Press.

Jacobus, Mary (1998), ' "The Science of Herself": Scenes of Female Enlightenment', in *Romanticism, History, and the Possibilities of Genre: Re-forming Literature 1789–1837*, Cambridge: Cambridge University Press, pp. 240–69.

Johnston, Kenneth (1984), *Wordsworth and* The Recluse, New Haven, CT, and London: Yale University Press.

Johnston, Kenneth (1998), *The Hidden Wordsworth: Poet, Lover, Rebel, Spy*, New York and London: W. W. Norton.

Keach, William (1984), *Shelley's Style*, New York and London: Methuen.

Keating, Geoffrey (1723), *The General History of Ireland*, trans. Dermod O'Connor, London.

Kelly, Gary (1989), *English Fiction of the Romantic Period 1789–1830*, London and New York: Longman.

Kelly, Gary (1993), *Women, Writing, and Revolution 1790–1827*, Oxford: Clarendon Press.

Kelly, Gary (1997), 'Last Men: Hemans and Mary Shelley in the 1820s', *Romanticism*, 3, pp. 198–208.

Kelly, Gary (2000), 'Politicizing the Personal: Mary Wollstonecraft, Mary Shelley, and the Coterie Novel', in *Mary Shelley in Her Times*, ed. Betty T. Bennett and Stuart Curran, Baltimore, MD: Johns Hopkins University Press, pp. 147–59.

Kersey, M. E. (2001), ' "Where are the Originals?" Britishness and Problems of Authenticity in Post-Union Literature from Addison to Macpherson'. Unpublished doctoral thesis, University of Leeds.

Kierkegaard, Søren (1983), *Fear and Trembling; Repetition*, trans. and ed. Howard V. Hong and Edna H. Hong, Princeton, NJ: Princeton University Press.

Kilgour, Maggie (1995), *The Rise of the Gothic Novel*, London and New York: Routledge.

Klancher, Jon P. (1987), *The Making of English Reading Audiences, 1790–1832*, Madison: University of Wisconsin Press.

Kristeva, Julia (1982), *Powers of Horror: An Essay on Abjection*, trans. Leon S. Roudiez, New York: Columbia University Press.

Labbe, Jacqueline (1998), *Romantic Visualities: Landscape, Gender and Romanticism*, Basingstoke: Macmillan.

Lalanne, Maxime [1866] (1880), *A Treatise on Etching. Text and Plates*, trans.

S. R. Koehler from 2nd French edn, London. First French edn, *Traité de la gravure à l'eau forte*.

Langbaum, Robert (1957), *The Poetry of Experience: The Dramatic Monologue in Modern Literary Tradition*, London: Chatto and Windus.

Larrissy, Edward (1985), *William Blake*, Oxford: Blackwell.

Larrissy, Edward (1990), *Reading Twentieth-Century Poetry: The Language of Gender and Objects*, Oxford: Blackwell.

Larrissy, Edward (1994), ' "Self-Imposition", Alchemy, and the Fate of the "Bound" in Later Blake', in *Historicizing Blake*, ed. Steve Clark and David Worrall, Basingstoke: Macmillan, pp. 59–72.

Larrissy, Edward (1999), 'The Celtic Bard of Romanticism: Blindness and Second Sight', *Romanticism*, 5:1, pp. 43–57.

Law, Jules David (1993), *The Rhetoric of Empiricism: Language and Perception from Locke to I. A. Richards*, Ithaca, NY, and London: Cornell University Press.

Leask, Nigel (1992), 'Shelley's "Magnetic Ladies": Romantic Mesmerism and the Politics of the Body', in *Beyond Romanticism: New Approaches to Texts and Contexts 1780–1832*, ed. Stephen Copley and John Whale, London: Routledge, pp. 53–78.

Leatherbarrow, David (1985), 'Architecture and Situation: A Study of the Architectural Writings of Robert Morris', *Journal of the Society of Architectural Historians*, 44:1, pp. 48–59

Lecky, William Edward Hartpole (1892), *A History of Ireland in the Eighteenth Century*, 5 vols, London.

Lee, Edwin (1866), *Animal Magnetism and Magnetic Lucid Somnambulism*, London: Longmans, Green & Co.

Leighton, Angela (1984), *Shelley and the Sublime: An Interpretation of the Major Poems*, Cambridge: Cambridge University Press.

Lennon, Colm (1981), *Richard Stanihurst the Dubliner 1547–1618: A Biography with a Stanihurst Text*, On Ireland's Past, Blackrock: Irish Academic Press.

Levinson, Marjorie (1986), *Wordsworth's Great Period Poems: Four Essays*, Cambridge: Cambridge University Press.

Levinson, Marjorie (1988), *Keats's Life of Allegory: The Origins of a Style*, Oxford: Blackwell.

Lister, Raymond (1975), *Infernal Methods: A Study of William Blake's Art Techniques*, London: G. Bell and Sons.

Liu, Alan (1989), *Wordsworth: The Sense of History*, Stanford, CA: Stanford University Press.

Lucas, E. V. (1907), *The Life of Charles Lamb*, 4th edn, London: Methuen.

MacLysaght, Edward (1979), *Irish Life in the Seventeenth Century*, 3rd edn, Blackrock: Irish Academic Press.

Maxwell, Catherine (2001), *The Female Sublime From Milton to Swinburne: Bearing Blindness*, Manchester and New York: Manchester University Press.

Mayhead, Robin (1967), *John Keats*, Cambridge: Cambridge University Press.

McClelland, Fleming (1996), 'Does Madeline Sleep, or Does She Wake? The Hoodwinking of Porphyro', *Keats–Shelley Review*, 10, pp. 31–4.

McGann, Jerome (1976), *Don Juan in Context*, London: John Murray.

McGann, Jerome (1996), *The Poetics of Sensibility: A Revolution in Literary Style* Oxford: Clarendon Press.

Medwin, Thomas (1847), *The Life of Percy Bysshe Shelley*, 2 vols, London.

Meigs, Cornelia (1969), *A Critical History of Children's Literature*, London: Macmillan.

Mellor, Anne K. (1988), *Mary Shelley: Her Life, Her Fiction, Her Monsters*, New York and London: Routledge.

Miall, David S. (1993), 'Coleridge's Debt to Hartley', in *Coleridge's Visionary Languages: Essays in Honour of J. B. Beer*, Cambridge: D. S. Brewer, pp. 151–63.

Mitchell, W. J. T. (1969), 'Poetic and Pictorial Imagination in Blake's *The Book of Urizen*', *Eighteenth-Century Studies*, 3, pp. 83–107.

Moore, John Robert (1925), 'Wordsworth's Debt to Macpherson's "Ossian"', *PMLA*, pp. 362–78.

Moorman, Mary (1965), *William Wordsworth: A Biography: The Later Years, 1803–1850*, Oxford: Clarendon Press.

Muir, Percy (1954), *English Children's Books 1600–1900*, London: B. T. Batsford.

Muldoon, Paul (1990), *Madoc: A Mystery*, London: Faber and Faber.

Murphy, Peter T. (1986), 'Fool's Gold: The Highland Treasures of MacPherson's Ossian', *English Literary History*, 53, pp. 567–91.

Newlyn, Lucy (1986), *Coleridge, Wordsworth, and the Language of Allusion*, Oxford: Clarendon Press.

Nichols, Ashton (1998), *The Revolutionary 'I': Wordsworth and the Politics of Self-Presentation*, Basingstoke: Macmillan.

O'Neill, Michael (1989), *The Human Mind's Imaginings: Conflict and Achievement in Shelley's Poetry*, Oxford: Clarendon Press.

Owen, A. L. (1962), *The Famous Druids*, Oxford: Clarendon Press.

Paley, Morton D. (1978), *William Blake*, London: Phaidon Books.

Paley, Morton D. (1983), *The Continuing City: William Blake's* Jerusalem, Oxford: Clarendon Press.

Paley, Morton D. (1993), '*The Last Man*: Apocalypse without Millennium', in *The Other Mary Shelley: Beyond* Frankenstein, ed. Audrey A. Fisch, Anne K. Mellor and Esther H. Schor, New York and Oxford: Oxford University Press, pp. 107–23.

Paley, Morton D. (1999), *Coleridge's Later Poetry*, Oxford: Clarendon Press.

Panofsky, Erwin [1939] (1972), *Studies in Iconology: Humanistic Themes in the Art of the Renaissance*, New York: Harper and Row.

Parker, Reeve (1987), 'Reading Wordsworth's Power: Narrative and Usurpation in *The Borderers*', *English Literary History*, 54, pp. 229–31.

Patterson, Charles I. (1970), *The Daemonic in the Poetry of John Keats*, Urbana: University of Illinois Press.

Paulson, Ronald (1983), *Representations of Revolution (1789–1820)*, New Haven, CT, and London: Yale University Press.

Paulson, William T. (1987), *Enlightenment, Romanticism and The Blind in France*, Princeton, NJ: Princeton University Press.

Perry, Seamus (1999), *Coleridge and the Uses of Division*, Oxford: Oxford University Press.

Pfau, Thomas (1993), ' "Elementary Feelings" and "Distorted Language": The Pragmatics of Culture in Wordsworth's Preface to *Lyrical Ballads*', *New Literary History*, 24, pp. 125–46.

Phillips, Michael (1994), 'Blake and the Terror 1792–93', *The Library*, 6th series, 16, pp. 263–97.

Pickering, Samuel F. Jr (1981), *John Locke and Children's Books in Eighteenth-Century England*, Knoxville: University of Tennessee Press.

Piper, H. W. (1962), *The Active Universe: Pantheism and the Concept of the Imagination in the English Romantic Poets*, Cambridge: Cambridge University Press.

Pottle, Frederick A. (1970), 'The Eye and the Object in the Poetry of Wordsworth', in *Romanticism and Consciousness: Essays in Criticism*, ed. Harold Bloom, New York: W. W. Norton, pp. 273–87.

Pratt, Lynda (1996), 'Revising the National Epic: Coleridge, Southey and *Madoc*', *Romanticism*, 2, pp. 149–63.

Prickett, Stephen (1970), *Coleridge and Wordsworth: The Poetry of Growth*, Cambridge: Cambridge University Press.

Radcliffe, David Hill (1992), 'Ossian and the Genres of Culture', *Studies in Romanticism*, 31, pp. 213–32.

Raine, Kathleen (1969), *Blake and Tradition*, 2 vols, London: Routledge and Kegan Paul.

Rauch, Alan (1995), 'The Monstrous Body of Knowledge in Mary Shelley's *Frankenstein*', *Studies in Romanticism*, 34, pp. 227–53.

Rawlinson, Nick (2003), *William Blake's Comic Vision*, Basingstoke: Palgrave Macmillan.

Rée, Jonathan (1974), *Descartes*, London: Allen Lane.

Rée, Jonathan (1999), *I See a Voice: A Philosophical History*, London: HarperCollins.

Richardson, Alan (1994), *Literature, Education and Romanticism: Reading as Social Practice*, Cambridge: Cambridge University Press.

Richardson, Alan (1999), 'Coleridge and the Dream of an Embodied Mind', *Romanticism*, 5, pp. 1–25.

Richardson, Alan (2001a), *British Romanticism and the Science of the Mind*, Cambridge: Cambridge University Press.

Richardson, Alan (2001b), 'Keats and Romantic Science', in *The Cambridge Companion to Keats*, ed. Susan J. Wolfson, Cambridge: Cambridge University Press, pp. 230–45.

Riskin, Jessica (2002), *Science in the Age of Sensibility: The Sentimental Empiricists of the French Enlightenment*, Chicago and London: Chicago University Press.

Rix, Robert W. (2002), 'Healing the Spirit: William Blake and Magnetic Religion', *Romanticism On the Net*, 25 (February: 37 pars, 20 http://users.ox.ac.uk/~scat0385/25rix.html>).

Robinson, Charles E. (1976), *Shelley and Byron: The Snake and Eagle Wreathed in Flight*, Baltimore, MD, and London: Johns Hopkins University Press.

Roe, Nicholas (1988), *Wordsworth and Coleridge: The Radical Years*, Oxford: Clarendon Press.

Roe, Nicholas (1992), 'Revising the Revolution: History and Imagination in *The Prelude*', in *Romantic Revisions*, ed. Robert Brinkley and Keith Hanley, Cambridge: Cambridge University Press, pp. 87–102.

Roe, Nicholas (1997), *John Keats and the Culture of Dissent*, Oxford: Clarendon Press.

Roe, Nicholas (2002), *The Politics of Nature: William Wordsworth and Some Contemporaries*, 2nd edn, Basingstoke: Palgrave.

Rogers, Pat (1985), 'Gulliver's Glasses', in *Eighteenth-Century Encounters: Studies in Literature and Society in the Age of Walpole*, Brighton: Harvester Press, pp. 1–10.

Rosenblum, Robert (1967), *Transformations in Late Eighteenth-Century Art*, Princeton, NJ: Princeton University Press.

Rousseau, G. S. (1991), *Enlightenment Crossings: Pre- and Post-Modern Discourses*, Manchester: Manchester University Press.

Ruthven, K. K. (1976), 'Keats and *Dea Moneta*', *Studies in Romanticism*, 15, pp. 445–59.

Scott, Peter Dale (1979), 'Vital Artifice: Mary, Percy, and the Psychopolitical Integrity of *Frankenstein*', in *The Endurance of Frankenstein*, ed. George Levine and U. C. Knoepflmacher, Berkeley, Los Angeles and London: University of California Press, pp. 172–202

Simpson, David (1982), *Wordsworth and the Figurings of the Real*, London and Basingstoke: Macmillan.

Spufford, Francis (1996), *I May Be Some Time*, London: Faber.

Stabler, Jane (2001), 'Space for Speculation: Coleridge, Barbauld, and the Poetics of Priestley', in *Samuel Taylor Coleridge and the Sciences of Life*, Oxford: Oxford University Press, pp. 175–204.

Stabler, Jane (2002), *Byron, Poetics and History*, Cambridge: Cambridge University Press.

Stafford, Barbara (1991), *Body Criticism: Imaging the Unseen in Enlightenment Art and Medicine*, Cambridge, MA: MIT Press.

Stafford, Fiona J. (1991), ' "Dangerous Success": Ossian, Wordsworth, and English Romantic Literature', in *Ossian Revisited*, ed. Howard Gaskill, Edinburgh: Edinburgh University Press, pp. 49–72.

Stieg, Elizabeth (1990), 'Reinterpreting the Old Testament: Blake's Tiriel as Prophet', *Studies in Romanticism*, 29, pp. 273–96.

Taylor, Charles (1989), *Sources of the Self: The Making of the Modern Identity*, Cambridge, MA: Harvard University Press.

Tessier, Thérèse (1981), *The Bard of Erin: A Study of Moore's* Irish Melodies *(1808–1834)*, trans. George P. Mutch, Salzburg: Institut für Anglistik und Amerikanistik.

Thurley, Geoffrey (1983), *The Romantic Predicament*, London and Basingstoke: Macmillan.

Trott, Nicola Zoe (1994), 'Wordsworth, Milton, and the Inward Light', in *Milton, the Metaphysicals, and Romanticism*, ed. Lisa Low and Anthony John Harding, Cambridge: Cambridge University Press, pp. 114–35.

Trott, Nicola Zoe (forthcoming), *Wordsworth's Second Sight*, Oxford: Clarendon Press.

Trumpener, Katie (1997), *Bardic Nationalism: The Romantic Novel and the British Empire*, Princeton, NJ: Princeton University Press.

Turner, John (1986), *Wordsworth: Play and Politics: A Study of Wordsworth's Poetry 1787–1800*, London and Basingstoke: Macmillan.

Vail, Jeffery (2004), 'Thomas Moore in Ireland and America: The Growth of a Poet's Mind', *Romanticism*, 10, pp. 41–62.

Vine, Steven (1993), *Blake's Poetry: Spectral Visions*, Basingstoke: Macmillan.

Viscomi, Joseph (1993), *William Blake and the Idea of the Book*, Princeton, NJ: Princeton University Press.

Waldorff, Leon (1990), 'The Silent Work of Imagination', in *Critical Essays on John Keats*, ed. Hermione de Almeida, Boston, MA: G. K. Hall, pp. 183–205.

Walsh, William (1994), *Locke, Literary Criticism and Philosophy*, Cambridge: Cambridge University Press.

Watson, J. R. (1970), *Picturesque Landscape and English Romantic Poetry*, London: Hutchinson Educational.

Weinbrot, Howard D. (1993), *Britannia's Issue: The Rise of British Literature from Dryden to Ossian*, Cambridge: Cambridge University Press.

Welch, Robert (1980), *Irish Poetry from Moore to Yeats*, Gerrards Cross, Buckinghamshire: Colin Smythe.

Welch, Robert (1988), *A History of Verse Translation from the Irish, 1789–1897*, Gerrards Cross, Buckinghamshire: Colin Smythe.

Welsford, Enid (1966), *Salisbury Plain: A Study in the Development of Wordsworth's Mind and Art*, Oxford: Clarendon Press.

Westbrook, Deanne (2001), *Wordsworth's Biblical Ghosts*, New York and Basingstoke: Palgrave.

Wheeler, K. M. (1981), *The Creative Mind in Coleridge's Poetry*, London: Heinemann.

Winch, Donald (1996), *Riches and Poverty: An Intellectual History of Political Economy in Britain, 1750–1834*, Cambridge: Cambridge University Press.

Wind, Edgar [1958] (1967), *Pagan Mysteries in the Renaissance*, 2nd edn, Harmondsworth: Penguin.

Wordsworth, Jonathan (1982), *The Borders of Vision*, Oxford: Clarendon Press.

Wu, Duncan (1993), *Wordsworth's Reading 1770–1799*, Cambridge: Cambridge University Press.

Wylie, Ian (1989), *Young Coleridge and the Philosophy of Nature*, Oxford: Clarendon Press.

Yeats, W. B. (1994), *Later Essays*, ed. William H. O'Donnell, New York: Charles Scribner's Sons.

Index